HOW COACHING WORKS

HOW COACHING WORKS

WORKS

THE ESSENTIAL GUIDE TO THE HISTORY AND PRACTICE OF EFFECTIVE COACHING

JOSEPH O'CONNOR AND ANDREA LAGES

A & C BLACK • LONDON

First published in Great Britain 2007

A & C Black Publishers Ltd
38 Soho Square, London W1D 3HB
www.acblack.com

A CIP record for this book is available from the British Library.

ISBN: 9-780-7136-8261-8

This book is produced using paper that is made from wood grown in managed, sustainable forests. It is natural, renewable and recyclable. The logging and manufacturing processes conform to the environmental regulations of the country of origin.

Design by Fiona Pike, Pike Design, Winchester
Typeset by RefineCatch Ltd, Bungay, Suffolk
Printed in the United Kingdom by Caligraving

For Amanda

CONTENTS

CONTENTS

INTRODUCTION

A QUEST

This book is the story of our quest for the soul of coaching. We set out with hope down a road that looked clear as far as we could see, the sun was shining and we did not foresee any problems, although we know every quest will have them. And, of course, the quest was more complicated than we thought, the soul of coaching was not so easy to discover, and what we found was different from what we expected. This book is our journal of our quest.

We are coaches. We love our profession and we enjoy working with people to help them learn, change and develop. And we are happy to learn and change as we work, as well. We have been coaching for over ten years in many countries. When we started out, business coaching and life coaching were well known in Europe, but barely known at all in South America. Andrea worked as a business coach in Brazil and had a business card with her name and the profession 'coach' printed on it. Most people who saw it asked her what she did; many thought she was in the tourist industry or was employed by a football team.

Sports coaching is well established. (A sports coach is a player with experience who motivates and trains a team or an individual athlete.) We started writing this book in a football World Cup year and it has been fascinating to see the rise of the celebrity football coach. The camera lingered on his face as well as on the players' faces after a goal, a missed chance or a questionable decision. The coach's emotion was broadcast to the world and suddenly he or she became visible and important. Coaches are now transferred between teams and countries for sums of money that only players enjoyed in the past.

Times change, and life coaching and business coaching have grown remarkably in the last decade. Many people are now engaging a life coach to help them make the most of their opportunities, and now admitting to having a life coach tends to attract curiosity rather than pity. Life coaching has invaded the domain of psychologists and counsellors, although there are signs that these professionals are slowly reclaiming their territory, because many life coaches have little in the way of credentials. The greatest growth of coaching has been in business. You do not need to be a psychologist or an academic to coach businesspeople, and businesses are often not enamoured with the academic world, which (to outsiders, at least) seems removed from the rough and tumble of the real world. There has also been an increase in financial coaching, career coaching and relationship coaching. The bandwagon is rattling along and even television is jumping on board, with the celebrity life coach appearing on chat shows in the United States. We have even seen a programme featuring a hapless client being 'coached' through hidden earphones on how talk to an attractive girl whom he felt too shy to approach. This is confusing and it is not coaching. Today, anyone who helps or advises others on anything seems to be using the title 'coach' where ten years ago they would probably have called themselves a 'consultant'. While many people describe themselves as coaches, what they do and the way they do it may vary considerably, and yet there must be some core idea, some basic concept and method at the heart of coaching; the term must surely describe something distinctive? What is a coach? What do coaches do? Is 'coaching' a profession? Or a flavour-of-the-month business idea? Should it be described as a profession? An activity? A discipline? Or an area? Can coaching be defined at all? Does definition mean restraint and control and, if so, who will be the controller? If it is a methodology for change, then how does it work and what type of change can it generate? These are the key questions we are trying to answer in this book.

During the last ten years, we have also trained and talked to coaches from over 30 countries, and we believe that coaching has a soul and a distinctive methodology. We believe that it has an identifiable core set of mental models and methodologies, and numerous individuals and organizations are working with them all over the world. Coaching is a methodology, not an ideology. It is a methodology for change, to help people (and through them, businesses) to learn, develop and be the best they can be. It is a practical way of working that can be used in conjunction with other methods.

We believe coaching is here to stay and not a a short-lived fashion. A fashion is great – for a month or so, and then it fades as the next fashion replaces it. Coaching is more than a passing bandwagon that businesses are quick to jump on and quicker to jump off. It is showing every sign of continuing to grow and becoming an established way for people and companies to change.

Business is notoriously pragmatic, and to be sustainable, coaching must link with other established disciplines. It needs to be embraced by other established methodologies for change. Coaching needs to be backed by research that shows it is effective. Does coaching deliver what it is supposed to deliver? Without consensus on what activity we are measuring and evaluating in relation to other disciplines, the evidence for coaching will remain fragmented and anecdotal. One of the goals of this book is to put some boundaries around the field to help this process of evaluation.

Our quest took us to many different countries and methods of coaching. We considered the fundamental premises of coaching. What has to be true for the coach and the client for the method to work? What sort of relationship do they build?

There are many different types, brands, schools and approaches to coaching. We have chosen to explore six of the best-known and most representative approaches, to see the core principles they share. Of course, the presentations and interpretations of the various coaching methods are ours. We looked for points of agreement: where, for example, an integral coach would agree with a behavioural coach and an NLP coach could see the value in how an ontological coach works, and all would see how their work fitted with the Inner Game, the GROW model and Positive Psychology. We wanted to find out what works, not what does not work.

We believe we have built a coherent and consistent system that brings together the most important points of all coaching schools of thought. We have tried to be inclusive and not exclusive. We did not know what we would find when we began, so we have not confirmed any existing prejudices. The only assumption we made was that there was a heart and soul to coaching that all the main approaches would agree on. We use this integrated model ourselves in our coaching and coaching training.

Why did we write this book? Because we believe it is needed. We wrote it because we value coaching and want it to succeed. We wrote it because we want to add something worthwhile to current coaching literature and help coaching to grow and develop. And we wrote it to learn more about coaching. Writing a book is a quest in itself; you do not know exactly how it will turn out, and the finished book is both surprising and familiar at the same time. People would ask us, 'What is coaching?', and we had to think every time. We would often say, 'It would take a book to answer that question.' This is that book. It contains many ideas about coaching, but coaching is a means to an end, not an end in itself. It is a means to help people to live their lives in happiness and fulfilment, achieving their potential and developing to the greatest extent they can. It is about living a full life. What drives us is to create this full life for our clients and ourselves.

There are many models and ideas here that will make your coaching more effective, but this is not primarily a 'how to' book. It is for all coaches: executive coaches, business coaches, life coaches and sports coaches. If you are already a coach, then we hope that this book will help you have a greater insight into your profession and be more effective with your clients. If you are in training, it will give you an invaluable view of the fascinating profession into which you are entering. For managers, teachers, psychologists and therapists, we believe this book will widen your skills and knowledge. For newcomers to coaching, there is a bewildering variety of brands, claims and varieties of coaching available. We hope this book sheds light on them all, shows you what drives them and the soul that inspires them.

We have written a distillation of coaching, taking the best from every approach, making as complete a model as we can. The test of a model, of course, is whether or not it works. Models are not true or false, just successful to varying degrees, depending on the results you get from them. We have tested this model with coaches in over thirty countries and we know it works.

AN OVERVIEW

The book has three parts. Part One, 'Coaching on the Edge of Chaos', is a review of the present state of coaching. In fact, the edge of chaos is not a bad place to be; it is continually creative. However, it is unstable, tending to flop first of all into rigid definitions of what coaching is or should be – the dead hand of orthodoxy – or to dissolve into a Wonderland where coaching is whatever anyone says it is. This part of the book contains many definitions of coaching, and also briefly explores the boundaries between coaching and other professions. It also has a short historical overview of how coaching grew. History is made by people working in a particular context, so we have written about both the people and the cultural conditions that fostered coaching. We believe that you can understand coaching well only if you understand its origins, otherwise you simply have a snapshot that tells you little of where it came from and less of where it is going. There are links between coaching and other established disciplines such as humanistic psychology, human developmental psychology and business practice, so it has a respectable intellectual and cultural pedigree.

Part Two opens with a world tour of the dominant types of coaching. We explain the main ideas and consider integral coaching, ontological coaching, neuro-linguistic coaching, positive psychology coaching, the inner game, coactive coaching and the GROW model, as well as behavioural coaching. As you read these, you can share our quest and our curiosity to find what they have in common. At the end of this part of the book we will give our model of the common core of all these approaches – the key elements of coaching. You will see how the key ideas of each coaching approach fit together, overlap and how they contribute to the overall model. They are like the primary colours of light, all different but when they blend together, you get another colour completely – white light that takes in and expresses the whole spectrum.

In Part Three, there is a chapter on how to measure the results of coaching from different perspectives to give evidence that it works, both in business and in life coaching. We also introduce two important ideas that are growing in the coaching field at the moment. First, there is the developmental aspect. Coaching currently lacks a developmental dimension, and is applied to every adult in the same way. However, there is considerable evidence showing that adults go through a sequence of developmental stages as their thinking changes and matures. What does this mean for coaching? How does the level of the coach influence the client? Can a coach help if they do not understand where a client is in their developmental cycle? What happens when there is a mismatch between the developmental level of coach and client? When is coaching transactional, rearranging the client's mental furniture, and when is it transformational, making them move house completely?

Second, there is the post-modern aspect of coaching. Our experience is formed and informed by our language, culture and other people. We do not see our links with others but they are there. How can you coach someone from another culture? What implications does this have for coaching? Finally, we speculate a little on the future of coaching with a dream and two nightmares of possible futures.

We wanted this book to be as inclusive as possible, and to this end we invited several writers and coaches to contribute a short reflection on coaching from their point of view. These are interspersed throughout; each has a unique view and the many different voices give a harmony to the book it would otherwise lack. We thank the contributors for their generosity in making this book richer.

Welcome to the quest. You will find a varied cast of characters here – writers, thinkers, academics and activists. Coaching was developed and is being developed by many different kinds of people.

We found important markers and clues in all the different types of coaching, and this reminded us of an experience in Colorado, USA in August 2003. Colorado is a beautiful state and we were high in the Rocky Mountains one day driving along the road as it wound its way up the steep rise. The sun was shining, there was a slight chill in the air, but the snow was reassuringly far away, a frosty crown on the heads of the largest mountains in the distance. As we drove along, we noticed that wooden poles, about 2 metres high, were stuck in the ground on both sides of the road at regular intervals. They looked strange, so we asked our friend and host what they were for.

'Well,' he said, 'right now the sun is shining and the road is clear, but come the winter, the first snowfalls can cover this road completely. It just disappears; everything is white. How do you think the snowplough knows where the road is? It ploughs between the posts.' And from that we learned to set up our markers in advance, because things may not be as clear later as they are when you begin the journey.

A few practical comments. We use some real coaching cases in this book, but with the names changed. Also, we debated how to refer to the person who is coached. We decided on the name 'client' to bring coaching into line with other professions that use the same terminology, and we also think that the word 'coachee', like most artificial words, is rather ugly. For both coaches and clients, where necessary we use 'he' or 'she' without discrimination.

ACKNOWLEDGMENTS

First of all, to all the writers and coaches who generously contributed their thoughts to this book: Lars-Eric Uneståhl, Sir John Whitmore, Robert Dilts, Anthony Grant, Fernando Flores and Carol Kauffman.

Also to all our clients, who have helped us to be better coaches. Our clients are our best teachers. Many thanks also to all the coaches we have trained in the last five years. Their insights have helped us to understand coaching better.

Many thanks to Sandy Vilas, Pamela Richarde and Laura Whitworth, who helped us in our research, and to Otto Laske, who helped our thinking considerably in developmental coaching.

Our thanks also to our editor at A & C Black, Lisa Carden, for supporting the book throughout.

Special thanks to our daughter, Amanda, who will be two when this book is published, for being such a wonderful coach for us.

And finally, as always, there was some music that we particularly enjoyed during writing this book. Our thanks in particular to Damien Rice, Nara Leão, Iron and Wine and J. S. Bach for inspiring us.

Joseph O'Connor and Andrea Lages
São Paulo, July 2007

PART ONE

1 COACHING ON THE EDGE OF CHAOS

'If we treat people as they are, we make them worse. If we treat them as they ought to be, we help them to become what they are capable of becoming.'

Goethe

In 2004 we gave our first coaching course in Santiago, Chile. The group consisted mostly of managers, who were keen and attentive. A weak sun shone through the white curtains that covered windows of the Radisson Hotel, and outside, the Andes that form such a wonderful backdrop to the city were struggling to assert themselves through a polluted autumn mist. On the first morning of the course, we gave an overview and short history of coaching. 'Coaching,' we began, 'comes from an old Anglo-Saxon word for a carriage, something that takes you from where you are to where you want to be.' A hand went up in the group; someone wanted to comment.

'It also comes from the old French word "*coche*", meaning a carriage,' said François, a participant who was to become a good friend. The temptation for Joseph to fight for the historical pride of England against the

French was tremendous, but he managed to resist. We thanked François for this extra piece of new information. Later, as we further researched the origin of the word 'coaching', we discovered something even more interesting.

There was a town called Kocs in medieval Hungary, near the walled town of Komárom. It held a strategic position in the transport network and was the Heathrow airport of its day. Many carriages stopped at Kocs on their way through central Europe and, because of its position, it was a lively trading centre. Not surprisingly, it started to make carriages. During the 15th century, the wheelwrights of the town began to build a horse-drawn vehicle with a steel spring suspension. This 'kocsi szeker', as the Hungarians called it, or 'cart of Kocs', very soon became popular all over Europe. It was the business-class way to travel through central Europe, comfortable and stylish. Soon these carriages were known by the name of the town that made them. A 'kocs' was a superior carriage, an elegant way to make a journey in quick time. This is the origin of the word 'coach', and similar words appeared in most European languages. Both Joseph and François were right and we discovered a great metaphor, because coaching is not just a way to reach your destination, but also the best and most elegant way to travel.

WHAT IS COACHING?

Let's start with this question, before looking at how coaching works. Coaching is a form of consultation to help the client. There are three main forms of a helping consultation based on how much responsibility the client has in the process.

First, there is the *expert model*, where the client buys expertise and has no responsibility for the outcome. For example, you buy the services of an architect to design your house and project-manage the construction. He does all the work, hiring the builders and decorators. You pay the bills and then you live in your house.

Second, there is the *medical model* of doctor and patient, where the client has a limited responsibility. Usually this is to take any prescribed medicine and follow instructions.

Third, there is the *process consultation model*, where the client has complete responsibility. Process consultation is defined as 'The creation of a relationship with the client that permits the client to perceive, understand

and act on the process events that occur in the client's internal and external environment, in order to improve the situation defined in the problem' [1]. This is an excellent definition of coaching, because it deals with relationship and process. Coaching is a form of process consultation [2] where the coach's main task is to help clients understand their way of generating problems, not to solve them.

Coaching is a means to an end, to help people lead a full and satisfying life, and has many possible definitions. To get the most comprehensive view of coaching, we need to take a number of perspectives. There is a broad consensus in the many books and schools of coaching, with the following being some typical definitions:

⇨ '. . . Sustained cognitive, emotional and behavioural changes that facilitate goal attainment and performance enhancement in one's work or in one's personal life' [3].
⇨ '. . . The art of facilitating the performance, learning and development of another' [4].
⇨ '. . . Equipping people with the tools, knowledge and opportunities they need to develop themselves and become more effective' [5].
⇨ '. . . Coaching is unlocking a person's potential to maximize their own performance. It is helping them to learn rather than teaching them' [6].
⇨ '. . . Coaching is a powerful relationship for people making important changes in their lives' [7].
⇨ '. . . Helping a person change in the way they wish and helping them go in the direction they want to go. Coaching supports a person at every level in becoming who they want to be and being the best they can be' [8].
⇨ '. . . Coaching is about learning. . . the coach and coachee enter into a learning partnership together' [9].

There are many more definitions like these. They are pointers to help you look in the right direction; they give clues, not answers. What are they pointing at? What can we take from these definitions? They are all abstract, because they are taken out of context, but they show a common idea, a basic architecture of coaching. These definitions contain four important elements in coaching – change, concern, relationship and learning. We will take a brief look at each in turn.

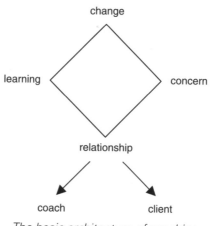

The basic architecture of coaching

CHANGE

Change implies direction and development, moving towards something better, either because you do not like what you have, or because you are attracted towards something better. Clients may seek change or have it forced upon them. Either way, they need to manage it in the best way. They may not know how to do this or have tried and failed. What needs to change in the client to deal with an outward change of circumstances? Thinking, emotions and behaviour.

CONCERN

Second, clients have a concern; some imbalance in their life, a problem, issue or goal they want to achieve. Life has made a demand that their current habits of thinking, feeling and behaviour cannot meet satisfactorily. They are not where they want to be and it bothers them. Many clients are not at all clear where they want to be, but they know very well they are not there yet.

> *You cannot separate the concern from the person who has it.*

RELATIONSHIP

Thirdly, coaching creates a powerful relationship – a partnership. Every client is unique, and the coach needs to treat him or her as such. The relationship needs to be one of trust, and the quality of the relationship coach and client create together is a determinant of how successful the coaching will be.

> *Coaches deal with clients, not problems.*

LEARNING

The fourth support is learning. Coaching helps clients learn and to become better learners in two different ways: first, learning a particular skill, or how to solve a particular problem; second, learning how to learn, how to be a problem solver. Coaching fosters the capacity for self-directed learning and personal growth as well as helping clients to solve problems, make decisions or achieve goals. Unless clients become learners and look at the world with new eyes, they will always be dependent on someone else for guidance, whether it be parent, teacher, boss or coach. Clients need to be able to generalize from a problem; they need not just to solve the problem that is confronting them, but to look critically at their thinking that gave rise to the problem in the first place. We shall discuss both types of learning in depth later in the book.

THE COACH AND CLIENT

Coaching does not happen without people; coach and client must be included in any definition of coaching. The coaching process is created moment by moment as they work together. Shared expectations are crucial. For example, if clients demand that the coach tells them what to do and threaten to leave if the coach does not comply, then clearly coaching cannot happen. Similarly, the coach should behave like a coach, and not tell clients what to do or give them solutions. A coach also needs to have certain supporting beliefs and values to help clients make the changes they want. Coaches need skills, a presence and a level of development to help their clients.

Coaches ask questions rather than give answers, because questions lead to learning and answers may not. Perhaps the first coach was the Greek philosopher Socrates (469–399 BC), who, rather than arguing with people, would ask them questions that led them to examine their own position and assumptions, thereby changing their own thinking for themselves.

This basic architecture is common to many other helping professions such as therapy, teaching and mentoring. The differences between coaching and these other professions is explained in the Appendix.

THE BOUNDARIES OF COACHING

Coaching is not normally used for young children, and for good reason. Coaching assumes the client can reflect on their own thinking and assume social responsibility. Young children cannot do this; they are not sufficiently developed.

Coaching is also not suitable for clients with serious mental or physical health problems. It is not a form of psychotherapy nor a substitute for it. Clients need to be functioning in their life and work before they consult a coach. They may not be functioning very well, but they will have concerns rather than breakdowns. Coaching is about mental development, not mental health. If clients are physically ill, then they should see a doctor to deal with their symptoms. They may take decisions about their illness as a result of the coaching, but coaching is not designed to deal with physical illness directly.

A coach should never deal with clients with serious emotional or psychological problems. These individuals need a therapist.

SPECIALIST KNOWLEDGE

The coach does not need to have specialist knowledge or expertise in the field in which the client operates. The client is the expert in that domain. In business coaching this means that the coach is like a consultant who can operate in many different types of company. Coaches can go from a software company to a linen manufacturer, from a restaurant owner to a librarian; they do not need to know exactly how the client's business works. They do need to know how a business operates in general, but the client is the expert on the specifics.

However, in practice, both formal and informal research suggests that executive clients look for a coach who has experience at their own management level, and if possible within their business, or one similar. They pay more attention to this than to certification. So, an experienced coach can find a niche in an industry; pragmatism reinforces success.

Knowledge of the client's business may seem like a good thing, but it can make coaching more difficult. If you have experience in a field, you may be tempted to give ready answers out of that knowledge instead of *listening to the client*. Then you will be coaching a problem instead of your clients. For example, we have had clients who wanted to write a book. We have written several, so it would be easy to start giving advice: 'Well, have you thought of writing down your goals for the book, imagine what the publisher wants, what the reader will get. . . etc.' This is floating expertise; it comes from the coach and is directed at their idea of the problem and may not help the clients write the particular book they want to write in the particular way they want to write it.

Expert knowledge and experience can be a barrier for the coach, who must listen to clients and deal with their concerns in the way that works for the client, not the way that worked for the coach. The coach's solution was in the past. The client is in the present.

Expertise in the area of the client's problem can make coaches take things for granted. They may assume they understand the problem and will 'fill in the blanks' from their own experience without realizing. A coach needs a 'beginner's mind'. They need to challenge the clients' assumptions about the concern and they can't do that if they share the same assumptions. It is a considerable challenge for the coach to use any specialist knowledge they have as a resource, rather than a barrier to their coaching.

> *You cannot separate the skill from the person who has it.*

COACH CREDIBILITY

This brings us to coach credibility. Clients need to respect the coach. They must be convinced that the coach is both sincere (keeps promises) and reliable (delivers what is promised). When the coach does both of these consistently, the client will trust the coach. The word 'trust' comes from an Old Norse word meaning 'support'. Someone you trust is someone you know will support you; they have demonstrated that they are strong enough to do so. Trust is not a thing, but a process, a relationship, something that is renewed and re-created from session to session. It takes time to build but may be lost in an instant. While a good relationship can sometimes be built in minutes, trust usually takes much longer.

Trust is created from two elements. First, the coach needs to be *sincere*, that is, genuine in their actions and intentions, with no hidden agenda. When they say 'yes' out loud, they are also saying 'yes' in their head and in their body.

Second, the coach needs to be *reliable*. This means they are able to do what they say, in the time agreed, to a satisfactory standard. Both are necessary for trust. A person who is reliable and not sincere will make a lot of promises but not really mean them. A person who is sincere but not reliable will genuinely want to help, but not be capable. For example, a child may be very sincere in his wish to operate a lawnmower, but with no experience, and therefore no competence, it would be dangerous to let him try on the basis of sincerity alone.

Trust is also specific to a particular domain. You can trust someone to do a great negotiation in a meeting, but not necessarily to be on time for it.

The coach's credibility also depends on whether they are a role model for the kind of changes that the client wants to make. The coach's whole way of being has an effect on the client. Coaches need not have gone through the same problem as their clients, but if they have, they need to have dealt with it in a way that worked for them. Then they become an embodiment of the change that the clients wish for. Example is the most

Sincerity ⟶

Low sincerity, high reliability Low trust because while the coach is able to keep promises, he does not.	*High sincerity high reliability* Trust established. The coach is both capable and willing to keep his promises.
Low reliability, low sincerity No trust; coach not willing and not able to keep promises.	*Low reliability, high sincerity* Little trust; coach wants to keep promises but is not able to.

Reliability

powerful form of leadership. It is one way that clients judge reliability. 'If they can't make it work for them, how can they help me?' is the client's unspoken question. If a coach keeps vacillating and is unable to make a decision, then clients will not be convinced a coach can help them with their own decision-making. If a coach is trying to deal with the same problem as a client brings, then it is both ethical and intelligent for the coach to decline to take on that client.

THE STATE OF COACHING NOW

At the time of writing, executive coaching is a billion-dollar industry. Eighty-eight percent of European companies and ninety five percent of UK companies use coaching according to a recent survey [10]. Forty percent of *Fortune 500* companies also use coaching, and ninety-five percent of these companies say that their use of coaching has increased in the last five years. Ninety-nine percent of organizations polled said coaching can deliver tangible benefits to individuals and organizations. Ninety-six percent said coaching is an effective way to promote organizational learning. Ninety-two percent said that when coaching is managed effectively, it has a positive impact on the organization's bottom line. The number of coaches working worldwide is in the region of 70,000. There are over 200 coach-training organizations in the world and this increases every month. [11]

Coaching is growing, then – but where did it come from? We will explore the history in the next section.

REFERENCES

1 Schein, E. (1988) *Process Consultation, Lessons for Managers and Consultants Volume 1 and 2*
2 Schein, E. (1999) *Process Consultation Revisited*
3 Douglas, C. & McCauley, C.D. (1999) *Formal Developmental Relationships: A Survey of Organisational Practices*, Human *Resource Development Quarterly* 10
4 Downey, Myles. (1999) *Effective Coaching*
5 Peterson, D. and Hicks, M. (1999) *Strategic Coaching, Five ways to get the most Value, Human Resources Focus* Volume 76, No.2

6 Whitmore, J. (2002) *Coaching for Performance*
7 Whitworth, L., Kimsey-House, H. & Sandahl, P. (1998) *Co-Active Coaching*
8 O'Connor, J. & Lages, A. (2004) *Coaching with NLP*
9 Sieler, A. (2003) *Coaching to the Human Soul*
10 Auerbach, Jeffrey. (2005) *Seeing the Light: What Organisations Need to Know About Executive Coaching*
11 www.peer.ca/coachingschools.html

2 THE HISTORY OF COACHING: THE PEOPLE

'The world is full of magical things patiently waiting for our wits to grow sharper.'

Bertrand Russell

THE EVOLUTION OF COACHING

Coaching involves two people meeting to grow and learn psychologically, so there have always been coaches. Socrates was a forerunner – his method of asking questions to help seekers find an answer for themselves still bears his name (the Socratic method). But many people have filled the role of coach through the ages: priests and philosophers, artists and professors, and, of course, parents.

The coaching movement as we now know it did not spring up from nothing, but has evolved as a methodology for change since the 1980s. The present is moulded from the past, and to understand coaching we need to look at its history. As animals evolve to adapt to their environment, so social movements like coaching evolve to fit into an environmental niche. In this and the next chapter, we will explore some of the history, the fossil record that will help us understand what coaching is today. There is surprisingly little published about the origins of coaching, perhaps because coaching is too young to be concerned with its past.

However, there are several ways that we can explore coaching's history. One way is to ask the people who helped make it and get their subjective reports. What did it mean for them? What do they remember of the time they were involved? What were they thinking and what were they trying to achieve?

A second way is to describe the process from the outside and get an overview. How did the structure of coaching evolve? What were the elements that went into it? This will be different from the subjective reports, because what people achieve does not always match what they *want* to achieve.

Finally, we can look at the context, the social environment in which coaching grew up. What were the social forces involved, what was it about the culture and the time that encouraged it to grow?

These three viewpoints will help us to understand how coaching evolved, and perhaps give us a clue about the direction it will take. We will use all three methods to consider coaching in this and the next chapter.

COACHING AS A MEME

The evolutionary biologist Richard Dawkins [1] coined the term 'meme' to describe a unit of cultural information that can be transferred from one mind to another. Simple examples are fashion and music; the ideas get transmitted and people act accordingly. People come into contact with them, like them, use them and pass them on, both by example and by telling others.

Coaching was (and still is) a meme. Memes spread just like biological mutations: if they fit with the cultural mores and values, they flourish; if they are at odds with the times, they wither and become extinct. They are like seeds that will grow if they are given the right environment. They also need a means by which to travel; not all methodologies of change have spread so far and so fast and with so much success to other countries.

COACHING IN SPORT

Jumping five centuries from our Hungarian town, during which people helped each other learn and develop under a variety of names, we arrive in the 20th century, when coaching centred on sport. A coach was a skilled trainer who helped athletes, a kind of sports teacher. You didn't have a teacher of tennis or squash – you had a 'coach', who was a mixture of mentor, motivator and mental trainer. Teams also had coaches. They were always good players, although not necessarily the best, because the skills of training and motivating others do not always go with high achievement in a sport.

THE INNER GAME

A sports coach would tell players what to do, monitor the result, give feedback, and 'coach' them to be better, with a mixture of encouragement and structured tuition. Then, in 1974, an extremely influential book was published – *The Inner Game of Tennis*, by Timothy Gallwey [2]. This was a tipping point for the start of coaching as we know it today.

Gallwey's book was revolutionary in its approach to tennis, and he subsequently applied a similar approach to many different fields. *The Inner Game of Work*, of *Golf* and of *Music* have since been successfully published, all authored or co-authored by Gallwey.

In *The Inner Game of Tennis*, Gallwey argued that the tennis player faces two opponents. One is the outer opponent on the other side of the net. Your job is to beat him, and his job is to bring out the best in you. The inner opponent is much trickier and harder to defeat, because it knows all your weaknesses and problems. This inner opponent has an arsenal of weapons such as self-doubt, distraction and inner conversations which stop players performing at their best. It whispers in your ear, 'Oh no, my opponent is looking good, I am not doing well, I might lose. . .' or sometimes, 'Hey! I am playing really well, I think I am going to win this. . .' Both take you from the present moment when you need to concentrate on hitting the ball coming at you from the other side of the net. Any top athlete will tell you that congratulating yourself for being in 'the zone' is exactly what pops you out of it. Your inner opponent distracts you, sabotages you and tells you how to play instead of simply letting you play. The inner game is played in the mind of the player and the opponent is himself or herself.

Gallwey's book brought together elements from humanistic psychology, Buddhist thinking, sports psychology and the idea of programming your unconscious, in a skilful blend of practical advice with a simple structure. It had enormous influence and arguably was the first tentative step of the infant coaching profession. However, Gallwey never went on to train coaches; that was for others.

ESALEN AND EST

Gallwey was a graduate of Harvard University majoring in English literature, where he also captained the tennis team. After serving as an officer in the US navy, he worked as a tennis coach in the 1970s. He started what he called 'yoga' tennis at the John Gardiner Tennis Ranch at the sports centre that was part of the Esalen Institute. Surrounded by spectacular mountain forest scenery in Big Sur, south of San Francisco on the Pacific coast in California, Esalen was the most important centre of humanistic psychology and multidisciplinary studies at the time. It was (and still is) the spiritual home of the human potential movement, was founded in 1962 by Michael Murphy and Dick Price, and soon became well known for running experiential workshops using a blend of eastern and western philosophies. Teachers at the Institute included Aldous Huxley, Abraham Maslow, Carl Rogers and B. F. Skinner. The three main influences on neuro-linguistic programming, Fritz Perls, Virginia Satir and Gregory Bateson, all taught there, as did Richard Feynman, Moshe Feldenkrais, Joseph Campbell, Carlos Castaneda, Fritjof Capra, Deepak Chopra and Bob Dylan.

Here is the Esalen statement of purpose:

'Esalen Institute exists to promote the harmonious development of the whole person. It is a learning organization dedicated to continual exploration of the human potential, and resists religious, scientific and other dogmas. It fosters theory, practice, research, and institution-building to facilitate personal and social transformation and, to that end, sponsors seminars for the general public; invitational conferences; research programs; residencies for artists, scholars, scientists, and religious teachers; work-study programs; and semi-autonomous projects.'

In 1971, Werner Erhard established EST training at Esalen. EST (Latin for 'it is') was an awareness-training programme for large groups. It was very popular, was attended by approximately a million people, and ran until 1981, when it was replaced by 'The Forum'. In this new training, people coached each other on a one-to-one basis. It then became known as 'The Landmark Forum'. Landmark Education purchased the intellectual property of Werner Erhard and Associates, and continues to run training sessions in many countries. Fernando Flores was involved in EST and knew Erhard. Flores' ideas were later developed by Julio Ollala and became the basis of ontological coaching.

Werner Erhard's ideas and approach to self-development training were very important at the time. One of his sayings was 'Create your future from your future, not your past.' Timothy Gallwey was Erhard's tennis coach. However, although Erhard introduced the word 'coaching' into EST, he was not interested in training coaches. Werner Erhard has been described as the second most important influencer of coaching of all time [3]. Only one person in the coaching world gets more testimonials, and that is Thomas Leonard.

THOMAS LEONARD

Thomas Leonard [4], who arguably did the most to found the discipline of coaching, was Budget Director for Landmark Education in the United States in the early 1980s and was thoroughly familiar with their training. However, Landmark worked with groups, and Leonard wanted to work with individuals. Leonard was a financial adviser by profession, and when he worked with individuals on their finances, he found that they wanted more than just financial advice. Finances were often just the tip of the iceberg. People wanted their lives sorted out as well as their finances. Leonard started to work with clients on a one-to-one basis to help them better themselves, and he used his psychological knowledge from many different fields. And, in his experimentation, a coaching methodology began to form.

In 1988, Leonard began teaching a course called 'Design Your Life' and founded what he called the 'College for Life Planning' the following year. Coaching developed from life planning and was not research based; it grew out of the creativity of a group of like-minded people led by Thomas Leonard at the beginning of the 1990s. They worked on the theme of coaching and they were passionate about it. Among these people were Laura Whitworth, who was at Thomas Leonard's first life planning seminar in 1988, and who also worked in the EST accounts department, Henry Kimsey-House, Katherine House, Frederick Hudson, Cheryl Richardson, Sandy Vilas, Peter Reding, Terrie Lupberger, Pam Weiss, Kathleen Merker, Pamela Richarde and Fran Fisher. Julio Olalla began the Newfield Network in 1991 and together with Rafael Echeverria worked with ontological coaching, which has spread throughout Spain and South America.

Coaching developed mainly in the United States during the 1990s, and spread mostly by word of mouth; there was little overt selling. Thomas Leonard was brilliant at creating ideas and theories; he was extremely analytical and also prescriptive in the way he applied them. A classic creative genius, he was prolific with ideas and would often withdraw for a time to recharge and recuperate. Leonard did not want to train coaches; he closed the Institute of Life Planning in 1991. A year later, Laura Whitworth opened the Coach Training Institute (CTI); this was when a group of professional coaches met for the first time. Leonard founded CoachU in 1992, creating an edge of competition and energy between it and CTI that kept them both on their toes, although Laura and Thomas remained friends as well as professional colleagues.

Leonard also started the International Coach Federation (ICF) in 1994, but a number of other people wanted a professional association of coaches and to take the ICF in a different direction to the one Leonard was interested in. So, Leonard withdrew from the ICF, which merged in 1997 with the Personal and Professional Coaches Association (PPCA) to create the ICF as it is in 2007. The vision of coaching as a professional organization was very important. There have been many personal development movements, but these were nearly all privately run and never gained the influence that coaching did. The Association of Coach Training Institutes (ACTO) [5] was founded in 1999 by eight of the original US training institutes.

At the outset, coaching and coach training was done mostly by telephone classes. This was innovative. Until then, most training had been carried out face to face in large groups using the EST model. With teleclasses, training could take place at a distance, and many more people could be trained for less effort and cost. Coaching continues to use teleclasses and now uses web conferencing too.

Although coaching developed first in the United States, it is far from being an American movement, and ontological coaching, in particular, is well developed in Spain and Latin countries. Sir John Whitmore took the inner game and coaching ideas to Europe and the United Kingdom during the 1990s and applied them specifically to business [6]. In 1999 the Coaching Academy was founded in the UK, in 2000 the European Coaching Institute was established and in 2001 the International Coaching Community (ICC) was founded in Brazil.

Thomas Leonard was an entrepreneur of ideas and founder of organizations, but once he had created them, he had little interest in running them. He sold CoachU in 1996 to Sandy Vilas, and founded Coachville in 2001. Both Coachville and CoachU are still operating as coach training institutes. Thomas Leonard died in 2003 at the young age of 47.

The ideas of coaching also started appearing in popular culture during the 1980s. For instance, the 1984 film *The Karate Kid* showed Daniel, a young boy being coached to become a karate champion by a mysterious Mr Miyagi. Mr. Miyagi is no ordinary sports coach. He teaches Daniel by giving him mundane tasks, like painting a fence and polishing a car, to develop his fighting skills. And, most importantly, he teaches Daniel that the greatest skill is the skill to master yourself; without that the others do not matter. He helps Daniel conquer his own pride and impatience, and only then does Daniel defeat his karate opponent, who is also the bully who has been tormenting him.

A popular book that took up the same theme of eastern martial arts was *Zen in the Art of Archery* [7], first published in 1953 and then republished in 1981 as coaching was growing in strength. The author was a German professor of philosophy named Eugen Herrigel who had taught philosophy in Japan in the 1920s and studied *kyudo*, the art of Japanese archery.

Herrigel says in his book, 'The archer ceases to be conscious of himself as the one who is engaged in hitting the bull's-eye which confronts him. This state of unconsciousness is realized only when, completely empty and rid of the self, he becomes one with the perfecting of his technical skill, though there is in it something of a quite different order which cannot be attained by any progressive study of the art.' Herrigel's ideas fit perfectly with coaching – defeating the inner opponent in order to achieve the highest performance.

THE TIPPING POINT

The idea of a 'tipping point' was introduced into popular culture by Malcolm Gladwell [8]. A tipping point is a critical event that makes a meme spread widely. It is the start of the meme epidemic, and comes from a proportionally small cause or causes. The change seems to happen in one dramatic moment. At the tipping point there is a sudden and seemingly unexpected increase in popularity; the meme spreads exponentially.

In his book *The Tipping Point*, Gladwell distinguishes three types of people who are necessary for the rapid and successful spread of an idea: connectors, mavens (experts, in other words) and salespeople.

Connectors are people who know a lot of influential people. It looks as though Werner Erhard was a connector. He knew and brought together a galaxy of humanistic psychological stars.

Mavens know a lot; they accumulate knowledge. Thomas Leonard, as well as being a highly creative person, seems to have been a maven. He had knowledge from many different fields and he brought it together in new and interesting ways.

Salespeople are good at selling. But selling is more than making a good speech about your product. It is the ability to appeal to another's values, to show them how your product benefits them from *their* point of view. There are no obvious salespeople in the history of coaching, because coaches deal with other people's values and goals. We think coaching sold itself through its coaches. With an intangible product, the salesperson represents the product, and the coaches did not just sell coaching, they embodied it.

The tipping point for coaching was probably when it moved inside business organizations around 1995 both in the United States and in Europe. IBM was the first large company to use coaching, and this took coaching from being a personal development vehicle for individuals to a way of developing people in business. Until then, the humanistic psychologies seemed useful to help individuals be happier in their life, but there was little or no business interest. Business was not hostile to these psychological ideas – a happier and more developed employee would probably work better and be more productive, but this seemed impossible to prove. In many ways, business coaching is the human potential movement gone corporate.

DIVERSE CULTURAL INFLUENCES

What else helped the coaching tipping point? Well, we know that coaching was influenced by many different elements, both geographic and cultural. We have an obvious United States influence from Timothy Gallwey and Thomas Leonard, together with a western practical and utilitarian approach. Gallwey in turn was strongly influenced by Buddhist philosophy, especially in his emphasis of unjudgmental awareness. So, there is an influence of eastern thinking in coaching, with its balancing emphasis on *being* as well as *doing*. Other schools have taken this up, the ICC and ontological coaching being two examples. John Whitmore's book and the GROW model have been influential from the UK. Fernando Flores, Francisco Varela and Humberto Maturana have all influenced the development of ontological coaching. All three were Chilean, although Varela lived in Paris and took French nationality. So, coaching has a South American influence, too.

These many and varied influences make coaching more grounded than many business approaches. There have been many 'flavour of the month' management approaches, but they are limited – to a month. Coaching has been self-sustaining; it has never made any unrealistic or outrageous claims, nor has it been held up as the panacea for all management ills (although this is now beginning to happen, unfortunately).

Coaching has no gurus – no charismatic figure spreading the word so that people associate the method with one figurehead rather than with the results. Charismatic gurus attract attention and can spread their ideas quickly, but no one is perfect, and if you look closely enough, all gurus have feet of clay or even baser material, because they are human. So, their followers perpetuate not just the good things about the guru, but also the bad. The situation is usually even worse if there are two founders, because they inevitably split up and disagree, and then you have two parallel and hostile approaches both claiming to be the 'right' path. Even with only one guru, there tends to be an attitude of the 'one true church' of the guru, and this gives rise to factions and fighting. Coaching lacks gurus, and we believe this is a big advantage.

Another important influence was the acceptance of coaching by academia and professional education institutions. The people involved at the beginning in the 1990s had a vision and faith in their fledgling profession, so coaching has a common theoretical basis and a set of standards and ethics, two important criteria for a profession. Several coaching courses are now established at respected universities in America, Europe and Australasia. Today, what started as experiential and experimental is coming of age as being evidence based.

The Coaching Time Line

Before 1971	Coaching applied to training athletes on a one-to-one or team basis
1971	EST established by Werner Erhard at Esalen
1974	*The Inner Game of Tennis* published
1975	
1976	NLP founded
1977	Fernando Flores begins ontological coaching
1978–80	EST training replaced by Landmark Forum
1981–2	Thomas Leonard working as budget director of Landmark
1983–7	Thomas Leonard starts the 'design your life' course Laura Whitworth one of the first attendees
1988	Julio Olalla develops ontological coaching Julio Olalla founds the Newfield Institute
1989–90	Thomas Leonard establishes CoachU Laura Whitworth opens CTI *Coaching for Performance* published Inner game and coaching spread to UK and Europe
1991	Thomas Leonard founds the ICF
1992–3	Coaching accepted in business
1994	Thomas Leonard sells CoachU to Sandy Vilas ICF merges with PCCA. Thomas Leonard leaves ICF
1995–6	
1997	
1998–2001	Coaching established in Europe and spreads to Australasia Ontological coaching established in South America and Spain
2001	The ICC founded Undergraduate and postgraduate courses in coaching proliferate

2003	Thomas Leonard dies Integral models applied in coaching. Integral coaching begins
2004–07	Behavioural coaching established in business Positive psychology coaching started by Martin Seligman Increasing acceptance of coaching in universities in the United States, Europe and Australasia Increasing rise of evidence-based coaching

REFERENCES

1   Dawkins, R. (1976) *The Selfish Gene*
2   Gallwey, T. (1974) *The Inner Game of Tennis*
3   Brock, V. (2006) *Who's Who in Coaching – Executive Summary (Privately published)*
4   *www.thomasleonard.com*
5   *www.acto1.com/*
6   Whitmore, J. (1992) *Coaching For Performance*
7   Gladwell, M. (2001) *The Tipping Point*
8   Herrigel, E. (1953) *Zen and the Art of Archery*

3 THE HISTORY OF COACHING: THE TIMES

'All human beings should try to learn before they die what they are running from, and to, and why.'

James Thurber

The four disciplines at the centre of coaching
Humanistic psychology
Eastern philosophy
Constructivism
Linguistic studies

Many creative people were involved in starting and spreading coaching, and the cultural context helped them. Coaching grew rapidly and successfully not only because of the people involved and the strength of the methodology, but also thanks to the climate and culture which received it.

There have been several 'quasi-coaching' psychologies that never came close to replicating the success of true coaching.

The context is important. Malcolm Gladwell calls this the 'stickiness factor' in *The Tipping Point* [1]. Sometimes these factors can be small, seemingly insignificant aspects. On other occasions, the meme is a perfect fit into the context and fills the need at exactly the time the need is being created. This is what we believe happened with coaching, which grew in fertile ground to achieve the position it has now.

In the last chapter we looked at the growth of coaching from the inside – the people who created it and what they did. This chapter looks at coaching from the outside, the culture and context in which it grew, what influenced it, and how it fitted into similar ideas that were evolving at the same time. If coaching is now a big river, what were the tributaries that flowed into it and swelled it to the size it is now? The people who were working in coaching at the beginning could not take the same overview; they were brainstorming and working things out in practice as best they could. The outside view strips away the emotions and shows the shape and growth. What were the influences on coaching? What are the intellectual roots and what other social factors led to its growth? The depth of the roots will give us an idea about the height and strength of the tree.

HUMANISTIC PSYCHOLOGY

Humanistic psychology is one of the principal roots of coaching. It was called the third force because for the first half of the 20th century American psychology was dominated by two schools of thought: behaviourism and psychoanalysis. Behaviourism looked at human beings from the outside and studied what they *did* rather than what they *thought*. Psychoanalysts looked at the inside, the deep motives that were hidden even from the person himself or herself and how these shaped their behaviour. Neither branch looked at a person as they experienced themselves, their values and goals and what it felt like to be human. Psychologists in the 1950s headed by Carl Rogers and Abraham Maslow wanted to build a system of psychology that focused on how people felt and thought about themselves, and what was important to them subjectively. This study was humanistic psychology. It dealt with issues like self-actualization, health, hope, love, creativity and meaning – the understanding of what it means to be human.

Humanistic psychology has several fundamental principles. First, it takes an optimistic view of people. It assumes that people want to grow and develop, and the natural way for humans is to move forward. They want to self-actualize. Human nature is trustworthy, and not a seething mass of base impulses waiting for an opportunity to assert themselves. Abraham Maslow [2] summed it up like this: 'A musician must make music, an artist must paint, a poet must write, if he is to be at peace with himself. What a man can be, he must be. This is the need we may call self-actualization. . . It refers to man's desire for fulfillment, namely to the tendency for him to become actually what he is potentially: to become everything that one is capable of becoming.'

This means that helpers should facilitate their clients' own natural potential for growth, not impose an agenda or force them in any particular direction. This idea is strongly represented in coaching; the coach has no agenda for clients and believes in their ability to solve their own problems.

Principles of humanistic psychology

1 How people experience themselves is a valid psychological perspective.
2 An optimistic view of human nature – people want to self-actualize.
3 Each person is a unique whole.
4 Every person is unique and valuable.
5 Choice is better than no choice. Everyone has choices and wants to exercise those choices.

Humanistic psychology treats people as a whole. It is an integrative psychology, not an analytical one. While we acknowledge that splitting people into parts – mind, body and emotions – can be useful, you can never predict the qualities of the whole from a study of the parts. A study of anatomy will never allow you to understand a living, breathing person, only how the parts of the body are interconnected. Coaching also looks at people as a whole. Life coaching helps them make connections between different parts of their lives, while business coaching is more focused on the working aspect of the client's life.

Humanistic psychology also stresses the uniqueness of the individual. For coaching, there is no formula; one size does not fit everybody. The client is the expert in his or her own experience; everyone is different and those differences must be respected. And humanistic psychology believes that people have choices and want to exercise them. Coaches invite clients to be architects of their own future selves by taking choices and responsibility for those choices.

These principles were reflected in how humanistic psychologists (who were mostly involved in therapy) interacted with clients. Carl Rogers was the pioneer of this new way of relating to clients, which he called 'unconditional positive regard'. It means accepting and valuing clients as they are, and not imposing any of the therapist's ideas or choices on them. Rogers [3] said, 'If I can provide a certain type of relationship, the other person will discover in themselves the capacity to use the relationship for growth and change and personal development will occur.'

Rogers emphasized that the personality of the therapist was important. Therapists need to be genuine and authentic to help the client be authentic in return. 'It is only by providing the genuine reality within me, that the other person can successfully seek for the reality in him. I have found this to be true even when the attitudes I feel are not attitudes with which I am pleased, or attitudes which seem conducive to a good relationship. It seems extremely important to be real' [4]. Authenticity, empathy and valuing the uniqueness of the client are present in coaching; all models emphasize the importance of an open, trusting coaching relationship.

Rogers' ideas profoundly influenced how we think about the relationship between client and therapist, coach and client, parent and child, indeed between any two human beings. It is a relationship where each person is an end in themselves and not a means to an end.

Rogers tried to be completely undirective in his therapy. Coaching is more directive, but still the coach needs to value the person as another unique, equal individual. Coaches do not judge clients, although they do not necessarily agree with them. 'To understand,' as Rogers put it, 'is to forgive.'

Humanistic psychology was the basis of the human potential movement in the 1960s. All the important humanistic psychologists taught at the Esalen Institute: Maslow arrived in Esalen in 1962 and led many workshops there, and Carl Rogers also taught there in the 1970s. Humanistic psychology is one of the foundations of coaching, and Carl Rogers and Abraham Maslow are the grandfathers of coaching.

EASTERN PHILOSOPHY

Coaching initially grew in the United States, with its pragmatic western approach to change, focusing on goals and achievement, so it may seem strange that we count eastern philosophy as an influence on coaching, but we do so for many reasons.

The 1960s saw a tremendous resurgence of interest in Buddhism and eastern thought in the West, which coincided with the rise of humanistic psychology and the human potential movement. Most western philosophy and religion emphasized action and achievement, while the eastern approaches emphasized being. The western mindset looked for God outside in the material world (while also trying to subdue it). The eastern approach looked within the person and emphasized direct experience. The West looks to God outside, the East to God inside. The human potential movement was very sympathetic to the eastern approach. Many forms of meditation became popular, the most influential being transcendental meditation (TM) as a means for quieting the mind and finding the still, silent core of the self inside when all internal dialogue is silent. The eastern approach, especially Zen Buddhism, avoided outward trappings of worship and instead embraced self-awareness and paradoxical approaches.

Coaching has many direct and indirect links with eastern thinking. Many eastern approaches were taught at Esalen and integrated into western philosophy. Michael Murphy, a co-founder of Esalen in 1962, practised meditation at the Sri Aurobindo Ashram in south India in the 1950s. Timothy Gallwey, author of The Inner Game of Tennis [5], followed the eastern religious leader Maharaj Ji, now known as Prem Rawat, who founded the Divine Light Mission in the United States when he was a teenage boy in the 1970s. In fact, Gallwey even dedicated The Inner Game of Tennis to Maharaj Ji, as well as to his (Gallwey's) parents.

Ontological coaching (or the 'coaching of being'), which began with Fernando Flores and was further developed by Julio Ollala, uses many self-awareness exercises that are very Buddhist in form and intention. Self-awareness means observing in a non-attached way without identifying with any part of the experience that you are observing. Once you identify with it, you are caught by it. Non-attachment is the basis of Buddhism. In James Flaherty's book on ontological coaching [6] there is a section on self-observation that would not be out of place in a book on meditation. Coaching encourages clients to look inside themselves for answers. It emphasizes non-judgmental awareness. A Buddhist might say that coaching has developed as a way to release people from their self-created illusions and foster non-attachment to their problems.

CONSTRUCTIVISM

'Man does not have a nature, but a history. Man is no thing, but a drama. His life is something that has to be chosen, made up as he goes along, and a human consists in that choice and invention. Each human being is the novelist of himself, and though he may choose between being an original writer and a plagiarist, he cannot escape choosing. . . He is condemned to be free.'

Heinz von Foerster [7]

Constructivism develops the idea that we actively make or 'construct' our world from our experiences. We are not passive receivers of what is 'out there' but are active creators of our experiences. We are actors in the drama, not spectators in the wings. The idea that there is a reality out there just waiting to be discovered and you can be right or wrong about it is called 'the myth of the given'. We do not see the world as it is; we see the world as we are.

Scientific modernists see themselves as citizens of an independent universe, whose rules and customs they may eventually discover. Constructivists see themselves as participants in a conspiracy, whose customs, rules and regulations they are helping to invent.

Here is a scenario that illustrates this neatly.

Three tennis umpires are sitting in a bar drinking zinfandel and watching a game on television. They are bemoaning the fact that no one appreciates them or understands their work properly.

The first one says, a little hesitantly, 'When I am umpiring a match, I call things as I see them. That's all I do.'

The second one takes a sip of wine and says proudly, 'OK, but I call points as they are.' The first umpire looks at him admiringly.

They both look at the third umpire, who pauses for effect and then says, 'They ain't nothing until I call them.'

The first umpire is probably a subjectivist – nothing exists outside the human mind that is experiencing it. The second umpire believes in the myth of the given, even though he probably acknowledges he can be wrong about what is given.

The third umpire is a constructivist.

We are born into a strange world; we create it as we explore and discover it. We make meaning of our experiences and we interpret what happens through our history. We observe the world. A world without an observer is inconceivable. The world needs an observer, they go together; without the observer to observe and describe, what is there? And the observer is also part of the world that she observes.

We are not independent observers who watch the world go by; we are actors in the drama of mutual interaction, in the give and take of human relations. There is not one world to be known, so the coach does not try to give the client the 'right answer'; the coach does not know, from all the possible answers, which one is 'right' for the client. The right answer does not exist – either 'out there' or anywhere else. A coaching session is not a desperate search to find it. Instead, the answer comes into being and is constructed from the interaction of the coach and client, the learning they both make, and the understanding that comes from the client acting differently in the world.

Some coaching clients come to coaching feeling stuck, with little influence on the course of their lives. The coach does not try to make their life better, nor does he or she tell them how to make their life better, but helps them to see, first, that they are helping to create the life they are experiencing, and second, how they do that. Then they can change it by doing something different.

Constructivism has thoroughly undermined the idea of scientific objectivity, where the observer carries out an experiment but is not part of that experiment. Quantum physics has shown that the observer is part of *every* experiment. The clearest example is an experiment to try to discover the 'true' nature of light. An experiment set up to detect that light behaves as a wave shows that light *is* a wave. When an experiment is set up to prove that light consists of particles, then sure enough, that is the result. In quantum physics, an observer collapses a world of possibilities into one in the act of observation.

The human equivalent is called 'confirmation bias', which means we seek (and find) confirmatory evidence to support our existing beliefs and ignore or reinterpret other evidence. A Buddhist sees confirmation bias as one of the main pillars that maintain the illusion of certainty. What happens in the brain during confirmation bias was demonstrated by functional magnetic resonance imaging (MRI) by Drew Western and a team from Emory University. They carried out a study of 30 men before the 2004 US presidential elections [8]. Half of the test subjects described themselves as strong Republicans. The other half described themselves as strong Democrats. All the subjects were asked to assess contradictory statements by their preferred candidate, and while they did so, their brainwaves were scanned using MRI. The scans showed that the part of the brain associated with reasoning (the dorsolateral prefrontal cortex) was not involved when assessing the statements. The most active regions of the brain were those involved in processing emotions (orbit frontal cortex), conflict resolution (anterior cingulate cortex) and making judgments about moral accountability (posterior cingulate cortex).

Western summarized the experimental results as follows: 'None of the circuits involved in conscious reasoning was particularly engaged. Essentially, it appears as if partisans twirl the cognitive kaleidoscope until they get the conclusions they want, and then they get massively reinforced for it, with the elimination of negative emotional states and activation of positive ones. . . Everyone from executives and judges to scientists and politicians may reason to emotionally biased judgments when they have a vested interest in how to interpret "the facts". '

We construct our world and we have a vested interest in maintaining the construction we make. This is why we often have a secret satisfaction at a misfortune of another, provided we predicted it. We are not pleased at their misfortune, but we are pleased that we were right in our prediction.

Constructivism implies action, because acting will change not only the world but also yourself. Every time we act, we change the world, and we change ourselves. The only way to understand fully is to take action. Coaching has a strong emphasis on action. Insight is not enough. (Buddhists say, 'Insight is the ultimate illusion.') Coaches ask clients to act to change their circumstances and therefore themselves. This is why tasking (agreeing small action steps with the client) is so important in coaching.

What is the implication for coaching? The vision of our limits is the limit of our vision. We see our own limits, not the limits of the world. By looking further and further, beyond the horizon you see and the next horizon beyond that and the next, what happens? What do you see? The back of your head. The further we look, the more we are brought up against our own limits. The way to see further is to get ourselves out of blocking our own way.

What does this mean for coaching? It means coaches challenge their clients' confirmation bias. It means coaches must continually ask clients' to push through their perceived limits in order to better their circumstances and change their world. The coach must be a model in this respect. The limits of coaching depend to some extent on the limits of the coach. It is extremely difficult for coaches to help clients explore a level that they have not reached themselves.

LINGUISTIC STUDIES

Language is the way we communicate and is probably one of the most remarkable human inventions. Linguistic studies over the past 20 years have shown the crucial role that language plays in constructing our reality. It gives us great freedom – but this comes at a price. Through language, we communicate our experience in ways that depend on the construction of language itself, rather than on the experience that gave rise to it. We construct our world in terms of how things relate and what they mean by using language to communicate.

We see, hear, touch, taste and smell through our senses. Even as we write this, it is an example of how language distorts the world. What are 'senses'? Do they exist as separate entities apart from what we experience? They are shorthand for how we apprehend experience, they are abstractions plucked out of the flow of the world and used as if they are a pre-existing thing. We often mistake the word for the thing. I might say, 'You made me happy', but this is not the same as 'You made me a coffee' or 'You made the car turn right', even though the linguistic construction is the same. The coffee and the car had no choice, but people can choose their feelings. Although 'you' is the subject of that sentence, it really about the speaker's experience. Ontological coaching and NLP coaching, in particular, have rich models about how the way we use language both limits and expands our world.

How we experience the world depends on our interests, attention and health. We do not register everything we experience; some things we never notice, others we forget immediately. We interpret what we remember and force that rich sensory experience into a linguistic straitjacket, a dribble of words that needs both time and sequence to make sense.

Reflecting upon the magic of language is similar to thinking about how the brain works. You need a brain to think about the brain, and you need language to analyse language. Language truly weaves 'spells', and its sorcery will always stop you understanding its sorcery.

Many coaching clients are at the mercy of the way they verbally describe their experience. They are the servants, not the masters, of language. When coaching clients tell their story, coaches do not know, nor will they ever know, how it 'really' was, because the experience is gone for ever. Coaches listen to their clients describing their experience that has been created by language, with language itself. Coaches need to listen behind the language, to the underlying message and to the whole person – body language, voice tone, what is said, what is not said and *what cannot be said*. For coach and client, language is both the disease and the remedy. Coaches point this out explicitly or implicitly and also use words to generate new, more helpful distinctions. The job of the coach is to take the words and help clients to reflect on them, to get a different perspective, and thus see the world differently. Rephrasing is reseeing. When we can look at the words, they become objective – in other words, outside ourselves – and they no longer control us. So, what they represent does not control us either.

The language clients use reflects their reality. Some clients will describe their experience in the passive tense, saying things like 'This happened to me, that happened to me, I had bad luck.' They see themselves as pushed around by events and other people, without choice. The passive voice ('this was done') in the English language makes no reference to the speaker, whereas the active voice does include the speaker ('I did this'). In the Hebrew language, the word 'luck' is made up of two symbols, one meaning 'place' and the other meaning 'language'. This represents the interesting idea that using the right words at the right time in the right place makes you lucky. When clients use a lot of passive language, they have forgotten that they created their experience, and a coach will point this out, ask them to reflect on it and maybe ask them to use the active voice, to see what difference it makes.

When you learns a new language (and both authors have experience of this – Andrea with English and Spanish, and Joseph with Portuguese), you learn to make new distinctions and to see the world anew. Learning a new language builds another perspective on the world. We will return to this in Part Three when we consider cross-cultural coaching.

THE SPREAD OF COACHING

Business coaching and life coaching spread quickly without any charismatic figures to sell them and both spread mostly by word of mouth. What were the social trends that fuelled this growth?

Social trends that spread coaching
Social isolation
The sovereign individual
The rise of the Internet
Accelerated social change

First, people are looking for support, as traditional means of support have broken down. The importance of the family has declined in western culture. Roles are blurred and the typical family no longer consists of two parents and their children. Many people can no longer get the support they need from their family.

Organized religion has also dramatically declined; it no longer provides the certainty and meaning that it did in the past. There is increased pressure on people and substantial movement into big cities. All these are factors that have contributed to an increasing sense of isolation among many people in developed countries. In the past they might have gone to their priest, or their friends. Now they go to a coach. Coaching is one way that people can find meaning and connection, both as clients and by becoming coaches themselves.

THE SOVEREIGN INDIVIDUAL

This is the 'I' generation of the western world. People want to be recognized and have control over their lives. 'The sovereign individual', the person who has power over his or her own destiny, is an attractive proposition, and coaching offers the promise of achieving it. People want to invest both time and money in themselves; they feel they deserve it. They can invest in themselves without being seen as strange, or selfish, or feeling that there is something wrong with them that needs fixing. People want fulfilment and they feel that they deserve to be happy. They want to have meaning in their life. After a century where the emphasis has been on achievement, on self as an instrument to achieve something, now people want to enjoy themselves, find their own meaning in themselves and not in their achievements. This can be seen in the trend of 'downshifting' where people leave a lucrative but hard-working job for a simpler, much less well paid job where they can work for themselves doing something they love. People want to drive, not be driven.

Many people achieve their professional and financial goals, yet still do not feel fulfilled. Something is missing; they know they can do better and achieve more, so they seek coaching as a way to help them realize their personal potential. The increase in wealth in the United States, Europe and Australasia means that people can afford to pay for it, too.

Coaching rose from the self-development movement and is commercialized and packaged like many self-development courses. 'You deserve to live your dream – now!' has been a powerful message coming from many channels, and coaching has benefited. The coach is for you, for no one else, to work with you on your life, your goals to become who you want to be.

Another trend that feeds the desire to make the most of yourself is the increasing way that everyday life has become public. The state has acquired enormous power to observe, control and influence everyone over the last ten years. This is a powerful trend as governments try to control their citizens and it has been pushed further by terrorist actions, terrorist threats, and the increasing rise of organized crime and the huge amounts of money involved. Most countries see the curtailing of their civil liberties as the inevitable price to be paid for safety. Video and CCTV cameras are ubiquitous. 'Smile, you are being filmed' can be found in hundreds of languages in millions of buildings all over the world. A call to your bank is routinely recorded 'to monitor quality' or for 'training purposes'. Anyone wanting to deposit cash in their bank account is regarded with suspicion and, if the amount is large, automatically reported to state security.

We increasingly accept a blurring of the line between public and private, and so a private space for yourself is precious. Coaching is confidential, at least for the professional coaches who follow a set of ethical principles. There is tremendous growth and interest in online virtual worlds such as Second Life [9] where you can be whoever you want and act in ways you would never do in your 'first life'. Virtual worlds are a playground where people can experiment in safety. Coaching is a way people can explore themselves in safety and in confidentiality.

THE INTERNET

The rise of the Internet has exactly coincided with the rise in coaching. Coaching began using the high technology of its time – the telephone and fax. It grew and has benefited from the Internet in ways other self-development movements have not. Coaching has a very large proportion of its members promoting themselves on the Internet. Individual coaches, business coaching services and coach training courses are all marketed on the Internet. And a flood of e-mails bombards us with nonsensical claims that coaches can achieve a six-figure income in a short time. Although coaching has its share of these ridiculous claims, strange advertising and spam that the Internet has generated, the Internet has also helped legitimate coaching spread internationally in a way that no other self-development or commercial development methodology has done in history.

While the Internet spreads news quickly, it may not be accurate – rumours and inaccuracies spread rapidly, too. In the last five years a serious body of research has grown up to counteract this tendency. The research has been done by academics and research agencies rather than coaches or coaching organizations with an agenda, and this helps people form a better picture of coaching.

THE SPEED OF CHANGE

The Internet is both a signal and a driver of the historically unprecedented speed of change in virtually every field of knowledge in the last 30 years. Many people feel disconnected from what they know; the world they learn about at school bears no resemblance to the world that awaits them when they leave.

The syllabus for schools and colleges is prepared at least a year in advance, and so is often out of date before students even begin their study. Coaching provides 'just in time' help, where and when it is needed.

The speed of change has put stress on many people. Society demands more, technology means we can do more in less time, and soon this becomes normal. Ambiguity and paradox abound, and while there are vast amounts of information, it is often hard to find what is relevant to your question. Try typing 'coaching' into Google (when we did this, it returned over 78 million hits).

In turbulent times, knowledge becomes uncertain. Beliefs, both religious and secular, are challenged daily. We have to deal on a daily basis with circumstances that concern us but which we cannot influence. We need to adapt to shorter time spans and respond to new situations with no previous models to guide us. Adaptation and success are no longer dependent on what you have learned, but on your capacity and speed of learning. It is not what you have done that counts, but your creativity to keep doing it and to build on past success. With the Internet 'flattening the world' [10], there is even less job security; we have to run to stay in the same place. A coach can help people cope with this turbulence.

BUSINESS FACTORS IN THE RISE OF COACHING

Business factors in the rise of coaching
Corporate uncertainty
The need for innovation
Increasing time pressure
The need to develop people
The need to avoid replacement and retraining
The need for new skills for managers
The need for people to learn new skills fast
Targeted just in time individual development
Coaching to support training
Support for top executives

Why did coaching grow so quickly in the 1990s from individual help to an industry service? First, rapid change generates particular problems in business. In the words of management consultant Rosabeth Moss Kanter [11], 'The mean time between decisions is greater than the mean time between surprises' (which we will abbreviate to MTBD > MTBS). So, there is stress in the workplace. Corporate uncertainty has put increasing pressure on employees to work longer hours and achieve ever-greater results. In the past, the family might have helped and supported people under stress at work, but families are more fragmented now. There has always been a certain stigma for businesspeople in seeing a counsellor or a therapist. It implies that there is something wrong with them that needs fixing and that perhaps they cannot do their job well enough. Where do people go for support and help?

Coaching can help an individual deal with stress at work; stress coaching is one of the fastest-growing areas of coaching at the moment. Australians have the highest average number of working hours of any country in the world. They also have the highest growth rate of coaches. Coincidence?

Time pressure is a significant part of the stress. The ability to learn and adapt quickly is more important than being able to work quickly. Coaching is very specific and exactly targeted; it addresses this issue for key people and helps them to be more creative and adapt faster. People need to learn all the time and coaching can support different learning styles more easily than training. Managers are routinely expected to be able to coach their employees as well as do everything else they have done in the past. Sometimes coaching in the workplace is a way of outsourcing managers' responsibilities. This has led to many in-company coaching training courses and coaching being widely used in corporate universities.

People are no longer loyal to their company, but they are loyal to their own career. On average, people will change careers three times in their working lives. Paradoxically, the only way companies can get people to stay with them is to train them and equip them with skills, knowing full well that these skills can be employed in the service of their competitors. But if they do not provide development pathways, people will certainly leave. They need to make their company attractive to people, and also to keep the people they have. Recruiting and training skilled people is extremely expensive and if coaching can save this cost then it is worth it. The cost of finding and training a replacement and avoiding the inevitable drop in work quality that this entails is considerable and makes coaching a good investment. Coaching is also an excellent way of demonstrating a company's loyalty to its employees, developing them and making them more effective. It is a signal to the market that the company is caring.

FLAT ORGANIZATIONS

Flat organizations require targeted, just-in-time individualized development. Managers need to have a much broader repertoire of skills and deal with more people, and more diverse people. Newly promoted individuals have to learn new skills and take on new responsibilities, and they have to do it quickly. Businesses use coaching to help people adjust faster and more easily. A top executive cannot simply step into a new job and work at top-level performance from day one without any support. Coaching is a flexible, responsive approach to executive development, which can be delivered individually. Many executives are finding work as coaches or mentors for younger executives.

Also, coaching is increasingly being used to support training. A survey by the UK's Chartered Institute of Personnel and Development (CIPD) [12] showed that learning at work rather than in the training room was becoming increasingly popular. Coaching can focus on work issues and improve performance in the workplace. When people go off site for training, most of the time the changes are lost quickly when they return. The enthusiasm and new ideas do not survive the 'business as usual' mentality. Fairly soon (usually after a couple of months), the new initiative fades with the energy of the trainees, and things go back to what they were before the training. Management may think, quite unfairly, that the training was not good, so they embark on another type of training and the cycle continues. This is why so much training without subsequent coaching support gives disappointing results, whereas training gives much better results when it is followed up with coaching. It helps the participants keep the ideas and the motivation as well as looking for ways to change the system instead of being beaten by it.

THE IMPORTANCE OF TOP EXECUTIVES

At a time when top executives are traded between companies like football players, it is increasingly recognized that they make a tremendous difference to the success of an organization. The financial cost of a poorly performing executive is immense. Top executives need to make important decisions with little guidance, often with a lot of money hanging on them. They have few people they can confide in, and they are expected to know what to do rather than discuss any issues. It is lonely at the top, and an executive coach can provide an objective and critical sounding board for the executives' thinking. External executive coaches are being increasingly sought to help executives in their decision-making.

Coaching has evolved to fill the niche that the wide-ranging changes in business practice and way of working have created. In the next part of the book we shall look at six of the most widespread coaching models and distil them to find the heart of coaching, the methodology that works in every model.

REFERENCES

1 Gladwell, M. (2000) *The Tipping Point*

2 Maslow, A. (1998) *Toward a Psychology of Being*

3 Rogers, C. (1980) *A Way of Being*

4 Rogers, C. (1951) *Client-Centered Therapy: Its Current Practice, Implications and Theory*

5 Gallwey, T. (1974) *The Inner Game of Tennis*

6 Flaherty, J. (1999) *Coaching – Evoking Excellence in Others*

7 von Foerster, H. (1994) Ethics and Second-Order Cybernetics, *SEHR* 4(2): *Constructions of the Mind*

8 Western, D. (2006) Confirmation Bias (unpublished), presented to the 2006 Annual Conference of the Society for Personality and Social Psychology

9 www.secondlife.com/web

10 Friedman, T. (2005) *The World Is Flat*

11 Kanter, R. Moss. (1983) *The Change Masters: Innovation and Entrepreneurship in the American Corporation*

12 CIPD survey, March 2005, 'Who Learns at Work?'

COACHING FOR DEVELOPMENT

INTEGRATED MENTAL TRAINING
AND POSITIVE PSYCHOLOGY

by Lars-Eric Uneståhl

BACKGROUND

Coaching – and especially coaching for development – is based on the same philosophy and uses the same principles as positive psychology and integrated mental training (IMT). Differences are more in the methods of learning and development. Where coaching emphasizes 'action learning' and 'learning through feedback', positive psychology emphasizes 'reflective learning' and integrated mental training emphasizes 'unconscious learning'.

Positive psychology looks at human beings as self-organizing, self-directed, adaptive entities and steers psychology to focus on two neglected areas:

⇨ developing normal people to increased productivity and well-being
⇨ using developmental resources for problem prevention

IMT is a systematic, long-term developmental training of mental skills, attitudes and processes. It is a cognitive and emotional training with an emphasis on images rather than thoughts and with a focus on detecting resources and development more than problem solving. I developed IMT in the 1960s based on research in:

⇨ **alternative states of consciousness**
⇨ **relationship between body and mind**

The training programmes were tested in co-operation with the various Swedish national and Olympic teams during the 1970s and were introduced into the Swedish school system in the late 1970s as life skills training. They were applied to the areas of health and work in the 1980s and became popular among the general population as a method of personal development from the early 1990s.

Because studies show no correlation between success in school or university and success in life, mental training and coaching became the most important ways to transform abstract knowledge into real competence in dealing with life.

Coaching and IMT are both future oriented, solution focused, action directed and experiential based. Coaching for development is the integration we have made between IMT and coaching in the last decade.

COACHING FOR DEVELOPMENT VERSUS PROBLEM COACHING

These two approaches have different assumptions. Problem coaching assumes the client has all the resources needed to solve the problem. Coaching for development assumes the client often needs to develop new resources, skills and behaviour in order to reach the goal. Coaching for development is based on the same philosophy of change as is found in mental training and in positive psychology, while most areas of society still follow the problem-based or clinical model. In the problem-coaching model, people want to change because of a problem or crisis. Coaching for development is based on the sports model, meaning that you can be satisfied with the present and still want – and be working and training – to reach a better situation.

So, in the problem-coaching model the direction of change is away from the problem, meaning that sometimes the result can be still worse (out of the frying pan into the fire). The emotional basis for the change is mainly dissatisfaction, and there can be a strong resistance to change as clients experience suggestions for change as criticism.

In problem coaching, progress is followed by maintenance and problem solving is followed by inactivity. Coaching for development looks at life as a journey with continuous improvement.

In problem coaching, suggested changes often evoke resistance, as they are interpreted as blame, disbelief and that something is wrong. In coaching for development, safety and security are not in the client's comfort zone, but in the change itself. It also gives the necessary stimulation and challenge important for high quality of life.

Coaching is action oriented and has its basis in learning by doing. Tasking constructs experiences, which through feedback provide adequate changes. While the goal in problem coaching is to return to a 'pre-problem' situation (mostly with the help of retroactive actions), coaching for development uses proactive methods to create a situation which is not only better than the present but also better than the pre-problem conditions. This includes 'problem solving' but without having to work on the problems.

Our brains are more easily ensnared by problem thoughts and images. There are three reasons:

1 **An evolutionary survival mechanism**
2 **The emotional components (emotions like fear grab our mind very easily)**
3 **Problems are often more concrete than goals**

In order to change this perception, coaching for development works to decrease fear and other negative emotions and make goals clear and attractive. One part of that is to learn to think and talk in positive ways and to replace problem words with developmental ones.

COACHING FOR DEVELOPMENT AND PSYCHOCYBERNETICS

In order to make even better progress, coaching for development combines the use of mental training tasks with goal programming. While problem coaching often stops when the clients' goals are clear and value based, coaching for development translates the intellectual goals to images, after which the goals are integrated and programmed. This seems to start an automatic process. The client often reports being more creative, and that they find solutions in an effortless way without conscious problem solving. They reach goals without knowing what took them to the goals.

SUMMARY

Coaching for development and developmental self-coaching will complement ordinary coaching methods in a number of ways. For example:

⇨ Coaching for development works in the same way with clients with problems and clients looking for continuous improvement. Developmental goals often include automatic problem solving.

⇨ Coaching for development uses mental training tasks as homework to detect and develop the resources needed to reach attractive goals.

⇨ Coaching for development uses the imagination to program goals in order to start a cybernetic process as a complement to the action plan and the homework.

Lars-Eric Uneståhl PhD is President of the Scandinavian International University and Professor in Applied Psychology and Mental Training. He is the author of 18 books and many research articles. Lars-Eric has developed numerous training programmes for the development of individuals, teams and organizations.

PART TWO
OVERVIEW: MODELS
OF COACHING

'Sometimes one must travel far to discover what is near.'

Uri Shulevitz

When we began to write this book, we debated whether to go through the main models of coaching first and give the synthesis afterwards, or to give the synthesis first and then go through the models. The first choice would be inductive, getting a general model from specific examples. The second choice would be deductive, with the model first followed by the examples. The thinking process we went through was inductive. We started with the different coaching models and extracted a set of general principles from them. We read widely, we met and debated and talked with coaches from Shanghai to Sydney, from Seattle to Santiago, and we saw that underlying all the forms of coaching there is a shadowy shape that infuses them all.

So, we will give the models and then the conclusions we drew from them, as it is more natural for you to go through the same process as we did. You can follow the detective story that we experienced – although maybe a detective story is not the right metaphor, for no crime has been committed.

Maybe it is more like an Indiana Jones quest in search of treasure. Does the treasure exist and did we find it? Or did we create the treasure by embarking on our quest, believing it would be there? It doesn't matter. One thing was certain – coaching does work, all the different models worked and therefore there had to be a core methodology.

In the following chapters we will examine very different models of coaching which are important and representative of coaching at the time of writing. There are other models, but at the moment they are less prominent. All six have many experienced and committed practitioners, all are influential in the field internationally and inspire good coaching. Coaches follow the model that works for them; a coach must be congruent with the model that they are using.

Inevitably, all the models are much fuller and more sophisticated than our summaries will be able to show. Nevertheless, we will summarize the essential elements and give a reasonable overview of each. We have tried to be objective and let each model speak for itself; we want them all to be heard equally. However, we are simply describing the models, not trying to teach how to coach with them.

First we will look at the inner game, the GROW model and coactive coaching. We have grouped these together because they emerged at the same time and have many elements in common. Second is the integral coaching model, followed by the model of coaching based on neuro-linguistic programming (NLP coaching). The next model is based on the new discipline of positive psychology, then behavioural coaching and finally ontological coaching.

No model can be completely right and no model is wrong. They are like different lights, all illuminating the multifaceted discipline of coaching, each from a different angle with a different brightness.

After giving these models, we will summarize the common, core distinctions of coaching that we distilled from them and our wider research.

Here is a Sufi story to put you in the mood for what follows. Nasrudin, a Sufi holy man who appears in many Sufi stories, has been appointed as a judge, much to his surprise. His first case is the disputed ownership of a herd of camels. The case is heard in a panelled courtroom; he is the only judge, but he has an experienced legal adviser beside him as a recorder. All the friends and relatives of both parties are present in the courtroom and are noisily putting their points of view.

As is the custom, each plaintiff gets ten minutes to argue his case uninterrupted before the judge. The first man enters and is very eloquent. He tells Nasrudin how he bought the camels and gave them to his friend as security against a loan. Now he has repaid the loan, but his friend (no longer a friend) has kept the camels. He has several witnesses who swear this is what happened.

Nasrudin listens and is impressed. 'This man is right,' he whispers to the adviser. 'Maybe,' says the adviser, 'but you need to listen to the other man too.'

The second man comes in and is equally eloquent. He recites how he bought the camels from his friend at a fair price; he denies it was a loan. He has witnesses too.

Nasrudin is again impressed. 'This man is right!' he exclaims.

'But your Excellency,' hisses the adviser, 'both men cannot be right.'

Nasrudin pauses for a moment. 'You're right!'

He looks down. 'The truth is more difficult than it appears.'

At the end of each coaching model, we will use the same case study to give an idea of how each model would address the same problem. Here is the case study.

CASE STUDY

Brian is a 41-year-old manager in a new cosmetics company. A Korean working in a US company branch in London, he has anglicized his name to fit in. He took a degree in chemistry at college, worked in a pharmacy for three years, then for several drug companies before becoming a senior manager in his present company. He has been there five years and is in charge of a team of ten people developing a new product. The company itself is seen as a leader in the cosmetics market because of its innovative (although expensive) products.

Brian plays chess and reads a lot (mostly technical material) and also likes historical novels. He has joined a gym three times in the past five years but has never kept it up for more than two months and has let the subscription lapse every time.

Recently Brian has become distracted, and is increasingly wondering if he is in the right job. He used to enjoy his work but now he does not. He is constantly tired and there is one member of the team who always seems to be getting on his nerves. He believes that person is making a bid to replace him.

Brian was passed over for promotion last year and this year he doesn't know if he should leave or put himself up for promotion again. He does not know if he deserves promotion based on his recent work.

Brian was raised in a Korean family with a strong work ethic. He went to an English school and also to a Korean school on Saturdays, and he had flute and tennis lessons during the week.

He has been married to Anne, an Englishwoman, for 12 years and they have two children, a boy of eight and a girl of six. His wife trained as a dental hygienist and works part-time in a local dental surgery. She would like to work full-time when the children are older. Recently, she and Brian have been quarrelling, as his job has taken up more of his time and they are not seeing each other much except at weekends.

Brian is quiet, and seeks co-operation rather than confrontation, but if this does not work, he can lose his temper rather easily. Until now he has kept this under control, but recently he has been constantly irritated and feels stressed. His company has instituted a coaching programme for senior managers, and he has jumped at the chance to meet with a coach. He wants to feels less irritated and less stressed. He is thinking about looking for another job, but wonders if leaving the company would be a good move either personally or professionally.

1 COACHING IN EUROPE AND THE UNITED STATES: THE INNER GAME, GROW AND COACTIVE COACHING

'Every man takes the limits of his own field of vision for the limits of the world.'

Arthur Schopenhauer

The publication of *The Inner Game of Tennis* [1] by Timothy Gallwey was a major turning point in coaching. And the inner game methodology was one of the first coaching models to jump the barrier from sport to business. What is the inner game and why was it significant? Because it deals with the outer opponent and the inner opponent. Business knows all about the outer opponent – the competition – but up until then had not paid attention to its inner opponent. The Inner Game methodology is how you can get the most from yourself, and for business it translated into how to get the most from your people.

Here is the thesis of the inner game. Timothy Gallwey proposed the player is divided into two selves. He called self one 'the teller' and self two 'the doer'. Self one is judgmental, and is very good at spotting mistakes and telling you about them and how to stop them. Self one is the inner opponent; it is the ego mind, self-consciousness and the urge to control. Self two is unselfconscious, 'the wisdom of the body' that acts without reflexive thought and does well as long as it has learned what to do. The relationship between the two selves is most important point in the inner game.

As writers, we have experienced the perfect example of self one and self two. Self one is the editor, self two is the writer. Self two needs learning and practice, but the best way to write is to just . . . write and let the creative energy flow. Let self two do its job. This is easy to say, but not so easy to do. Every book on creative writing will tell you this and they all have suggestions to help you. The problem is self one, the internal editor who is always interfering. Self one wants the writing to be perfect first time; it tries to analyze each sentence as you write it, and tells you what is wrong with it almost before you have finished it. Very few authors write perfectly first time. The whole point of the first draft is to get the ideas down on paper *without editing*. Only after that should the editor come in and clean up. If self one (the editor) is always active, the writer will struggle and be self-critical, and maybe give up, (perhaps calling the problem 'writer's block'). The editor is essential, but it has to be controlled and allowed out at the right time. Much of the first draft may be rubbish, but self two needs permission to write rubbish and to make mistakes otherwise the good writing cannot flow. Only by allowing yourself to make mistakes can your writing go beyond the banal.

Another way of looking at the two selves is as horse and rider. The rider (self one) needs to set the destination and direction and let the horse (self two) do the work. It is not the job of the rider to tell the horse where to put its feet, yet this is exactly what happens when we try to use our conscious self one to do things that are best left to the unconscious self two.

The Chinese philosopher Chuang Tzu (c 350 BC) wrote about this long ago [2]: 'When you are betting for tiles in an archery contest, you shoot with skill. When you are betting for fancy belt buckles, you worry about your aim. And when you are betting for real gold, you are a nervous wreck. Your skill is the same in all three cases – but because one prize means more to you than another, you let outside considerations weigh on your mind. He who looks too hard on the outside gets clumsy on the inside.'

Self one makes the player clumsy on the outside as well as on the inside. Praise and compliments from the coach may work in the outer game, but they do not work in the inner game, because the client will try to live up to the coach's expectations and earn more praise. Praise is a subtle criticism; it implies there is something bad (even though you are not doing it now). Self one immediately takes hold of this and uses it.

The work of the coach in the inner game is to help the player program the two selves so that they work together in the best way. In practice this means getting self one out of the way at the critical times when the player is playing the shots. Gallwey created a simple model for getting the judgmental self one out of the way.

SELF-OBSERVATION

First, players must decide what they want to achieve, change or improve. They may have a very general goal – they want to be a better player – or a very specific one of improving a tennis stroke. Second, they need to observe what is happening in the present moment that could be stopping them getting the result they want. This seems easy, but it is difficult to do without judgment. Judgment applies a label; you do not see what happens, you only see the judgment: 'good' or 'bad'. It obscures what is happening, and unless you know what is happening, you will not be able to change it.

Open awareness gives you the best feedback. Then you know what is happening in that moment. How can you have this open awareness and get this high-quality, objective feedback when you really need it? This is a key issue for coaching. The coach needs to supply objective feedback, but, more important, the coach needs to help clients to develop a capacity to give objective feedback *to themselves*. Clients will model how the coach gives feedback, and the result of the coaching will be not only a change in the client as a result of that feedback, but also an enhanced ability to see themselves more clearly and therefore to rely less on the coach. Good coaching helps clients learn to become their own coaches. They learn the principles of feedback rather than just feedback on a specific issue.

The feedback must be objective and non-judgmental. The coach needs to bypass the player's self one, and this may not be easy. Many people have a strong habit of judging themselves in everything they do. Habits cannot simply be broken, because a lot of effort has already gone into establishing them. Brute force does not work; you have to apply mental aikido to get around them. However disturbing self one is, it does have a positive intention – it is trying to help the person do better, it is just not doing it very effectively.

Most tennis professionals tell a student to 'Watch the ball!' But students *know* they should watch the ball. They *try* to watch it, but the trying gets in the way of the watching. Then they play a poor stroke and draw the conclusion that they are not good players. The problem is that 'Watch the ball!' is too general. Watch it for what? How? Also, the ball they are watching is heavy with significance for their self-esteem as it hurtles towards them. Gallwey found a way to help them watch the ball objectively and without judgment, therefore bypassing self one. He would tell them to watch the seam of the ball as it approached to see which direction it was spinning in. This is a great instruction, because it works on several levels. First, it demands more concentration than usual. Second, the answer will be a description and not a judgment, because the answer does *not* depend on the stroke the student is planning. Their stroke will not distract them from the present moment. When they are not worrying about the quality of their shot and just watching the ball as keenly as they can, paradoxically their stroke will be better. Third, there is a direct feedback loop to the coach, who is also watching the ball spin. This non-judgmental awareness automatically helps the player to respond unselfconsciously – self two is engaged.

PROGRAMMING

Next, the player must change what they are doing, on the basis of the feedback. They must do something different. If they know what to do already, then they have to *let it happen* without interference. Letting it happen is not making it happen, so perhaps they need to learn and practise the stroke first. Gallwey refers to this learning as 'programming' self two, using the same vocabulary as neuro-linguistic programming, which was growing in popularity in California at the same time as the inner game.

Gallwey wrote that self two learns best by images and example. The player needs to see the stroke done by the profes-sional and then make a mental image of that. How could this apply to a coach working with a client on a cognitive skill? Again, it would be important for the client to see the coach demonstrate the skill in the session. A thousand words do not have the impact of a demonstration. A coach needs to model the skills they ask of the client. The way to program self two is to tell it what you want and then create compelling mental images of exactly that.

When you know what you want, and you know what you have without interference or judgment, and when you have programmed self two by images to do what you want, *then* you have to step aside and let it happen.

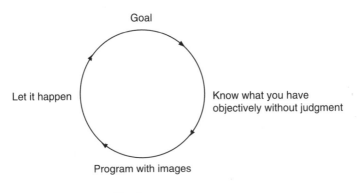

The inner game process

Players usually react to a mistake with self-criticism, heavy internal dialogue, and exhortations to do better. This is self one running riot, and it destroys concentration. Concentration is a mental skill that needs practice; Gallwey wrote that meditation practice off court could help.

The inner game methodology can be applied to anything. Goals are no longer things you achieve. They are the means of conquering *yourself*. An outside opponent gives us a challenge to develop ourselves. Only by being the best opponent possible does this opponent become a true friend. Whatever outer game you choose, whether it is tennis, golf, management, sales, leadership or coaching, you can still use it to play the inner game to develop yourself. Life is the biggest game of all. Another influential book at the time (which Gallwey quotes) is *The Master Game* by Robert De Ropp, published in 1968 [3]. De Ropp said that people do not primarily seek wealth, comfort or esteem; rather, they seek a game worth playing – and that depends on how you play it and what the stakes are.

In the inner game of coaching, the worthy opponent is the client.

THE SPREAD OF THE INNER GAME

The inner game swiftly spread to Europe. John Whitmore was a professional racing driver in the UK in the 1960s who trained with Timothy Gallwey. He took the inner game in the 1990s across the Atlantic to the UK and reworked the principles for business use. His book *Coaching for Performance* [4] is a business-focused book. The goal was to improve business performance through coaching by unlocking people's potential to maximize their own performance. Coaching helps individuals to learn rather than teaching them; it cuts across the controlling style of management. All businesses want high performance, but they do not agree on how to get it. As Whitmore says, 'Real performance is going beyond expected standards; it is setting one's own highest standards that surpass what others demand or expect.'

In the book, Whitmore also stresses awareness and responsibility to help clients achieve their best performance. Awareness is about knowing what is happening around you, and self-awareness means knowing what is happening inside you. Both are fostered by questions rather than statements or commands. When people are told something, they do not have to think, and it raises little awareness, motivation or creativity. Powerful questions raise all three. The business coach needs to find an equivalent question to 'Which way is the ball spinning?' to help business clients understand their situation internally and externally, objectively and without judgment. In his contribution to this book, John Whitmore develops these ideas and touches on the use of coaching in transpersonal psychology.

THE GROW MODEL

The GROW model is presented in *Coaching for Performance* as a basis for coaching. It was originally constructed by Graham Alexander, who also brought the inner game to Europe at the beginning of the 1980s. GROW is an acronym for **G**oal, **R**eality, **O**ptions and **W**hat (will you do).

'G' IS FOR GOAL

A goal is a dream with substance. A goal is what clients want, and implies a change. A life without goals is an empty desert with no future. There are two types of goal. The *end goal* is the final objective, but is not under your control. There are too many other people and larger systems involved. The *process goal* is the performance level you need to achieve the end goal.

We all have an area of concern, things we care about where many larger systems converge. Within that area of concern we have an area of influence, in which we can take action and make a difference. For example, we may be concerned about the state of the economy and the level of wages, but this is the result of many different systems, economic and political as well as local systems where we live and work, and industry-specific factors. However, we can vote, an action we hope will make a difference. We can lobby, join a political party, write articles for a newspaper, try to persuade friends to see our viewpoint and generally become politically active. These things are all inside our area of influence.

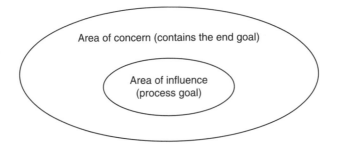

Area of influence and area of concern – end goal and process goal

A process goal is in the area of influence – it is the performance level you need to achieve to get your end goal. If your end goal is promotion to senior manager, you need to raise your performance to that level. Whitmore says the end goal is the inspiration; the performance goal is the specification. We would add that the performance goal means perspiration, too. Business coaching boosts performance by setting process goals at the performance level needed to achieve the business end goals.

Goal setting is an important part of business and there are many ways to formulate it. Many businesses use the SMART acronym – **S**pecific, **M**easurable, **A**greed, **R**ealistic and **T**imed (with a deadline). Whitmore adds the PURE acronym – **P**ositively stated, **U**nderstood, **R**elevant and **E**thical – and he also adds that the goals need to be challenging, legal, environmentally sound, appropriate and recorded.

The quality of the coach's questions is always important. Whitmore states, 'If a coach only asks questions and receives answers from the normal level of conscious awareness, he may be helping the coachee to structure their thoughts, but he is not probing to new and deeper levels of awareness.'

'R' IS FOR REALITY

You need to know what you have in order to change it, so you need to know where you start from. There is a joke about this. A traveller is walking along a long country road. A light rain taps insistently on his hat. He pulls out his map every few minutes, turns it around in exasperation and trudges on. He is clearly lost. A local under the shelter of a large tree watches him approach. The traveller spots him and hurries up. 'Excuse me,' he says, 'I am trying to get to Metatown. Can you tell me if I am on the right track?' The local looks down and rubs his head. 'Oh dear, sir. If I was going to Metatown, I certainly wouldn't start from here.'

But you have to start from where you are, so you need to know where you are without wishful thinking, judgments, opinions, hopes or fears that may blur your view. The coach helps define the clients' present reality as objectively as possible.

For example, imagine a client saying, 'I decided to go to the gym on Friday afternoon, but when it came to the crunch, I didn't. I stayed at home and watched TV. I felt tired.' This description is more objective than 'I really wanted to go to the gym on Friday but I didn't because I was lazy. I sat around and watched TV. What I need is self-discipline!' There is a proposed solution (self-discipline) without an appreciation of present circumstances or the goal. Such abstract self-discipline will always be elusive.

The more objective and specific the description of reality, the more it will help the client.

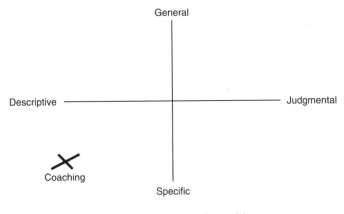

Specific – descriptive grid

The more the client understands their present state in descriptive and specific terms (bottom left of the grid), the better the coaching will be. If clients venture into other areas of the grid, then the coach must move them back into being descriptive and specific.

Tennis is a physical sport, but the inner game principles can be applied to any activity. Mind, body and emotions are connected. Thoughts carry emotion, emotions are reflected in the body, and bodily feelings trigger thoughts. High performance describes the results of behaviour, the actions people take. And the actions are triggered by their thinking and emotions. The primary focus for coaching is cognitive. Whitmore suggests that the coach may have to work on body awareness, but gives no details.

'O' IS FOR OPTIONS

The options step means brainstorming choices, not finding the right answer. Neither coach nor client knows the right answer at this moment. The object of this phase is to create more choices about what to do.

This stage can be difficult if clients have negative assumptions about what is possible, about their capability or about whether other people can be relied on. Clients may also doubt their own resourcefulness. They do not know if their negative ideas are true, but they still assume them. It is important for the coach to insist on a brainstorm: what could you do – *if there were no constraints?*

'W' IS FOR 'WHAT WILL YOU DO?'

Now we have a goal, a present state and some options. The final step is deciding what action to take. The coach will be asking many questions in this phase to help clarify the action and its consequences.

Once the action is decided, 'When will you do it?' is a key question. There are two types of answer. One is a definite date, for example 'I will do it on Wednesday.' The other type of answer is a deadline, for example 'I don't know exactly which day, but it will be before the weekend.'

'Will your action meet your goal?' is a useful question. The action is unlikely to achieve the goal completely. It should be a first step, and the client needs to connect the result of the action with the end goal. This question can also bring out any unexpected side-effects.

'What obstacles could you encounter?' is another valuable question. 'What support do you need and how you are going to get it?' is a practical inquiry to help the client actively seek resources if they need them.

Finally, when clients are clear about their action plan, the coach can ask them to rate their degree of commitment to the action on a scale of one to ten. If the answer is not ten, then coach and client need to explore the action plan a little more, or expand the deadline.

THE KOLB LEARNING CYCLE

The GROW model fits the Kolb learning cycle, which has been a basic model of experiential learning since it was proposed in 1984 [5].

There are four stages of learning in the cycle. The first stage is concrete experience, which provides the basis for the second stage – observation and reflection to understand what has happened and to generalize from the experience. These reflections are assimilated into abstract concepts – general principles that appear to govern what is happening and can be used to predict what will happen in future. The fourth and last stage is to plan a new action, to test the hypothesis, and so enter into the cycle again (but with more knowledge and experience).

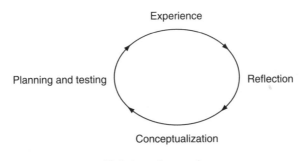

Kolb learning cycle

Kolb said that ideally a learner would engage fully in each of the four steps. He also suggested that different people have different learning styles and excel at different stages of the cycle (and so by inference are weaker at others).

How does the GROW model fit into this cycle? Goal setting is the proposed experience. Reality is explored by reflection and observation. Options come from conceptualization, and action is the planned experiment to test the hypothesis. The coaching process fits into the Kolb model, but only if the client takes action. Without action there is no feedback and no experience to test by reflection. The cycle stops dead without even completing one revolution.

COACTIVE COACHING

Coaching developed quickly and reached a stage in the United States that is summed up in another important book, *Co-Active Coaching* [6] by Laura Whitworth, Henry Kimsey-House and Phil Sandahl. The book has an introduction by John Whitmore. This book has been influential in the development of coaching in the United States and Europe. The book explores the particular sort of *relationship* that coaching generates, and focuses more on the client perspective, whereas *The Inner Game* and *Coaching for Performance* focus more on the coach's point of view. *Co-Active Coaching* translates the coaching relationship into a number of understandable tools that coaches can use. The emphasis has shifted from being a powerful coach to creating a powerful relationship with the focus on the client. And the power of a question does not reside in the question itself, but in its impact on the client.

The book begins from the client's point of view. Coaching is defined as a relationship of possibilities. 'Imagine a relationship where the total focus is on you. . . on what you want in your life and on what will help you achieve it. . . Imagine a relationship in your life with a person who is even more committed to what you want in your life than you are. . . Imagine a relationship with someone who will absolutely tell you the truth. . . This coaching relationship is one of trust, confidentiality and safety.'

The book lists the four cornerstones of coactive coaching:

1   The client is naturally creative, resourceful and whole.
2   Coactive coaching addresses the client's whole life.
3   The agenda comes from the client.
4   The coaching relationship is a designed alliance.

The book then lays out five contexts of coaching: listening, intuition, curiosity, action/learning and self-management.

LISTENING

Listening is not hearing. Hearing is a passive process. Hearing is what happens when sound waves rattle your eardrum so your brain registers the sound. Listening is active. You pay attention when you listen. And there are different levels of listening.

Listening at the first level makes everything personal. What we hear is tangled up in our associations and internal dialogue. 'What does this mean to *me*?' is the only question we ask at this level of listening. 'What brilliant question can I ask the client next?' is often what the coach is thinking at this first level of listening.

The second level is focused listening. You are focused on your clients, what they say and how they say it. You follow their lead.

The third level is defined as global listening. You listen to your clients and you are also aware of the environment and your own sensations and feelings. At this level, you are open to whatever there is to receive. You may feel vulnerable, but it gives more access to your intuition than level two, which leaves no mental space for messages from your unconscious.

As coaches listen at the deeper level, they will be able to articulate what is going on for their clients. Articulating is pointing out in a succinct way what their clients are concerned about. Doing something about it is the clients' job. With good listening, coaches can also clarify what their clients say. Many clients go round and round, getting caught in the metaphorical webs they weave. Sometimes they leave out information, jump to conclusions or make hasty judgments. Coaches clarify so their clients understand themselves better, and in the process coaches understand better and can follow their clients' stories.

INTUITION

With global listening comes intuition. It is interesting to see intuition defined as a coaching tool, when for most people intuition seems to be vague, uncontrolled and unsupported ideas. Intuition can be a tool, and coaches can learn to use it and trust it. Then their clients may also come to trust their own intuition.

What is intuition? Messages from the deep. An intuition is an idea stripped of the supporting rational back-up information that argues its case. But this does not make it wrong. When coaches are listening globally, they are receiving huge amounts of information that they are not aware of, or consciously responding to. This information gets processed at an unconscious level and the conclusions may pop up into the conscious mind as an intuition or hunch. It can be a gut feeling; it can be an internal voice. Is it right? Maybe. But that is the wrong question to ask. Intuition is not about right or wrong, it is a pointer. We can choose to pay attention to it and to put it into words. When coaches express an intuition, they will usually say something like 'I have a feeling that. . . ', I have a hunch that. . . ' or 'It may not make much sense, but think about this. . . '

CURIOSITY

Listening implies curiosity – exactly the attitude for a non-judgmental evaluation of reality. Coaches need to be curious to help clients set goals and see reality. Coaches do not have the answers; clients have the answers. If coaches are interested in their clients, this makes the clients interested in themselves. Sometimes clients do not take themselves seriously, maybe because other people do not take them seriously. A coach's attitude is crucial to help clients tell their story. Curiosity will also give rise to powerful questions that are judgment-free.

ACTION LEARNING

Learning comes from action, and coaches will always ask clients to take action. These actions are often called tasks or homework and are negotiated between coach and client. The coach may propose, but in the end the client must be committed to the task, and is accountable for both the task and the result. The task corresponds to the 'W' in the GROW process, 'What will you do?'

SELF-MANAGEMENT

Now the focus switches to the coach. Coaches need to be ready to play their part in the coaching relationship. This is not a step in the coaching process, but a step in the coaches' preparation. There are two aspects to self-management.

First, coaches need to be committed to their clients' success. It is no use asking for commitment from clients if coaches themselves are doubtful. Clients will pick up the incongruity, and the coaching will not work. Coaches must believe in their clients' potential. Coaches must also set their own boundaries. For example, they should not take on clients who they believe should see a medical doctor, therapist or mentor.

The second part of self-management is called 'clearing'. Coaches must keep their own unresourceful or negative feelings out of the process. Coaches listening at level one will take things personally. They will react to what their clients say, and agree or disagree. This is not relevant to clients. The feelings come from the coaches, and clients are pushing their buttons (without meaning to).

Clearing is realizing when this is happening and deliberately putting the feelings aside in order to concentrate on listening to clients. This might only take a few seconds; however, occasionally clients may talk about painful issues in a way that enmeshes the coach. Perhaps coaches have also been dealing with these same issues in their own life. When this happens, it is very difficult for coaches to remain professionally detached, and whether coaches feel they can continue to coach clients on this issue is an ethical question only they can decide. However, coaches will need to clear the emotions that have built up, perhaps at the end of a session by deep breathing or relaxation. Clearing is a personal skill for coaches to manage their internal state, not a direct coaching tool. Many coaches prepare a session with a short meditation or relaxation ritual and end a session the same way to ensure that they are in the best state to continue and that they leave the last client and their problems behind so they can focus on the next client.

COACHING FROM THE INSIDE AND OUTSIDE

Coactive coaching complements the GROW model. The GROW model focuses on the coaching procedure seen from the *outside*. GROW describes the process and structure of what is happening, whereas coactive coaching focuses on the *inside*. It deals with the attitudes and skills the coach needs to apply the GROW model or any other coaching model. Listening and curiosity apply to every step, while self-management sets up a feedback loop for the coach to stay in the most resourceful state.

The coactive coaching process seen from the outside would go like this:

1   Help clients to see they are looking at the issue from a limited point of view.
2   Help clients take other viewpoints. (This could be an interesting options step in the GROW model – choosing perspectives on the problem, not actions to solve the problem.)
3   Help clients to get inside the different viewpoints so they become real and not just an academic exercise.
4   Help clients choose the perspective they want.
5   Help clients create a plan that addresses the situation.
6   See clients commit to the plan.
7   Support clients to take action.

CASE STUDY

We can briefly look at Brian's situation with a combination of inner game, GROW and coactive coaching methodology to see the main ways they could help him. Who is Brian's inner opponent? It appears to be the one that distracts him, that makes him upset and irritated and not persist with his plans, like joining the gym. The first step for the inner game method would be to encourage Brian to be objective and non-judgmental about his situation. Is he very self-critical? What are his inner voices telling him? What exactly happens when he is irritated with his co-workers? Does he feel he should confront them? Does he think he should be more assertive? Brian needs to see past his self-criticism and self-judgment and describe what is happening objectively. He needs to be clear about what he wants. He needs to clarify whether he wants to stay with the company or leave, and if he does leave, what job exactly he would go to.

The GROW model will make these steps more definite. What is Brian's goal? What is most pressing? Does he want to work first on his tiredness and irritation and see if things improve, or does he really want to leave the company? If he wants to leave the company, then he needs to be clear what sort of job he wants. He needs to explore the reality of his situation at the moment, objectively and specifically. When he does this, he will probably feel better, because it will reduce his self-criticism, which is fuelled by his strong work ethic and sense of obligation. A coach will help him brainstorm his options in the situation and identify his resources, both personal qualities and also friends and family. Finally the coach will help him take specific actions to remedy the situation, and identify the obstacles that could block him and deal with them one by one.

Coactive coaching would help Brian develop his curiosity and intuition. Curiosity about himself – how does he see himself? Do his Korean family roots have anything to teach him? What does his intuition tell him about this situation when he looks at it objectively and stops his self-criticism?

Perhaps he feels a victim of events, rather than an active protagonist. What other viewpoint could he take? Future manager of the company? Husband? Father? Head-hunted executive? How does he feel when he imagines himself in these roles? What perspective does he want to take? Finally, like all coaching approaches, coactive coaching would help him form an action plan to address the various aspects of his situation, without pressuring him into making any decision until he was sure.

REFERENCES

1 Gallwey, T. (1974) *The Inner Game of Tennis*
2 Chuang Tzu. (1964) *Basic Writings*, translated by Burton Watson
3 De Ropp, R. (1968) *The Master Game*
4 Whitmore, J. (1992) *Coaching for Performance*
5 Kolb, D. (1984) *Experiential Learning: Experience as the Source of Learning and Development*
6 Whitworth, L., Kimsey-House, H. and Sandahl, P. (1998) *Co-Active Coaching*

REFLECTION ON COACHING

by John Whitmore

The coaching profession is reaching adulthood. Now it is time for it to get a job – and to get the job done. Coaching faces a choice between remaining a peripheral service to the workplace and becoming an example to the workplace. It has been inward-looking during its formative years; now it is time for it to come out and lead the way. It has had a very good start. It has the right credentials, as it represents the next evolutionary wave of psychology in action. Now coaching has to be integrated into management, into education, into leadership so it transforms the way those things are done and thereby their effectiveness.

Coaches have long held that coaches must honour and follow their clients' agenda at all times, and in practice they do, or often attempt so to do. However, a coach always influences both the process and the coachee by his or her very presence and the size of vision he or she holds. By analogy, when we taught skiing the inner game way, we always encouraged the learners to do what they liked with awareness, but we set the boundaries of the terrain they used, for safety's sake. So it is with workplace or life coaching. The bigger our vision, the more terrain our clients can play on, and learn from.

For this reason I believe that it is imperative for all aspiring coaches to learn to use transpersonal techniques, but they can't do that unless they themselves are on their own transpersonal journey. Transpersonal means 'beyond the personal', which is a whole-system approach that includes the spiritual realm of personal development. That is the inner stuff, but coaches also need to keep up with what is going on in the outer world, now that it is in constant change. How can we help clients if we do not have a deep understanding of the individual and collective evolution that humankind is in the midst of, and how that manifests in changes in society?

I commend this book, for it will serve the reader well to contextualize coaching, but I want to reinforce the importance of the bigger picture and add this point. Historically, most of the cultures with which we are familiar have been vertical hierarchical power or wealth structures, or both. The transition has begun, in many parts of the world, towards a flatter model of social behaviours with far more people being self-responsible and having decision-making opportunities. Humankind has reached this point in its collective social evolutionary journey. It is touching every sector of life in subtle ways, in education, in management, in psychotherapy, in child rearing, in the performing arts and in sport, but coaching is the first and only profession that fully embodies the principles by which we all will live in future. As such, the profession has a big opportunity and a big responsibility.

Corporate, public sector and political leadership is going through a parallel process, but it lags a decade or so behind. There is a growing bond and similarity between coaching and leadership. Coaches need not only to help to create new leaders, but also to become leaders themselves. Leaders of the future must have more than the cleverness that some of today's leaders have: they must be conscious too, something that very few are today. This requires continuous learning on both the inner and the outer planes. Coaches can initiate and provide ongoing support for that process.

To be a great coach is becoming more challenging but it is also potentially far more rewarding, as we may have inherited the task of being midwives for a very important period of social transformation. Yes, coaching has a great future, if we all have the courage to move into the mainstream, to own our power and to sustain our self-belief.

Sir John Whitmore is Executive Chairman of Performance Consultants International Limited. He has written five books on sports, leadership and coaching, of which *Coaching for Performance* is the best known.

He believes that our purpose as an organization is to share the best leadership, social responsibility and other people skills among different countries and cultures for a sustainable future for all.

2 INTEGRAL COACHING

'What we see depends mainly on what we look for.'

Sir John Lubbock

Our second model is integral coaching. The word 'integral' means complete, inclusive, balanced and comprehensive. Coaches of all persuasions would claim this for their coaching, but the term 'integral coaching' has become closely associated with the framework of the integral model, originating mainly from the work of the writer and philosopher Ken Wilber [1] [2] [3] [4] in the United States and developed by him and others since the 1980s. Many coaches are building their methodology and practice using this framework or a variation of it – the integral model has many useful distinctions for coaching.

Clients need to understand the distinctions of the integral model in order to get the most out of the coaching, so we will start by briefly describing some of its important points and then how they can be used in coaching.

The integral model aims to be a comprehensive model of the individual, society and culture. It starts from the simple idea of perspectives. There are three perspectives, or points of view, we can have in any situation, and nearly all languages make these distinctions, so it seems that they are deeply built into the human mind.

The first perspective is 'I'. This is the point of view of the observer, the person who is speaking, and is known as the first person.

The second is 'You', the person being spoken to. This is known as the second person.

The third point of view is 'him', 'her' or 'it' – the person or thing being spoken about. This is known as the third person.

When I speak to you, I want to share my understanding with you. If you listen to me and understand me, then you and I form a 'we'. 'We' are you and I in mutual understanding. This shared point of view is one that a coach wants to create with her client. This means that she must talk to the client as another person, a 'you' – someone different to 'I' but equal. Only then can the coach make a connection and explore the space of possibilities between herself and the client. This is quite different from treating someone as a third person, for if another person becomes an 'it' then there is a separation, not an understanding, and the other person becomes a means to an end, rather than an end in themselves.

In the integral model, the first-person view is linked to aesthetics, the beauty that is in the eye ('I') of the beholder. The second-person view is linked to morals, how we treat others. The third-person view is linked to objective truth, the world 'out there' that we fathom with the sciences. So, the three perspectives are linked with the good, the true and the beautiful.

The integral model then develops a four-quadrant model from these perspectives. There is a first person singular ('I') and first person plural ('we'), which incorporates the second person. There is also a third person singular ('it') and a third person plural ('they'). Each of these perspectives can be viewed from the inside or the outside. This gives us a model of four quadrants.

INDIVIDUAL PERSPECTIVE FROM THE INSIDE (UPPER LEFT)

The upper left is the interior individual space – looking at yourself from the inside, how you subjectively experience yourself. This is the realm of your beliefs, values, goals, feelings, hopes and dreams as you experience them.

This quadrant was colonized by humanistic psychology. Only you can understand *in this way* because only you have this privileged viewpoint. Coaching ventures to make this quadrant a more ordered and a more comfortable place to live in.

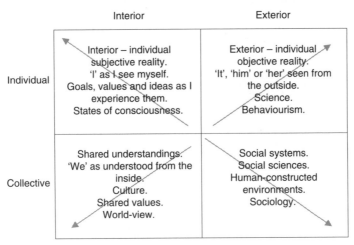

The integral model – the four quadrants

INDIVIDUAL PERSPECTIVE FROM THE OUTSIDE (UPPER RIGHT)

The upper right is the individual seen from the outside. This is what you can see, hear and feel – concrete reality as we normally think of it. This is the third-person quadrant 'it', 'him' or 'her' seen from the outside. It is the realm of observable behaviour, and the study of people in this quadrant is behaviourism. This is how we study the world with empirical science. Everything we experience in the upper left quadrant as subjective experience has a counterpart in the upper right that can be studied. Brain states can be described as alpha and theta waves and measured by an EEG machine. Moods and emotions can be tracked by levels of hormones and neurotransmitters. The internal feeling of telling a lie can be seen on a lie detector. Upper right remedies such as drugs can be used to treat depression and mental illness, as can psychoanalysis and cognitive therapy (which are both upper left remedies). We know that we can influence our states of mind by thinking differently, and we know we can influence our states of mind by taking drugs. We can even alter our state by eating different foods. One does not invalidate the other; every phenomenon in the upper left has some aspect that can be studied objectively in the upper right. No view is wrong; they are just looking from a different place.

We judge ourselves mostly by our intentions, which are found in the upper left quadrant. 'I didn't mean it; I didn't have a bad intention.' Other people judge us by our behaviour, the upper right quadrant: 'Look what you did to me.' They cannot judge our intentions, because they cannot see them.

COLLECTIVE PERSPECTIVES (BOTTOM LEFT AND BOTTOM RIGHT)

The bottom quadrants are points of view from more than one individual. They are the collective quadrants. The bottom left is collective from the inside, the realm of shared understanding and feelings, the 'we' quadrant. It is the cultural viewpoint.

The bottom right is the social system – we see it from the outside and it can be studied by the social sciences. The financial system goes in this quadrant, as well as systems of family relationships.

Everything on the right side can be seen. Everything on the left side must be interpreted.

COACHING IN THE QUADRANTS

Here is an example to illustrate the difference between the quadrants. We went to Denmark two years ago, and gave a coaching training session in a wonderful hotel set in pine forest north of Copenhagen. We were a little nervous as it was our first training session in Denmark. We wanted it to go well and it was important to us that it did. Our thoughts, feelings and values belong in the upper left quadrant. Joseph had a headache the first night from jet lag and felt restless. He relaxed by doing a visualization exercise (upper left), which helped, but later he took an aspirin (upper right).

The training went well from our point of view, and the feedback from the participants was very good. The session was videotaped and we viewed the tape afterwards. The written feedback and tape formed a record of the course in the upper right quadrant. All the manuals, paper, computer equipment and projectors that supported the training also belong in the upper right quadrant.

We are well aware that the social system of Denmark is very different from that of Brazil, where we live. People are more reserved, they want more time for reflection, and they are less overtly emotional and more punctual. We heard the sounds of the Danish language, but we did not understand it. Some of the Danish jokes when translated did not seem very funny to us, and some of our jokes were lost on our Danish audience. All this relates to culture and belongs in the lower left quadrant. The way the training was organized, the structure of the exercises for the participants, and the overall organization of the course belong in the lower right quadrant.

Every human experience has aspects in all four quadrants. The question from the integral coaching point of view is which one do you pay attention to and which one do you take action in? If someone were coaching us to help us make the best training possible, what sort of things would they consider?

Should we be clear in our own goals and values and prepare ourselves with a relaxation exercise? (Upper left.) Certainly.

Should we make sure that all the equipment is working well and make sure our behaviour and body language are in keeping with what we are saying? (Upper right.) Absolutely. Even the most interesting course can send people to sleep if delivered in a monotone by an boring speaker.

Should we make sure that everything is clear about how the training will be held, how the assistants work, when the breaks are, and how the finances will be dealt with? (Lower right.) Of course.

And maybe next time we should learn a few words in Danish to establish rapport, ask our Danish host about the important values in Danish culture and learn a little about Danish humour? (Lower left.) An excellent idea. An integral coach would consider all these approaches.

The four quadrants are also applicable to business coaching. At the moment there are four main theories of business management. Theory X, which stresses individual behaviour (upper right). Theory Y, which stresses individual motivation (upper left). Then there are cultural management, which deals with the business culture (lower left), and systems management (lower right), which deals with the business systems processes. Each clearly focuses on one of the quadrants. Which is right? Wrong question. The answer is all of them. Which one is most important at the time? It depends on the business context.

Coaching questions can be classified by quadrant. For example, if we were coaching a client to be a better salesperson using the integral approach we might ask questions like:

⇨ **What is important to you about this goal?**
⇨ **How will you feel when you have achieved it?**
⇨ **What internal qualities do you have that will help you?**
  (All upper left questions)
⇨ **What would you be doing differently?**
⇨ **Can you show me how you approach a client?**
⇨ **Have you read this study on what makes a good salesperson?**
  (All upper right questions)
⇨ **How do people define a good salesperson in this company?**
⇨ **How does your goal fit with the company vision and values?**
⇨ **How does your boss view your goal?**
  (All lower left questions)
⇨ **What system do you use to qualify your clients?**
⇨ **How do you manage your sales pipeline?**
⇨ **What do you do to liaise with other departments?**
  (All lower right questions)

In integral life coaching, a coach and client might discuss how to work in a balanced way on developing the client in all the quadrants. Work in the upper right quadrant could involve diet, yoga or vitamin supplements. Working on the upper left quadrant could involve visualizations, meditation and affirmations. A client might get involved in educational charities, or travel, or cultural studies for the lower left quadrant and working on their relationships and community service, as well as their career and financial status, for the lower right.

Quadrants are only one aspect of the integral model, which also deals with states, stages, lines and types. These are aspects of all the quadrants.

STATES

States are temporary states of consciousness and they change all the time. There are the three natural states that we experience – waking, dreaming and deep sleep. States are not all or nothing affairs; they shade one into the other. Many people are officially awake, but they are so deeply in their own reality that they are responding to their own ideas rather than what is going on around them – they are in a trance. Everyone has times when they 'wake up' to their surroundings. Moods are also states. They are the sum of everything that is going on in the person in every quadrant that influences them and makes them feel a particular way – happy, sad, excited, anxious etc. There are energetic states and depressive states. Moods are important in ontological coaching. We tend to have favourite moods that we fall into, not all of them pleasant; the more we indulge in them, the easier they are to access. We follow the path of least resistance.

An integral coach might work with clients in the different quadrants to change their mood, if the mood was unpleasant or affecting them or others in a bad way. There are many more types of states, including peak experiences where we get a glimpse of wonderful emotions and possibilities beyond our usual feelings, like a sudden gust of wind that opens the curtain for a moment for the sun to pour onto our face in the early morning. These peak experiences are explored in detail by positive psychology coaching.

STAGES

In the diagram, each quadrant is shown with an arrow going across it. This is because the integral model presupposes that there are developmental stages in each quadrant. Individuals and society evolve through definite levels. There is evolution and change in all the quadrants, and this evolution and change is assumed to be for the better. Stages unfold one after the other and they take time. Once you reach a stage then you have attained it permanently.

Cultures (lower left) develop through different world-views. The anthropologist Jen Gebser [5] has developed a classification of cultures as they move forward: archaic, magic, mythic, mental and integral. These parallel the development of human thinking.

Social structures (lower right) have advanced through hunter-gatherer to agrarian to industrial. Today, we are at the dawn of the informational age. In the upper right quadrant our language, science and behaviour become more and more co-ordinated and complex. Now seems to be the era of biotechnology.

Spiral dynamics is an important model of stages identified by prevailing values in societies and individuals, and is used in integral coaching, as well as in business consulting and political scenario planning. The best reference for this model is the book by Don Beck and Christopher Cowan [6] or the related website [7]. The model itself was developed from the pioneering work of the psychologist Clare Graves [8] [9].

In our internal world (upper left), we go through some well-defined states of consciousness as we grow up, before we are able to generalize and grasp abstract concepts. Maturity involves being able to see and respect other people's viewpoints. This leads to moral and social development. At the very least, we can say that a human being develops through three stages: egocentric (everything is referenced to self), conventional (learning and abiding by social norms of behavior) and post-conventional, when there is a concern for all people, not just the person's particular social group. Each stage incorporates the one below it and each is more complex than the last.

When we think in stages, there are two possible ways to change. The first is transactional. This means you become more competent and better adapted at the same stage. A good metaphor is that you are dissatisfied with your apartment, and want a change. Transactional change would involve moving the furniture around and maybe buying some new furniture, even adding another room, but staying in the same apartment.

The second way to change is transformational. This is when you move up a level, and this gives you a whole range of possibilities that were not present before. In our metaphor, it is like moving house. You can take some furniture with you, but the new place will never be the same as the old one. Adult stages of development are important and we will be looking at them in detail in Part Three, because while the integral model makes distinctions about stages, most coaching has neglected the important implications.

LINES OF DEVELOPMENT

Integral coaching also looks at lines of development. We all recognize that we are well developed in some areas and not in others. And most people are unbalanced in how they develop their talents – for example, the archetypal nerd living in his head while neglecting his physical health, or an athlete spending most of his time practising and missing out on a social life. A common example is the businessman who rises to the top of his profession while losing touch with his family. These are extremes; sometimes people choose them and sometimes they just seem to happen.

Howard Gardner [10] first mooted the idea of multiple intelligences, while emotional intelligence, from the works of Daniel Goleman [11], now dominates where intellectual intelligence held sway 20 years ago. There are different types of intelligences; we all develop them to a greater or lesser extent. When someone has a lot of one type of intelligence, they are usually said to be 'talented' in that area. Examples include musical intelligence, physical intelligence and mathematical intelligence. The integral approach lists five main intelligences, but clients could work on different ones if they wished. The main five are:

1   The cognitive line – the ability to think clearly and effectively.
2   The moral line – the ability to take the role of the other person and live with others in society.
3   The emotional line – the ability to manage and express emotions in a positive way.
4   The interpersonal line – the ability to get on with people, to communicate well, to be liked and be trustworthy.
5   The psychosexual line – the ability to have happy and healthy sexual relationships and integrate the sexual energy in a way that works for self and others.

All these are important. Integral coaching is often involved in balancing and developing clients in their areas of weakness.

Coaches and clients can design a psychograph of the important lines clients have in their life, where the clients give themselves a score on how far they feel they have developed that area. They can work on that area, and the psychograph provides a way of measuring the results. Here is an example of a psychograph:

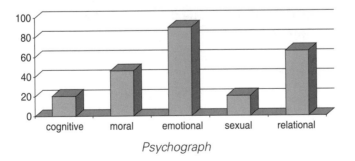

Psychograph

The psychograph shows potentials. What needs to be developed? This is the psychograph of a client who is very satisfied with his emotional life, but not so satisfied with his sex life. He feels that his cognitive line could be better developed. An integral coach could also do a psychograph along the same lines depending on how well they are developed and according to different criteria, not simply on subjective satisfaction (which is a measure only in the upper left quadrant). Integral coaching aims for balance, so it is not just about developing the weaker lines, but also about bringing all the lines into better balance and harmony.

The lines of development proceed through stages. For example, the emotional line develops through the egocentric stage, where all children's emotions are about satisfying their own needs. This is followed by the conventional stage, where they feel for the immediate members of their family and community, and then the post-conventional, where they feel concern for everyone, wherever they are.

It is important to note that you can have a state in these lines of development at any level; the states are fleeting but a stage is permanent. Once you have reached a stage, then you have it reliably and do not usually slide back from it (except perhaps in extreme circumstances). For example, you might have a state of intense musical appreciation even without playing an instrument or learning music, but you are not going to have a peak experience of being a concert pianist, because that involves many hours of practice and is a stage, not a state.

TYPES

A type is how we refer to a particular way of doing something. For example, we say someone is an extrovert type if they are very social, get along with people, and like to go out with others. There are many models of types. The major psychometric tests delineate different types, eg Disc [12], MBTI [13], Birkman [14]. Types show different ways of doing something; they do not show fixed and unchangeable identities. There is development neither in types nor in stages in types. No type is better than another; it is just different. Types can be useful in understanding how people think differently, especially in the business context.

One type affects everyone and is very important – gender. There is a growing and influential literature on evolutionary biology and how men and women think differently and have different values and interests, so we can say there are distinct masculine and feminine types or ways of thinking and behaving. Carol Gilligan [15], in particular, has written about the feminine type and brought out the value of the feminine when most of recorded history has overvalued the masculine way of doing things.

There are some generally agreed differences between masculine and feminine types. Masculine thinking tends to be abstract, objective and deductive, that is, working from a general principle to specific examples. Masculine thinking also tends to be centred on autonomy, justice and rights. Men tend towards individualism, women towards relationship. Feminine thinking is typically more centred on people, experiential and inductive, going from particular cases to the general principle. Feminine thinking deals with relationship, care and responsibility. Men hurt feelings to follow the rules, while women break rules to save feelings.

Masculine and feminine are two equal and different types. Balance and harmony are important; going to the extreme of any type is dangerous and pathological. In any aspect of life, it is possible to be too 'masculine', separating yourself and dealing only in principles and abstractions. This leads to extreme selfishness, domination rather than strength, alienation and fear of commitment rather than independence. Men and women can fall into this trap, but it is more common with men. Too far the other way becomes too feminine, being too influenced by people and their emotions, and this leads to losing yourself in other people's concerns. Again this is possible for men and women in any aspect of life.

Coaching is a secular activity, but the integral approach also deals with the spiritual side of being human – our ultimate concern and how we relate to other people and the world at the deepest level. We have seen that self-awareness is a strong value and an important skill in all coaching approaches. Integral coaching would ask, 'What self are you aware of?' Are you aware on the gross level of the physical body? Or the subtle level of the mind, or on the causal level of the spirit? What sort of awareness does each of these mean? Many clients engage an integral coach to help them in their spiritual development.

SUMMARY

The integral model was not developed as a coaching model – coaching is only one application. We have drawn out what we think are the important implications here. It was developed as a world-view, a framework from which to act, so it serves well as a structure from which to explore coaching. At its essence, the integral approach cultivates body, mind and spirit in the individual, as well as in culture and nature. It is important that the client understands the model and its distinctions in order to use it, so part of an Integral coach's work will be to explain the model so it is fully understood.

Integral coaching also makes some distinctions about gender, and therefore coaching for a man and coaching for a woman might be different. We shall return to this topic in Part Three. Anyone who is interested in furthering their spiritual development might seek out an integral coach.

The key elements of the integral model for coaching are taking different perspectives and balancing them. An integral coach will work with the client on those lines, levels and states where they have the most potential, in the expectation that this will make them a happier, more complete and fulfilled human being.

CASE STUDY

An integral coach would take a wide view of Brian's difficulties and goals, seeing how they fit into his life. First, they might look at how well his life is balanced in the different quadrants. Brian likes chess and reading (these are more introspective pursuits); he is neglecting physical exercise. An integral coach would be helping Brian to plan integral practice to help him in different areas. A relaxation or meditation exercise might help relieve his moods and irritation and would fit into the upper left quadrant. At the moment Brian does not do any physical activity, nor does he eat well, which could be contributing to his lack of energy and irritation. Starting some simple exercise like walking regularly and perhaps eating with his family in the evening at least twice a week might help in that area. An integral coach might also ask about Brian's Korean cultural background – what he knows of it, how he might honour it and how it might have some resources that would help him now.

An integral coach would also help Brian track his moods and be more aware of them, without necessarily trying to change anything at first. The coach would also help him rate and appreciate his different types of intelligences. Brian's cognitive intelligence is high, but his emotional intelligence is lower and so is his interpersonal intelligence. Some practices to help him understand his own moods and other people's feelings as well as learning communication skills to deal with his work colleague would be helpful. An integral coach would aim to balance Brian's areas of weakness and, in the process, make Brian more aware of himself, his emotions, other people and their emotions and how to deal with them. Out of this new balance and set of practices, Brian would probably become clearer about what he wants to do about his work.

REFERENCES

1 Wilber, K. (1995) *Sex, Ecology, Spirituality*

2 Wilber, K. (1996) *A Brief History of Everything*

3 Wilber, K. (1999) *One Taste*

4 www.kenwilber.com/web

5 Gebser, J. (1985) *The Ever-Present Origin*

6 Beck, D. and Cowan, C. (1996) *Spiral Dynamics*

7 www.spiraldynamics.org/web

8 www.claregraves.com/web

9 Graves, C. (1970) Levels of Existence: An Open System Theory of Values, *Journal of Humanistic Psychology*, November

10 Gardner, H. (1993) *Frames of Reference*

11 Goleman, D. (1997) *Emotional Intelligence*

12 www.discprofile.com/web

13 www.myersbriggs.org/web

14 www.birkman.com/web

15 Gilligan, C. (1982) *In a Different Voice*

3 NLP COACHING

'Reality is that which, when you stop believing in it, doesn't go away.'

Philip K. Dick

Neuro-linguistic programming (NLP) began in the mid-1970s at the University of Santa Cruz, California. John Grinder, an associate professor of linguistics, and Richard Bandler, a student of mathematics at the university, were intrigued by talent. How was it that some people were very good at something even with little formal training, while others struggled even with a lot of practice? 'Talent' is the easy answer, but that is a description, not an explanation. Bandler and Grinder started to model exceptional individuals to find out how they got their results [1] [2] [3] [4]. They studied Fritz Perls [5], the innovative psychologist and originator of Gestalt therapy. They also studied Virginia Satir [6], who pioneered systemic family therapy. They studied extensively with Milton Erickson [7], who founded an international school of hypnotherapy that still bears his name – Ericksonian hypnotherapy.

Bandler and Grinder also studied videotapes of Carl Rogers and Eric Berne [8], who began transactional analysis. Another strong influence on their thinking was their neighbour in Santa Cruz, Gregory Bateson [9]. Bateson was a founder member of the ground-breaking Macy conferences on systems theory in the 1950s and made important contributions to cybernetics, psychiatry and systems theory. All but Milton Erickson had taught at Esalen. From the studies of these people, NLP was born. NLP is another child of the human potential movement and has very similar roots to coaching. NLP coaches will seek to understand the inner world of the client, using many tools that have been developed through modelling exceptional individuals.

NLP is generally defined as 'the study of the structure of subjective experience', and as such belongs in the top left quadrant of the integral model. Internal experience is not random. You can understand yourself and others by studying the internal world of goals, beliefs and values. NLP says that everyone can learn to think in the same way as talented individuals and so get better results.

NLP spread from California in the 1970s and early 1980s at the same time as the inner game. NLP trainings encouraged communication skills, and because the original models were mostly in the field of psychotherapy, NLP therapy also spread. Today there are NLP institutes and programmes throughout the world.

NLP AND COACHING

NLP skills fit well into coaching, because NLP encapsulates three important elements in its title. 'Neuro' is the mind, our thinking. 'Linguistic' is language, how we use it to influence others and ourselves. 'Programming' is not about computers, but about how we sequence our actions to attain our goals. So, NLP in short is the study of how language affects how we think and therefore our actions. NLP proposes that change can be approached from three directions: by changing the way a person talks about an issue, by changing the way a person thinks about an issue and by changing his or her behaviour. NLP uses a number of distinctions that are helpful in coaching.

POINTS OF VIEW

One of the basic ideas in NLP concerns different perspectives, called perceptual positions. The first position is your point of view, your values, goals, beliefs, interests and preoccupations. The first position is 'I'.

The second position is how you imagine another person thinks and feels. It is the basis of empathy and rapport. When you take the second position, you speak for the person whose viewpoint you are taking. You also use the physiology and voice tone of that person if you know it.

The third position is the systemic position that can look at both first and second position. This is an objective view of the relationship between first and second, which you can adopt without identifying with either. Each position is another point of view, using a different physiology and different language for each.

NLP coaches help clients get in touch with their authentic values and goals through the first position. The second position helps clients understand other people's points of view, especially in relationship problems. The third position is used as an objective position where clients evaluate different relationships, see themselves 'from the outside' and can coach themselves. The third position is a useful tool to help clients describe their present state in specific, descriptive and unjudgmental terms.

First, second and third position can also be seen to represent different types. Some people are stronger in first position. This gives them strength of personality, but can make them selfish and unsympathetic to other people's concerns. Other people have a strong second position. This makes them very empathic; but they may consistently treat other people's demands as more important than their own needs. Others have a strong third position, giving them clarity, objectivity and analytical skills, but a lack of empathy. The NLP approach is to develop and balance all three positions. Clients are helped to see a problem from different perceptual positions to get a fuller understanding.

RAPPORT

Rapport is a word used to describe the quality in a relationship of trust and mutual influence. It is essential in coaching. NLP proposes that rapport is achieved by matching using second position. The intention of second position is to understand others from their point of view, and one way to do this is by matching, meaning taking on some aspects of their behaviour. People like people who are like themselves. People feel more at ease with others who match their body language and voice tone and rhythm. (Match as in a dance, not copy exactly, which is very annoying.) People match body language and voice tone naturally and subconsciously.

This has been demonstrated by the work of William Condon in the 1960s [10]. He analysed short videotapes of people talking together and found (as has been confirmed by many subsequent researchers) that the gestures were harmonized and the rhythms of the conversation matched.

Rapport is an essential skill for a coach, and an NLP coach can teach clients rapport skills to help them communicate better with others.

NEUROLOGICAL LEVELS

The concept of neurological levels is widely used in NLP, and is taken from the writing of the NLP trainer Robert Dilts [11]. In his contribution to this book, Dilts uses neurological levels to describe and illustrate different types of coaching.

The first neurological level is the environment – the place, the time, the people and things that are there to see. In the integral model, this would be the right quadrants. To get rapport at this level you need to be dressed correctly for the environment to meet other people's reasonable expectations. This level also deals with psychogeography. Psychogeography is how we use space to represent relationship, and this is very important for a coach to know. When a coach sits opposite a client, the psychogeography is 'opposition'. Of course, the coach does not intend that, but the client may feel uncomfortable. Bodies opposite each other might represent opposite ideas. Sitting side by side or at an angle of 90° is generally more comfortable. Also, most people have a subconscious preference for being on one side of someone else. The reason does not matter; the NLP coach will let the person sit on the side they prefer. Making a comfortable environment for the client is more than providing a chair and turning off the cell phone.

The second level is behaviour – what people do. Behaviour can be seen from the outside and is the result of the person's thoughts and emotions. Matching body language and voice tone is an example of matching behaviour. This is the upper right quadrant in the integral model.

The third level is capability – the level of skill and behaviour that is consistent, automatic and habitual. Skill cannot be seen except through behaviour. Coaches must have the skill to deal with each client's issue, or they will quickly lose rapport.

The fourth level is beliefs and values – beliefs are the principles that guide our actions, our models of the world. They give us security when we feel we can predict what will happen. We accumulate beliefs from experience and they both open and limit the experiences we allow ourselves. Values are what are important to us; they are our deepest motivation. Matching at this level means respecting the beliefs and values of clients, without necessarily agreeing with them. Both capability and beliefs and values belong in the upper right quadrant of the integral model.

The fifth level is identity – your sense of yourself and what defines your mission in life. Rapport at this level involves listening to clients as unique human beings and giving them a quality of attention that helps them to articulate their issue.

The sixth level is beyond identity – less well defined than the other levels, it encompasses ethics, religion and spirituality, and our place in the world and connection with others.

NLP coaches use neurological levels in a variety of ways. First, they help clients think through the different types of resources they have, and those they need. Second, neurological levels can be used as a framework to help clients pinpoint the level of the problem and clarify the level at which they need to take action. For example, they may need more information or help at the environment level; perhaps their goal will not get the support of other important people.

⇨ Perhaps they have the information they need, but do not know what to do (behaviour) about it, so they need to formulate an action plan with their coach.

⇨ Maybe they have the information and know what to do, but lack the skill. They will need to learn the skill.

⇨ It could be that they have the skill, the information *and* know what to do, but do not believe that it is possible or it is not important enough for them. The client and coach then will work on the client's beliefs and values that could be obstructing them

⇨ Finally, even if all the other levels are taken care of, it may not fit with the person's sense of self or spiritual beliefs. Neurological levels give the coach a frame to work with as well as building rapport.

THINKING ABOUT THINKING

When we pay attention on the outside we use our five senses – seeing, hearing, smelling, tasting and touching – to understand the world. NLP proposes that we think by using those same senses mentally. If you check out your thinking at the moment, you will probably find it is a mixture of hearing (you hear these words as you repeat them to yourself) and visualizing. When we ask you to imagine a bunch of blue flowers, you will probably make a picture of them. If we ask you to think about a strong cup of coffee, your memory will probably bring back the taste and smell of the coffee. The quality of our thinking is influenced by how well we use our senses on the inside (called representational systems in NLP vocabulary).

This has many coaching applications. NLP proposes that we all have a preferred representational system; in other words, we prefer to think either in pictures, or in sounds, or with feelings. This means that we will be good at some things but not others. For example, if clients rely heavily on their visual representational system, then they will pay a lot of attention to what they see but may not listen very carefully. Coaches can help clients become aware of this and work on the less well-developed system, thereby helping their thinking to become more flexible. Some professions need to have a particular sense well developed, not only on the outside, but also on the inside in the person's thinking. For example, musicians need to listen carefully, but they also need the ability to hear sounds clearly in their minds to progress in music. NLP coaching can help clients refine and develop their thinking to get better results.

NLP also proposes that we use a sequence of representational systems for all our thinking, learning and decision-making. NLP coaches can discover the way clients are making decisions and help them to develop a better decision-making strategy which will improve the quality of all their decisions. People take their thinking patterns and strategies for granted; they assume everyone thinks in the same way and that these patterns are not changeable. NLP coaches can move them to a different view, where they can reflect on their own thinking process and improve it.

How do NLP coaches become aware of the way clients are thinking? Watching their clients' body language (especially involuntary eye movements) can tell coaches *how* clients are thinking (pictures, sounds or feelings), but not *what* they are thinking. Also, NLP coaches pay attention to the words clients are using. As words are a direct reflection of thought, if a client says something like 'I can't *see* beyond this problem', then they are using a visual metaphor and that is how the client is thinking about the problem. The coach can then respond in the same representational system ('Let's *see* if we can broaden the horizon a little') to establish rapport and then perhaps work to help the client develop other ways of thinking to solve the problem.

THE INNER QUALITIES OF THINKING

When clients use their senses internally, they must be making the same sorts of distinctions on the inside as they do on the outside. For example, mental pictures will have colours, size, distance and brightness, just as they do on the outside. Mental sounds will have rhythm, pitch and volume, while mental sensations will have warmth, pressure and direction. When clients change the qualities of their thinking, they change the meaning of what they are thinking about. These qualities are known as submodalities.

One of the most important submodalities is whether a thought is associated or dissociated. When you are inside the thought, you are associated. For example, imagine eating a fruit. You will experience the feelings and the taste as if it were real. When you are outside the thought, you are dissociated. You see yourself in a situation, which gives mental distance from the event, so you will not get the same sensations as if you were there. Make a picture of someone eating a fruit and you will not get the taste; you are dissociated from the experience.

NLP coaches can help clients learn from experience using these tools. If a past experience is bad, then they will help clients to evaluate while staying dissociated, so they do not experience the bad feelings again. Once is enough! They can review the experience objectively and learn from it. But if it was an enjoyable experience, coaches will help clients to associate into the memory. To build motivation, NLP coaches will encourage clients to think about the desired goal as if it was already achieved, so they are inside the picture, associated so they get all the good feelings.

Some clients have problems managing their time, in which case the NLP coach can help them take a dissociated view of time, so they will be aware of time passing, instead of being associated in the moment.

LANGUAGE

Words are how we communicate our mental pictures, sounds and feelings to other people. But our thoughts are not the experience and our words are not our thoughts, so our experience can get badly distorted when we speak about it. We forget, we misunderstand what happened, but the words can appear to be reality even if they are only pale reflections of it. Words are twice removed from the actual experience (once from the experience itself and once again from the mental representations of it), yet the judgments that we make and the way we describe things take on a quality of truth. According to Alfred Korzybski's famous saying, 'The map is not the territory', but clients believe that their maps (what they say, what they remember and interpret about what happened) are the territory (real objective events agreed by everyone who was there). So, language is the raw material with which we create reality for ourselves and for others. NLP shares a constructivist approach with coaching.

NLP has a set of distinctions known as the Meta model for helping clients. The Meta model is a model of language on language, using language to clarify language. It consists of a series of questions to help clients untangle the way they speak about their experience. Words can be manipulated and spun in many ways when clients put problems into words. So, coaches need to solve the *linguistic* tangle clients create, before helping them take action. NLP coaches will help their clients untangle the language from the experience and help them find a better map of their problem.

For example, one of the Meta model patterns is to challenge judgments that the client makes by asking who makes the judgment and by what standards. Many clients make judgments about themselves (usually bad), which NLP coaches can challenge. Some clients feel emotionally at the mercy of other people; they do not experience any choice when they feel angry or sad or unresourceful, but feel pushed around like a billiard ball. There are Newton's laws of motion, but not Newton's laws of emotion. Clients may say that someone 'made' them feel angry, but that is a manner of speaking. No one can force another person to be angry. NLP coaches will help clients to have a choice about how they feel.

Lastly, many clients labour under a suffocating weight of 'shoulds' and 'shouldn'ts' in their lives. They feel torn, under an obligation, yet somehow wanting to break free; they have internalized other people's commands, and experience them as their own. In this case, NLP coaches can help clients think through what they really want to do. Together they can turn obligations into goals, 'shoulds' into 'wants'.

Clients want to achieve their goals, but there are obstructions, otherwise they would not consult a coach. These obstructions are usually in the client's mind rather than in the outside world. Clients have limiting beliefs about themselves, their resources or other people. NLP, like all other coaching methodologies, does not treat beliefs as the truth (although they seem true for the client), but as best guesses based on previous experience. These limiting beliefs act as self-fulfilling prophecies. When we believe something, we follow it, so we never gather feedback to question it, because we always act as if it is true. Everyone believes in gravity, so we do not try to fly unaided or the feedback would be very painful, if not fatal. However, beliefs about ourselves, others, how men and women should treat each other are very different from beliefs about gravity. They are learned or copied from significant adults in our childhood and adolescence and are not true. They become true when we act as if they are. Beliefs are learned, so they can be unlearned. We are not born with all the fears and restrictions we carry into adulthood. When beliefs are limiting clients, NLP coaches can help clients see them differently, get feedback and change them if they wish.

Coaching is about change, and NLP considers two types of change – simple change or generative change.

Simple change is on the level of behaviour or capability. Managers learn a skill, know when to use it and when not to, and increase their efficiency and their effectiveness. Celebrations all round. We can represent simple change like this:

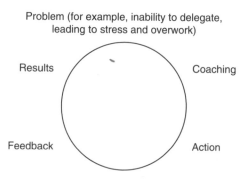

Simple change

This is known as single-loop coaching. There is a problem in this example: stress and overwork caused by an inability to delegate. The manager delegates with the help of their coach. They monitor feedback, get different results and the problem diminishes until everyone is happy. The coach's work is done.

The second type of coaching works at the neurological level of beliefs and values. The coaching makes clients question their beliefs, not just build a new skill. A limiting belief may be stopping them from learning.

This is called double-loop coaching, because coaches help their clients get feedback on the belief, not just the problem. Coaches would not try to disprove the belief or argue about it, but help the client get better feedback by taking small experimental steps. There is always a limiting belief at the back of a persistent problem. Double-loop coaching does not just solve the problem, but also changes the thinking that gave rise to the problem in the first place and has maintained that thinking subsequently.

METAPROGRAMS

Metaprograms in NLP are ways in which we filter our experience. We cannot process and respond to all the possible sensory experience; there is too much. So, we habitually pay attention to certain parts of it and not to other parts. There are various Metaprogram patterns. The best-known ones are 'proactive' (a proactive person will initiate action) and 'reactive' (a reactive person will analyse and wait for others to make the first move).

Another Metaprogram pattern is 'general' (focusing on the overview, then diving into the details) as opposed to 'detail' (going from the details and building the big picture from those). Some people notice similarities, others notice differences. Metaprograms are not about identity and one pattern is not better than another; it depends what you want to accomplish. NLP coaches will notice the Metaprogram patterns of their clients to understand how and why their clients act the way they do, and frame their coaching in the way that is best for the clients.

APPLICATIONS OF NLP COACHING

NLP was not developed specifically for use in coaching and has been used extensively in therapy. However, coaching provides a good vehicle for many NLP tools and shares many of the same intellectual roots as NLP. What does NLP contribute to coaching? NLP is pragmatic and concentrates on 'how to do' as well as 'what to do'.

First, NLP can be used to model good coaches. What distinguishes the best coaches from others? By exploring their thinking patterns, language, values and beliefs, NLP can generate some useful ways to train coaches.

Second, it can be used in building rapport with clients at every neurological level, by paying attention to psychogeography, matching body language and voice tone in a respectful way, as well as respecting values and beliefs. Matching language helps to build rapport. If clients use a visual metaphor about their problem, for example, 'I can't see a way forward', then coaches will match their visual language in talking about the problem. This will reassure clients that their coach is respecting the way they think. NLP coaches also use a technique known as backtracking. This means reflecting back what a client says, using the same key words and gestures. A backtrack is not a paraphrase. A paraphrase distorts what the clients have said by using the coach's words, and these will not mean the same thing to the client.

The NLP Meta model of language is also useful in surfacing the assumptions behind questions. For example, '*If* you get this goal, what would it achieve for you?' is one possible question, but the word 'if' implies uncertainty. '*When* you get this goal, what will it achieve for you?' implies certainty, and so from the NLP point of view helps to focus the client's mind on getting the goal, therefore aiding them to answer the question. 'Do you have any resources?' is a closed question and does not assume resources. 'Of the resources that you have, which would be the best ones to deal with this situation?' is more useful, because it focuses the client on the resources they have.

NLP coaches might suspect that the way their clients are thinking about an issue is hindering them from a solution, so they can encourage them to use different representational systems. For example, to make pictures of the future may be more useful than having a feeling about the future, and it will certainly be more specific.

NLP also uses the concept of an 'anchor'. An anchor is a sight, sound or feeling that is associated with a particular response or emotion in the past, and so triggers the same feeling in the present. The feeling may be good or bad. We have all experienced times when a familiar smell evokes a memory, or how a specific piece of music reminds us of a special time (most couples have a special song that reminds them of when they met). Equally, a voice tone may make you cringe because it reminds you of a person you do not like. Sometimes we relate to people not in terms of who they are now, but in terms of who they remind us of in the past. NLP coaches help clients see what anchors are in their life at that moment and whether these are triggering unresourceful states. If they are, coaches will help them become aware of these anchors and so they will lose their power. Knowledge of anchors helps coaches build reminders for their clients (often called structures) to help them remember a task, action step, or change in perspective they need to take to move forward.

CASE STUDY

An NLP coach could help Brian in a number of ways. To begin with, they could explore the three perceptual positions. Does Brian have a strong first position? Is he clear about what he believes and what he wants? Second, how empathic is he? How good is he at going to second position? The problems Brian has with workmates and with his wife suggest that this could be his weak point. An NLP coach would help Brian take second position with his wife, children and work colleagues in order to understand them and their points of view better. This will give him better information on which to build his decisions about his future. The coach would also encourage Brian metaphorically to step outside the problem and look at it from third position. From there, he will be able to coach himself because he will feel more resourceful.

An NLP coach might use neurological levels to help Brian understand the problem. Does he have the resources he needs at the different levels? Does he have the information he needs, does he know what to do? Does he have the skills? What is important to him about his present position? What does he want from another job? Can his spiritual beliefs be a resource for him in this situation? When he has identified the weak point, he can take action to solve it.

An NLP coach could also teach Brian some rapport skills of matching body language and voice tone to help him in his relationships. They would also help him understand his decision-making strategy. In NLP terms, a strategy is a sequence of representation systems leading to an outcome, in other words a sequence of internal pictures, sounds and feelings. What is Brian's decision strategy? What is his sequence of thinking? Does it serve him well? A poor decision-making strategy will give poor-quality decisions; it will not take in all the necessary information he needs in the right order.

Brian would learn to look back on his quarrels from a dissociated position and learn from them, and he could also identify any anchors in his environment that trigger him into an unresourceful state like anger or irritation. Once he is aware of these anchors (it could be a tone of voice, or a particular situation), he can avoid them, and have more choice about how he responds to them. Brian might be using a 'detail' Metaprogram and also be reactive. An NLP coach could help him look at the bigger picture and be more proactive in his life.

REFERENCES

1 Bandler, R. and Grinder, J. (1975) *The Structure of Magic* Volume 1, Science and Behavior Books

2 Bandler, R. and Grinder, J. (1976) *The Structure of Magic* Volume 2, Science and Behavior Books

3 Grinder, J. and Bandler, R. (1975) *Patterns of Hypnotic Techniques of Milton H. Erickson M.D.* Volume 1, Meta Publications

4 Grinder, J. and Bandler, R. (1976) *Patterns of Hypnotic Techniques of Milton H. Erickson M.D.* Volume 2, Meta Publications

5 Perls, F. (1969) *Gestalt Therapy Verbatim,* Real People Press

6 Satir, V., Bandler, R. and Grinder, J. (1976) *Changing with Families,* Science and Behavior Books

7 Erickson, M. and Rossi, E. (1975) *Hypnotic Realities,* Irvington

8 Berne, E. (1964) *Games People Play,* Penguin

9 Bateson, G. (1972) *Steps to an Ecology of Mind,* Ballantine Books

10 Condon, W. (1982) Cultural Microrhythms, in M. Davis (Ed.) *Interaction Rhythms: Periodicity in Communicative Behavior,* Human Sciences Press

11 Dilts, R. (2003) *From Coach to Awakener,* Meta Publications

NLP AND COACHING
WITH A CAPITAL 'C'

by Robert Dilts

In general, *coaching* is the process of helping people and teams to perform at the peak of their abilities. It involves drawing out people's strengths, helping them to bypass personal barriers and limits in order to achieve their personal best, and facilitating them to function more effectively as members of a team. Thus, effective coaching requires an emphasis on both task and relationship.

Coaching emphasizes generative change, concentrating on defining and achieving specific goals. Coaching methodologies are outcome-oriented rather than problem-oriented. They tend to be highly solution focused, promoting the development of new strategies for thinking and acting, as opposed to trying to resolve problems and past conflicts. Problem solving, or remedial change, is more associated with counselling and therapy.

ORIGINS OF COACHING

A 'coach' is literally a vehicle that carries a person or group of people from some starting location to a desired location.

The notion of coaching in the educational sense derived from the concept that the tutor 'conveys' or 'transports' students through their examinations. An educational coach is defined as 'a private tutor,' 'one who instructs or trains a performer or a team of performers', or 'one who instructs players in the fundamentals of a competitive sport and directs team strategy'. The process of being a coach is defined as 'to train intensively (as by instruction and demonstration)'.

Thus, historically, coaching is typically focused towards achieving improvement with respect to a specific behavioural performance. An effective coach of this type (such as a 'voice coach', an 'acting coach', a 'pitching coach') observes a person's behaviour and gives him or her tips and guidance about how to improve in specific contexts and situations. This involves promoting the development of that person's behavioural competence through careful observation and feedback.

THE COACHING REVOLUTION

Since the 1980s, the notion of coaching has taken on a more generalized and expanded meaning. Coaching in organizations involves a variety of ways of helping people perform more effectively and overcome personal limitations. Organizations have realized that limitations in employees limit the company. There are several common types of coaching in organizations. *Project coaching* involves the strategic management of a team in order to reach the most effective result. *Situational coaching* focuses on the specific enhancement or improvement of performance within a context. *Transitional coaching* involves helping individuals move from one job or role to another.

Another rapidly developing area of coaching is that of life coaching. *Life coaching* involves helping people to reach personal goals, which may be largely independent from professional or organizational objectives. Similar to transitional coaching, life coaching encourages individuals to deal effectively with a variety of performance issues that may face them as they move from one life phase to another.

LARGE 'C' AND SMALL 'C' COACHING

Clearly, personal coaching, executive coaching and life coaching provide support on a number of different levels: behaviours, capabilities, beliefs, values, identity and even the spiritual level. These new and more general forms of coaching – executive coaching and life coaching – can be referred to as capital 'C' Coaching.

Small 'c' coaching is more focused at a behavioural level, referring to the process of helping another person to achieve or improve a particular behavioural performance. Small 'c' coaching methods derive primarily from a sports training model, promoting conscious awareness of resources and abilities, and the development of conscious competence.

Large 'C' Coaching involves helping people effectively achieve outcomes on a range of levels. It emphasizes evolutionary change, concentrating on strengthening identity and values, and bringing dreams and goals into reality. This encompasses the skills of small 'c' coaching, but also includes much more.

FROM COACH TO AWAKENER – NLP AND COACHING

The skills and tools of neuro-linguistic programming (NLP) are uniquely suited for promoting effective coaching. NLP's focus on well-formed outcomes, its foundation in modelling exceptional performers, and its ability to produce step-by-step processes to promote excellence make it one of the most important and powerful resources for both large 'C' and small 'c' coaches.

Common NLP skills, tools and techniques that support effective coaching include establishing goals and well-formed outcomes, managing internal states, taking different perceptual positions, identifying moments of excellence, mapping across resources and providing high-quality feedback.

The task of the capital 'C' Coach is to provide the necessary support and 'guardianship' which help clients successfully to develop, grow and evolve at all these levels of learning and change. Depending on the situation and needs of the client, the coach may be called upon to provide support at one or all of these levels, requiring that he or she takes on one of several possible roles [1].

GUIDING AND CARETAKING

Guiding and caretaking have to do with providing support with respect to the *environment* in which change takes place. Guiding is the process of directing a person or group along the path leading from some present state to a desired state. It pre-supposes that the 'guide' has been there before, and knows the best way (or at least a way) to reach the desired state. Being a caretaker, or 'custodian', involves providing a safe and sup-portive environment. It has to do with attending to the external context and making sure that what is needed is available, and that there are no unnecessary distractions or interferences from the outside.

TRADITIONAL COACHING

Traditional coaching (ie small 'c' coaching) is focused at a behavioural level, involving the process of helping another person to achieve or improve a particular *behavioural* performance. Coaching methods at this level derive primarily from a sports training model, promoting conscious awareness of resources and abilities, and the development of conscious competence. They involve drawing out and strengthening people's abilities through careful observation and feedback, and facilitating them to act in co-ordination with other team members. An effective coach of this type observes people's behaviour and gives them tips and guidance about how to improve in specific contexts and situations.

TEACHING

Teaching relates to helping a person develop *cognitive skills and capabilities*. The goal of teaching is generally to assist people to increase competences and 'thinking skills' relevant to an area of learning. Teaching focuses on the acquisition of general cognitive abilities, rather than on particular performances in specific situations. A teacher helps a person to develop new strategies for thinking and acting. The emphasis of teaching is more on new learning than on refining someone's previous performance.

MENTORING

Mentoring involves guiding someone to discover his or her own unconscious competences and overcome internal resistances and interferences, through believing in the person and validating his or her positive intentions. Mentors help to shape or influence a person's *beliefs and values* in a positive way by 'resonating' with, releasing or unveiling that person's inner wisdom, frequently through the mentor's own example. This type of mentoring often becomes internalized as part of a person, so that the external presence of the mentor is no longer necessary. People are able to carry 'inner mentors' as counsellors and guides for their lives in many situations.

SPONSORING

'Sponsorship' is the process of recognizing and acknowledging ('seeing and blessing') the essence or *identity* of another person. Sponsorship involves seeking and safeguarding potential within others, focusing on the development of identity and core values. Effective sponsorship results from the commitment to promote something that is already within a person or group, but which is not being manifested to its fullest capacity. This is accomplished through constantly sending messages such as: *You exist. I see you. You are valuable. You are important/special/unique. You are welcome. You belong here. You have something to contribute.* A good 'sponsor' creates a context in which others can act, grow and excel. Sponsors provide the conditions, contacts and resources that allow the group or individual being sponsored to focus on, develop and use their own abilities and skills.

AWAKENING

Awakening goes beyond coaching, teaching, mentoring and sponsorship to include the level of *vision, mission and purpose*. An awakener supports another person by providing contexts and experiences which bring out the best of that person's understanding of love, self and spirit. An awakener 'awakens' others through his or her own integrity and congruence. An awakener puts other people in touch with their own missions and visions by being in full contact with his or her own vision and mission.

SUMMARY

In summary, the overall goal for coaches is to help their clients learn skills and apply tools at different levels of change. The purpose of these skills and tools is to help clients build the future that they desire and activate the resources necessary to reach that future. The role of the coach is to help clients learn to apply the needed skills and tools for themselves. As clients become more proficient with each tool in the toolbox, they are able to utilize those tools for themselves with progressively less dependence on the coach for their success. In doing so, clients become truly empowered to live fuller and more effective lives.

REFERENCES

Dilts, R. (2003) *From Coach to Awakener*, Meta Publications

Robert Dilts has been one of the foremost developers, trainers and consultants in the field of neuro-linguistic programming (NLP) since its creation in 1975 by John Grinder and Richard Bandler. Dilts also studied personally with Milton H. Erickson, MD and Gregory Bateson. He is the author of 18 books on NLP.

4 POSITIVE PSYCHOLOGY COACHING

'Ask yourself if you are happy and you cease to be so.'

John Stuart Mill

Positive psychology follows closely in the footsteps of Maslow's psychology of self-actualization. Positive psychology concentrates on the qualities of mental health, happiness and well-being rather than dealing with problems, and so it takes a different perspective on the model of mental health from that followed by many systems of psychology. In the usual models, behavioural and emotional problems are diagnosed, treated and cured. Then the patient returns to normal. This does not fit coaching, which tries to make 'normal' into exceptional. Coaching based on positive psychology is often called authentic happiness coaching (AHC).

Positive psychology researches how we have positive emotions and what we can do to get more of them. It models individuals who are happy and fulfilled and then explores how they build more and lasting positive emotions into their life. Then the coach can help others to do the same. These questions have been generally neglected by the disciplines of psychology.

Positive psychology has been developed primarily by Martin Seligman [1] and focuses on three main areas. The first is positive emotion. The second is positive character traits, strengths and virtues of mind, body and spirit that support the positive emotions. The third is the study of positive institutions that support the character traits. The discipline is built on well-validated scientific research.

Coaching with positive psychology means identifying and cultivating clients' basic strengths and values and using these in their personal and professional lives. Positive psychology assumes that generally we want to be happier and more fulfilled. This means cultivating positive emotions as well as dealing with negative ones. Negative emotions are a defence against external threats; they are a signal to act, to move away from a dangerous situation, but they do not make us happy. They help us to balance our life by moving us out of danger or repairing a breakdown. People who seek coaches are usually doing well; they want to realize even more of their potential, and they know that they do not have to be sick to get better. Happiness is not just the absence of misery, in the same way that health is not just the absence of illness.

HOPE AND OPTIMISM

When clients consult authentic happiness coaches, what happens?

The coach will first explore how the person thinks and feels about their experience and how they make sense of what happens. There are two distinct ways of making sense of events, termed 'attributional styles' by Seligman and his colleagues at Pennsylvania University in the 1980s [2]. They are the pessimistic style and the optimistic style. Each has three components.

First, people thinking in the pessimist style will assume a misfortune is their fault. They blame themselves. They make it personal. And when something good happens, they do the opposite and attribute the good fortune to something beyond their control.

Second, they think a bad situation will persist. However, when something good happens, they think it will not last. Third, they think that a bad experience will be pervasive and affect many other areas of their life. If the experience is a good one, they expect it will not have such a pervasive effect. So, for example, a pessimist has a quarrel with a friend. He will blame himself; he will think that the friendship is over and that his friend will tell many other people about what happened. If he meets a new person and they become his friend, he will be put that down to how nice the other person is, but it probably will not last and anyway will not make much difference to his quality of life. Some people think pessimism is somehow more 'realistic'. 'Expect the worst,' they say, 'and you won't be disappointed.' However, pessimism is no more 'realistic' than optimism.

The optimistic style is the complete opposite. An optimist will not take blame for bad situations, and they will take personal credit for good ones. They see bad situations as transient, but good situations as persisting. And when something bad happens, they see it as an isolated incident, but agood experience they see as pervasive and helping them in other areas of life.

These two styles are tendencies, and people tend to lean one way or the other; it is rare to find an extreme type.

Optimistic attribution style	Pessimistic attribution style
1 Personal ⇨ Take credit for good events but do not blame themselves for bad situations.	1 Personal ⇨ Blame themselves for bad events but do not take credit for good ones.
2 Temporal ⇨ Believe good things will last, but bad things will not.	2 Temporal ⇨ Believe bad situations will last, but good ones will not.
3 Pervasive ⇨ Believe good things will have an effect on the rest of their life, but bad experiences will not affect other areas of their life.	3 Pervasive ⇨ Believe bad experiences will have an effect on the rest of their life, but good experiences will not affect other areas of their life.

Optimistic people see good events as having permanent causes and bad events as being temporary. This means that they recover from bad events quickly and keep the warm glow of good events for longer. They make very specific explanations for bad events but universal ones for good events. They let their triumphs cut across many areas of their life, but keep the failures in their own box. Optimism and pessimism as described here are extreme positions. Most people fall between the two.

What difference does this make? A big difference. A study done over 35 years at Harvard [3] showed that, overall, men who used optimistic explanations for bad events in their 20s were healthier later in life (over 40) than men who favoured pessimistic explanations. The health of the pessimistic group showed a marked deterioration that could not be accounted for through any other variable (lifestyle, smoking, eating habits etc). The upshot is that optimists had 19% greater longevity. The results were statistically significant; there was a less than 1 in 1,000 chance of its being a random association. There are toxic and harmful thought patterns just as there are toxic and harmful foods. Given that optimism is just as realistic as pessimism, it obviously pays to think optimistically (while taking appropriate steps to cover any unnecessary risks.)

Optimism and its companion, hope, have been the subject of many research studies. They give better resistance to depression when bad events do happen, better performance at work, especially in jobs that are challenging, and better physical health. Best of all, contrary to popular belief, they can be learned. A positive psychology coach will help clients to make their thinking more optimistic. This will help with whatever problem is confronting them and will also have long-term benefits.

Seligman [1] describes a simple process for recognizing and disputing pessimistic thinking, which he calls the ABCDE model – **A**dversity, **B**eliefs, **C**onsequences, **D**isputation and **E**nergization.

ADVERSITY

Adversity refers to the experience, especially if it was negative. How was it a challenge? For example, you have a coaching session and you don't feel very inspired and the client doesn't seem to make progress. At the end of the session they say they don't feel they have made any change.

This can be seen from many points of view. It is easy to hop from event to explanation, skip from explanation to judgment and then jump to conclusion – that it was a bad coaching session, or even, you are a bad coach. This would be the classic pessimistic conclusion.

BELIEFS

⇨ **What do you believe about what happened?**

⇨ **Was it your fault?**

⇨ **Will the next session be as bad?**

⇨ **Are you losing your skill?**

⇨ **Will the client continue with the coaching?**

CONSEQUENCES

What are the consequences of the pessimistic belief? Maybe insecurity about coaching, and a worry that this client will stop the coaching and tell all their friends and important business partners. Maybe the supply of business clients will dry up. Perhaps you need some more supervision.

DISPUTATION

Disputation is the key step. Look carefully and objectively at the event and its surrounding circumstances, the belief and the possible consequences. Cross-examine your pessimistic part; don't let it off the witness stand without justifying itself. What evidence do you have about this? What are the other explanations? An event does not have only one cause; it is always a combination of circumstances. For example, first you might remember that you did not sleep very well the previous night and felt a little under the weather before the session. You were also worried about your son's school report; he does not seem to be doing as well as last term. This was a nagging worry and you forgot to do your short relaxation/clearing ritual before the session, because the previous session ran late. The worry about your son must have still been bubbling under the surface. It would not be realistic to expect you to be at your best under those circumstances. Also, remember that the client has been happy with their coaching up until now. Everyone has off days; you have had sessions like this before, maybe once a month but hardly a pattern.

So what are the implications? You are human. You have off days. Even if the client stopped the coaching, that would say as much about his commitment as about you. Pessimistic thinking is not reasonable.

ENERGIZATION

Disputing the negative belief and the pessimistic thinking gives energy. What can you learn from this? You do not have to be perfect, your performance will fluctuate from time to time; that is natural. If it goes below normal, then it can also go above normal. Maybe you had an excellent session with a demanding client the same week that led to some remarkable insights for her and a big breakthrough. Could that mean you are becoming a better coach and she will recommend you to her business contacts?

Your work is good most of the time and sometimes it is excellent, but it is useful to monitor your performance and notice patterns. At the next session with the problem client, you could start with a review of the last session and see what they think about it, and progress from there. You might also go back over your notes on the session and see what better questions you could have asked. Coaching is not always onwards and upwards. There are little detours and obstacles, and that just makes the breakthroughs even more pleasant.

This ABCDE process is easily learned and helps clients not only to deal with a problem but also to change their habitual way of thinking. Longer life is not usually considered as a benefit of coaching, but perhaps it is.

HAPPINESS

Happiness is a state – one we seek in different ways throughout life, despite problems, difficulties, illnesses and tragedies. There is no fixed formula for happiness. Leo Tolstoy wrote as the first line of his novel *Anna Karenina*, 'Happy families are all alike; every unhappy family is unhappy in its own way.' This idea makes interesting fiction, but it is only half right. Everyone and every family are also happy in a unique way.

Seligman identified three pathways to happiness:

⇨ **through the emotions**
⇨ **through connection with an internal or external activity**
⇨ **through personal meaning**

Everyone is different and has different capacities and needs and different ways of being happy. Authentic happiness is being happy in your own way. The coach helps you to do that by identifying your strengths and potentials and helping you to develop them. Happiness is not the same as hedonism. Hedonists want as much pleasure as possible. But happiness is not the same as pleasure. What is happiness and can we measure it?

THE HAPPINESS FORMULA

Happiness is a multifaceted word, and although everybody would agree it is desirable and they prize it and seek it, it can be elusive. Until the mid-1990s it was generally assumed that a capacity for happiness was set like a thermostat at birth. Some people were just naturally happier than others and there was not a lot they could do about it. Good or bad events would change your level, but then it tended to revert back to its pre-set level. But now we know happiness is not completely controlled by genetics.

Here is the positive psychology happiness formula:

$$H = S + C + V$$

H stands for your enduring level of happiness. We all have moments of happiness, but they do not always last.

S is the set range. This is genetically determined to a large extent. We do habituate to new circumstances and after a while what made us happy in the past becomes part of normal living. We then set new goals that we hope will make us happy. And they do – for a while. We achieve, enjoy and then take for granted all the good things that come our way in life.

C is for circumstances. We can change our circumstances, but it is not easy. Money does not buy happiness. In wealthy nations where everyone has a social safety net, increase in income scarcely affects the happiness level at all. Even the most wealthy people in the United States are reportedly only slightly happier than average. Age, education, climate, race and gender do not seem related to happiness. Circumstances come from the outside; enduring happiness can only come from the inside – and this we can control.

V is for what you can do voluntarily. This is under your control. For example, optimistic thinking patterns are something we can bring about voluntarily to increase our happiness level. Yet happiness is something of a paradox. It is a state, and you can only be happy in the present moment. It is not like a possession that you can carry around with you, so that if you had it yesterday, you will wake up with it today. The more you try to grasp it, the more it eludes you. It is like a shy friend that needs to be tempted into your house. If you grab them and try to force them across the threshold they will run away and stay away.

PLEASURE

Positive psychology makes a distinction between happiness, pleasure and gratification. 'How can I be happy?' is an ambiguous question. Happiness has two distinct elements, pleasure and gratification. Pleasure is sensory; it is immediate and emotional. Pleasure feels good (although guilt and other negative emotions may sometimes follow). The raw pleasures of sex, laughter, a hot bath or a cold shower, a wonderful piece of music or a piece of chocolate are all wonderful. Cognitive appreciation can enhance a pleasure, for example listening to music or wine tasting. Add to this list at your leisure. Pleasures, at least the basic sensory ones, vary little from person to person, as our bodies are similar biologically, wired for pain and pleasure in the same way. Pleasures are unselfconscious; you do not question them or try to analyse them, and if you do, they dissipate.

The trouble is that pleasure fades. It is subject to the law of diminishing returns. The first glass of wine may be delicious, but the taste buds do not register the same pleasure for the tenth. Each pleasure detracts something from the one that follows. We habituate to pleasure; it often takes more and more of the same stimulus to get the same pleasure, and this is the basis of addiction. Pleasures need to be spread out and savoured for the best effect. In that sense a coach can educate the client to get the most from their pleasures.

GRATIFICATION AND FLOW

Pleasure is mostly passive; you lie back and enjoy it. Gratifications are active. They engage us fully, and if there is pleasure, we are not always directly aware of it. It creates what has been described as the 'flow state'. You are in a 'flow state' when you are vitally engaged and grounded in what you are doing. The activity has meaning and a sense of purpose, and positive psychology coaching helps clients to achieve meaning and purpose by helping them to achieve more flow in their life. Flow has been studied primarily by Mihaly Csikszentmihalyi [4]. It is not a state of grace accessible only to the chosen few, but something everyone experiences at one time or another, given the right circumstances. It can be cultivated, and positive psychology coaching helps clients to cultivate it.

What are the conditions of flow? The first is inner clarity. Everything seems clear; there are no doubts. The second is being completely in the present moment. There is little self-consciousness. You are there, but you are not aware it is 'you'. You are part of the flow of life. The moment you think, 'Wow, isn't this great, I am in the flow', you are out of it. 'Flow' is another name for what athletes call 'the zone'. Athletes in the zone are at their very best, but are not thinking how well or badly they are playing, but just responding in the moment to whatever is happening. They become empty, so their skill just flows through them. This is exactly the state that the inner game is trying to cultivate.

There is a great sense of control in the flow state, and the sense of doing flows into what is done; there is action, but no actor. When you are in flow there is very little sense of the passage of time. A long time may elapse and yet for the person caught up in the state, it seems only a few seconds or minutes.

These qualities (inner clarity, being in the present and time distortion) are consequences of the flow state – they are not controllable. You cannot try to do them; in fact, trying makes them impossible. However, there are two things that clients can control about the flow state, and the coach can help them do so.

The first is balancing the level of skill versus challenge for the clients. Flow needs a high level of skill meeting a high challenge. It is the clients' perceived level of challenge and skill that counts, not an absolute level of challenge and skill. If they think the challenge is too great, they will go into not a flow state, but an anxiety state. If they think their skill is more than adequate to meet the challenge then they will be bored.

The other aspect of flow that is under clients' control is motivation. No one goes into a flow state doing something they do not like doing. Coaches will help clients search for activities that they value and enjoy for their own sake. Flow cannot be bribed, forced or pulled. It needs to be invited and attracted.

Coaches can help their clients to find flow and gratification as follows:

⇨ **By giving clear and immediate feedback about their activities, and helping them to identify how and where they can get clear feedback from others. The**

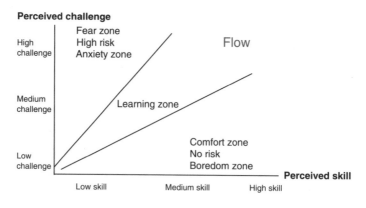

Perceived challenge

Flow, skill and challenge

feedback should be supportive and positive, but not too much, as too much positive feedback is counterproductive.

⇨ By helping clients to reflect on their experience. How are they spending their time? What are they doing? If time was money, what are they investing in? Are they truly making time in their life for activities that they value and that give them happiness?

⇨ By respecting clients' views of their level of skill and challenge, and by helping them find the right balance between the two – always pushing them a little beyond their comfort zone, but never far enough to leave them anxious, doubtful or frustrated.

⇨ Perhaps most important of all, making clients aware of their internal dialogue, which may be very judgmental. Many clients judge themselves harshly and are constantly giving themselves negative feedback inside their heads. This negative feedback may overpower anything positive that comes from the outside. Clients need to be aware of their internal conversations and make them as supportive as possible.

VALUES, VIRTUES AND STRENGTHS

Positive psychology coaching focuses on helping clients connect with what is important to them and what they are good at. Chris Peterson and Martin Seligman [5] have developed a classification of character strengths called the values in action (VIA) survey. A character strength is a natural capacity for

The basic core virtues endorsed by nearly all cultures and major religious traditions
Wisdom
Courage
Humanity
Justice
Temperance
Transcendence

behaving, thinking or feeling that lets people function in an optimal way to achieve their goals and perform at their best.

Coaches can guide clients through this survey to identify their character strengths. Coach and client then work together on developing these strengths and using those qualities more in their everyday life. There are 24 strengths, which derive from six basic core virtues that are endorsed by every major religion and cultural tradition. These virtues are wisdom, courage, humanity, justice, temperance and transcendence. These core virtues can be developed and they are valued as ends in themselves. There is a free VIA survey of your strengths that you can take on the Internet [6].

When clients are acting from a signature strength, they feel authentic and energized and want to find more ways to use it. It is a tool for bringing out the best performance. Profiles of clients' strengths show what they are like at their best and what motivates them. The coach uses their clients' values to help them build gratifications and flow and link them to these universal virtues.

POSITIVE PSYCHOLOGY AND TEAMS

There are many business implications for positive psychology. People want to be happy in their work, feel part of a team and enjoy what they do. When they bring their signature strengths to their work, their performance will improve. Positive emotions energize and motivate people to more creative work. There is a research study by Losada on the results of 60 business teams [7]. It found that positive feelings played a very big part in how the teams functioned and the results they achieved. During their meetings, the researchers measured the ratio between the number of positive (that is, approving or supportive) statements that were made, and the number of negative (disapproving or critical) statements that were made. The teams were evaluated according to profitability and customer satisfaction and given a high, medium or low rating. The results showed that the high-performance teams had a ratio of roughly three positive support statements to every one negative, disapproving statement. The lower the positive to negative ratio, the lower the team rating. Just because there were more supportive comments did not mean that there was no criticism or challenge; these are obviously important in getting a team to give its best.

Later research [8] showed that you can have too much of a good thing. When the ratio of positive to negative comments goes over 12 to 1 the team does not do well, and individuals become inflexible and unthinking. This has implications for coaches who work with business teams as well as life coaches. Be supportive, yes, but only up to a point. Too much support makes the person less responsive and proactive.

In summary, positive psychology coaches work with clients on their strengths and values, helping them to achieve their best performance through their natural strengths. They help clients to think in an optimistic style and also give tasks to support clients in this way of thinking, to increase positive emotions, their engagement in their activities and their sense of purpose. For example, an exercise to increase positive emotion would be for clients to set aside a short period of time to devote to their favourite pleasurable activity. Clients will savour the moment, get absorbed in the activity and appreciate this pleasure in a new way. It can be woven into their life on a regular basis. Positive psychology takes concepts that until a few years ago were considered too subjective to study, such as happiness, flow and character strengths, and uses them in a pragmatic and meticulously researched way to help people lead fuller lives.

CASE STUDY

How would a positive psychology coach help Brian?

First, he or she would invite Brian to focus on his strengths and achievements rather than what was wrong, without denying that things could be better. Clients like Brian often let the problems of the present completely cloud their mood, so they lose sight of their strengths and achievements. This creates an unresourceful mood that leads to further unhappiness and problems. The coach would work with Brian to increase his hope, first by showing him what he can do and helping him see that he does have influence in the situation, and second by helping him formulate a clear action plan that will form a pathway to success.

The coach would also help Brian assess his optimism by helping him to think about his situation in a positive way. The coach would take him through the ABCDE process to help him see the present difficulties as isolated and as being able to be resolved in the near future. The coach would also help him to be aware of any blaming internal dialogue that might be running in his head. And he or she would help him formulate what he wants to happen and see how he can directly achieve that, making it long-lasting and affecting other aspects of his life in a positive way. The coach would help him look at the problems now – to see what he believes about them, the consequences of those beliefs, to challenge those that are making him unresourceful and unhappy – and to move forward in a positive, hopeful way.

The coach would explore the dynamics of his team and how he works with them to see if the amount of positive supportive feedback could be increased. He would also help Brian to find ways to get useful feedback from others, as Brian's problem suggests that he is rather isolated and finds it difficult to ask for and get good feedback.

The coaching would explore Brian's values and help him cultivate his personal strengths. What is important to him about chess? About reading? About his family, his wife and children? What does he really care about? What things give him the greatest pleasure and gratification? The coach would encourage Brian to find ways to do more of those things in his life. The coach would give Brian homework to do some pleasant and pleasurable activity on a regular basis.

Brian would also take a Values in Action survey to identify his character strengths. From this profile, the coach would help Brian use his main strengths in his situation and explore how these special resources could be used to make a difference. Finally, the coach would help Brian to see how he could best use his strengths and make the important decision about his future.

REFERENCES

1   Seligman, M. (2003) *Authentic Happiness*
2   Peterson, C. and Seligman, M. (1984) Causal explanations as a risk factor for depression, *Theory and Evidence Psychological Review* 91 (3)
3   Peterson, C., Seligman, M. and Valliant G. (1988) 'Pessimistic Explanatory Style Is a Risk Factor for Physical Illness: A Thirty Five-Year Longitudinal Study', *Journal of Personality and Social Psychology* 55.
4   Csikszentmihalyi, M. (1991) *Flow: The Psychology of Engagement with Everyday Life*
5   Peterson, C. and Seligman, M. (2004) *Character Strengths and Virtues: A Handbook and Classification*
6   www.authentichappiness.sas.upenn.edu
7   Losada, M. (1999) 'The Complex Dynamics of High Performance Teams: Mathematical and Computer Modeling.' *American Psychologist* 30
8   Frederickson, B. and Losada, M. (2005) 'Positive Affect and the Complex Dynamics of Human Flourishing', *American Psychologist* 60

FROM CLINICAL TO POSITIVE PSYCHOLOGY

MY JOURNEY TO COACHING

by Carol Kauffman

When I discovered the profession of coaching and the academic field of positive psychology, I felt like a bird being released from a cage. At last, I had intellectual frameworks and supportive colleagues to help me transcend the artificial constraints accidentally set in place within clinical psychology. New possibilities soon emerged, both for myself and for those I am privileged to work with.

As a clinical psychologist, my job is to delve into the client's pain, to follow the trail of tears towards inner healing, interpersonal recovery and improved functioning. It's rewarding work. Helping people progress from −10 to 0 is obviously important. But I yearned to go further, to spark a progression from 0 to +10. I found the opportunity to do so through positive psychology and coaching. In contrast to clinical therapy, coaching involves following the 'trail of dreams' and co-creating a journey towards optimal life satisfaction and performance. Healing often occurs along the way, but it's a side-effect of discovering strengths, feeling more joy, and falling back in love with one's work, one's life and one's self.

Like many therapists-turned-coaches, I spent my early career tilting towards coaching without quite identifying what was incomplete about 'psychology-as-usual'. My first job in psychology, as a research assistant, began in 1974. I ran a study of children at high risk for pathology, all of whom had (very) psychotic mothers. During my first meeting with my new bosses I asked, 'Why are we only looking at what's wrong with these children? Can I study the kids who are doing well despite their mums' psychoses?'

These open-minded Harvard professors allowed me, at 21 years old, to add this work to their ongoing research. Years later, my findings were the most significant results to emerge from the six-year study. My professors stepped aside and let me be the lead author. To my surprise, 'Superkids: Competent Children of Psychotic Mothers' was published in the *American Journal of Psychiatry* [1].

I went on to become a clinical psychologist specializing in trauma. I had a full-time private practice and taught at McLean Hospital, a teaching hospital of Harvard Medical School. My early interest in strengths stayed with me. In the dozens of seminars and hundreds of research meetings I had attended, I had always been aware that we lacked the language to describe what's right with people. We only discussed what was wrong, missing or pathogenic. When I mentioned strengths and human potential, colleagues were tolerant but uninterested. Without a theoretical framework, and hundreds of studies to support that framework, my comments carried little weight. I was seen as a psychologist who looked on the bright side, but the bright side wasn't considered important. Although there were studies on resilience and creativity in the psychological literature, they certainly were not mainstream.

That changed in January 2000 with the official launch of positive psychology, and the publication of a special issue of the *American Psychologist* on optimal functioning. I remember the moment vividly. I loved my clients, but was disheartened by my profession. A colleague's copy of *American Psychologist* caught my eye. It had the words 'Special Issue on Optimal Human Functioning' on the cover. Standing alone in the post room, I began reading. The door to the cage swung open.

Positive psychology is a science that can support coaching in many ways. It is defined as the empirical study of positive individual traits, positive subjective experience and positive institutions [2]. Another definition – which feels most closely aligned with coaching – states, 'Positive psychology is the study of the conditions and processes that contribute to the flourishing or optimal functioning of people, groups and institutions' [3]. What does coaching offer, if not that?

Positive psychology has provided the framework needed for psychologists to take strengths seriously. There are now hundreds of studies helping to validate coaching as a 'real' profession. For me, it was important to have a scientific foundation for the kind of work I had been interested in doing. We're no longer on our own; there's now excellent research demonstrating the merits of a strengths-based approach, and solid data suggest the long-term benefits of positive affect. Studies have revealed that specific ratios of positive to negative experience spark creativity and well-being (such as that by Fredrickson & Losada [4]), and specific conditions that facilitate states of flow and being in the zone of optimal performance [5] [6]. We now have a range of positive psychology assessment tools (eg Lopez & Snyder [7]), and we have empirical studies demonstrating the efficacy of coaching and positive interventions (eg Seligman et al [8]). The science – in addition to the art – can now be at the heart of coaching [9] [10].

How do I pull this all together? I'm working on it (see Kauffman [11]). When I work with a client, I apply the basic tenets of positive psychology in five steps. In a workshop or group setting, these steps are presented in an organized manner, with accompanying interventions. More often, however, I use a less structured client-driven model. Interventions are often implicit and interwoven into the coaching process through powerful questions, inquiries or requests. Whether explicit or implicit, I cover the following areas:

⇨ **reversing the focus**
⇨ **positive assessment**
⇨ **enhancing well-being**
⇨ **fostering hope**
⇨ **attaining peak performance**

Space doesn't permit much elaboration, but here is a brief explanation of the science behind these five areas.

REVERSING THE FOCUS

We are trained – and probably wired – to focus on what's wrong with ourselves and others. Our brains process unresolved issues (such as failures) more vividly than resolved ones (such as successes and positive experiences). Research suggests that reversing this focus leads to greater creativity, big-picture thinking, increased productivity and enhanced well-being.

POSITIVE ASSESSMENT

Research also suggests that being able to articulate and use one's strengths leads to enhanced well-being, decreased depression, and increased self-worth. There are numerous assessments of strengths (VIAStrengths.org; AuthenticHappiness.org; Peterson & Seligman [12], for example), optimism (Carver & Scheier [13]), happiness, life satisfaction, courage, hardiness and hope (Lopez and Snyder [14]). These invaluable tools help us chart progress as we navigate towards our goals.

ENHANCING WELL-BEING

Fredrickson's research [14] [15] [16], for example) demonstrates that the impact of positive experience goes far beyond the moments in which one feels good. Small increases in positive experience can enhance functioning by broadening and building our repertoire of thoughts, skills and behaviours. One meta-analysis of more than 250 studies also revealed that happiness leads to success – not vice versa – and that happiness may also cause enhanced health and improved performance (Lyubomirsky, King & Diener [17]).

ESTABLISHING HOPE AND HARDINESS

Supported by a great deal of evidence (such as Lopez et al [18]; Synder et al [19]), hope theory suggests that there are two components of hope: agency (a belief that one is able to achieve valued outcomes) and pathways (an understanding of what steps are needed to achieve them). Having both is ideal. People can have great confidence in their abilities to achieve goals without having any idea of how to achieve their goals. Others may know exactly what steps are necessary to move from point A to point B, but lack confidence in their ability to take those steps. Data suggest that hope is a strong predictor of athletic, academic and professional success. There are now many strategies available to increase hope (such as Lopez et al [18]).

ATTAINING PEAK PERFORMANCE

Once considered the exclusive domain of Olympic athletes, flow states are in fact available to us all. Hundreds of studies have revealed the conditions that facilitate flow. One key is a balance of skill and challenge. Applying highly developed skill to an unchallenging activity yields boredom. Facing tremendous challenge without skill, on the other hand, yields anxiety. There are numerous coaching techniques that can tweak either side of the equation to foster flow and peak performance.

These steps may initially seem daunting. In practice, however, the interchanges and explorations are lively and fun, with many of those wonderful 'aha!' moments. Growth and laughter are common. Weaving the foundations of positive psychology into coaching practice is invigorating. The process can be transformative both for ourselves and for our clients.

REFERENCES

1 Kauffman, C., Grunebaum, H., Cohler, B. & Gamer, E. (1979). 'Superkids: Competent Children of Psychotic Mothers', *American Journal of Psychiatry,* 136 (11), 1398–1402

2 Seligman, M.E.P. & Csikszentmihalyi, M. (2000). 'Positive Psychology: An Introduction', *American Psychologist,* 55 (1), 5–14

3 Gable, S. & Haidt, J. (2005) 'What (and why) is positive psychology?', *Review of General Psychology,* 9 (2), 103–110

4 Fredrickson, B. & Losada, M. (2005). 'Positive affect and the complex dynamics of human flourishing', *American Psychologist,* 60(7), 678–686

5 Czikszenthmihalyi, M. (1991) *Flow,* Harper

6 Czikszenthmihalyi, M.(1997) *Finding Flow: The Psychology of Engagement with Everday Life,* Basic Books

7 Lopez, S. & Snyder, C.R. (2003) *Handbook of Positive Psychological Assessment: A Handbook of Models and Measures,* American Psychological Association

8 Seligman, M.E.P., Steen, T., Park N. & Peterson, C. (2005) 'Positive Psychology Progress: Empirical Validation of Interventions', *American Psychologist,* 60 (5), 410–421.

9 Kauffman, C. (2004) 'Toward a Positive Psychology of Executive Coaching', in A. Linley and S. Joseph (eds.), *Positive Psychology in Practice,* Wiley

10 Kauffman, C. (2006) 'The Science at the Heart of Coaching', in D. Stober and A. Grant (eds.), *Evidence based Coaching Handbook: Putting Best Practices to Work for Your Clients,* Wiley

11 Kauffman, C. (2007) 'The Practice of Positive Psychology in Coaching.' Invited Keynote Address, to be presented at the Second International Coaching Psychology Conference, British Psychological Society, London, Dec 2007

12 Peterson, C. & Seligman, M. (2004), *Character Strengths and Virtues,* American Psychological Association

13 Carver, C.S. & Scheier, M. (2003). 'Optimism', in S. Lopez and C.R. Snyder (eds.), *Positive Psychological Assessment: A Handbook of Models and Measures,* American Psychological Association

14 Fredrickson, B. (2001). 'The Role of Positive Emotions in Positive Psychology: The "Broaden-and-build" Theory of Positive Emotions', *American Psychologist,* 56 (3), 218–226

15 Fredrickson, B. (2006). 'The "Broaden-and-build" Theory of Positive Emotions', in F. Huppert, N. Baylis, and B. Keverne (eds.), *The Science of Well-being,* Oxford University Press

16 Cohn, M. & Fredrickson, B. (2006). 'Beyond the Moment, Beyond the Self: Shared Ground Between Selective Investment Theory and the Broaden-and-build Theory of Positive Emotions', *Psychological Inquiry,* 17 (1), 39–44

17 Lyubormirsky, S., King, L., & Diener, E. (2005). 'The Benefits of Frequent Positive Affect: Does Happiness Lead to Success?', *Psychological Bulletin,* 131 (6), 803–855

18 Lopez, S., Snyder, C.R., Magyar-Moe, J., Edwards, L., Pedrotti, J. T., Janowski, K., et al (2004). 'Strategies for Accentuating Hope', in A. Linley and S. Joseph (eds.), *Positive Psychology in Practice,* Wiley

19 Snyder, C.R., Harris, C., Anderson, J., Holleran, S., Irving, L., Sigmon, S. et al (1991). 'The Will and the Ways: Development and Validation of an Individual', *Journal of Personality and Social Psychology*, (60) 4, 570–585

Carol Kauffman PhD, PCC maintains an active coaching practice and is an Assistant Clinical Professor at Harvard Medical School where she teaches positive psychology and is founder of the Coaching Psychology Institute. She co-edited a special issue in positive psychology for the *International Coaching Psychology Review* and will be co-editor in chief of the new journal, *Coaching: International Journal of Theory, Research and Practice*. For more information, visit: www.PositivePsychologyCoaches.com as well as www.CoachingPsychologyInstitute.com

5 BEHAVIOURAL COACHING

'The shortest distance between two points is under construction.'

Noelie Altito

Behavioural coaching shifts the focus from the client's inner goals, values and motivations to their external behaviour. The root of the word 'behaviour' is from Middle English: 'be' and 'have', that is, to bear oneself in a particular way. Behaviour is what people do and say, their actions and reactions to what happens. If people were coached for many months and still did everything exactly as they always had done, you would question the effectiveness of the coaching. Effective coaching always results in changed behaviour. It helps people do things differently; the results are observable in actions that have an impact on the external world. These actions can be seen from the outside; but the thoughts and emotions that lie behind them cannot; they have to be inferred. Behavioural coaching focuses on the behaviour, not the thinking and emotions that give rise to it.

Coaching changes clients' internal world, too, their values, emotions and thinking. There is no external behavioural change without internal subjective changes (except in zombies!). Changes in thinking and emotions will necessarily lead to different actions. All coaching affects behaviour, although not all coaching approaches focus primarily on behaviour. The assumption behind behavioural coaching is that behaviour is learned, and what is learned can be unlearned, relearned or modified.

Behavioural coaching seeks sustainable, measurable changes in behaviour, through validated techniques in the behavioural sciences. The behavioural sciences are disciplines like sociology, anthropology and the different branches of psychology (personal, clinical and industrial). It does not incorporate developmental psychology, because that branch of psychology focuses on changes over time and how they relate to each other. Behavioural coaching focuses on behaviour rather than what that behaviour means or what gives rise to it.

There must be a way to measure the behaviour before and after the change, otherwise the change is impossible to evaluate. Change is clear and unequivocal when it can be measured. You can't change what you can't measure and you can't measure what you can't see. The behavioural coach takes an outside perspective on change. It needs to be visible and it needs to be measured.

BEHAVIOURAL COACHING IN BUSINESS

Behavioural coaching is mostly applied in a business context. Business demands high performance, and high performance only makes sense if it can be measured and contrasted with other levels of performance. When an individual's performance improves, the whole organization benefits. Behavioural coaching is used as a means of increasing the performance of individuals and to increase the performance of the business. People will learn and grow as a result of their coaching in the workplace, and this learning and growth needs to contribute to making the business more effective and efficient, achieving corporate goals and furthering the vision, mission, values and profitability of the business. Coaching that results in a person becoming disillusioned and leaving the organization is not deemed a success (although it may well be the best outcome, given the circumstances). Coaching that leads to a person being happier without any improvement in their work cannot be deemed a success either.

Behavioural coaching is mostly used with managers and executives to help them develop their skills, remove personal blocks and achieve valuable and lasting changes in their professional and personal life. The models of behavioural coaching are based on definitive, proven modelling and management principles and should lead to objectively measurable results. Clients' changes need to be translated into an action plan that is part of an ongoing development plan for them in their work.

The main proponents of behavioural coaching are Suzanne Skiffington and Perry Zeus, who have written a number of books exploring the behavioural approach [1] [2] [3]. The overall goal of behavioural coaching as defined by Skiffington and Zeus is to 'help individuals increase their effectiveness and happiness at work, in education, in health care settings and in the larger community'. They set out a six-step methodology for behavioural coaching interventions in business. The steps are: education, data collection, planning, behavioural change, measurement and evaluation. The model aims to change behaviour; and gather behavioural feedback to measure progress and evaluate the result, based on behavioural changes leading to business goals. This methodology deals mostly with the structure of coaching and how it needs to be set up from the outside in order to work at its best. As such, it fits into the right-hand quadrants in the integral model.

STEP ONE: EDUCATION

Coaches need to educate clients about coaching, what it does and how it will be evaluated. They need to manage the expectations of their clients, both individual and corporate, and to dispel any mistaken ideas about coaching. Often a Coaching Needs Analysis is done at this stage.

This step is where confidentiality issues arise. Confidentiality is essential. A coach and their client must work together, and the client must be sure that what they say is not fed back to their managers. If they think it will be, then they will not say what they think, and will probably withhold information. The coach must be independent of managerial pressure. If coaches are seen as management pawns and people think that what they say will be reported back to their managers, then the coaching will not be effective. The coaching process will fail from the start if coaches do not gain the trust of their clients. Coaches need to find a way to respect the confidentiality of the individual client, while fulfilling their contract and obligation with the organization. There is potential conflict because the client is not the same as the employer. The company employs them to coach a manager in the organization, and it is the manager who is the client. Coach, client and organization need to come to an agreement about this right from the beginning. There are two main ways to approach this:

⇨ **The coach and client may agree to give a regular written report to the manager, and this report is always seen and signed off by the client.**
⇨ **The feedback to the business is the behavioural changes of the client and the improved business results, provided there is an agreed way of measuring them.**

The business does not need to know in detail what happened in the session, only the behavioural result, because that is what it is paying for.

STEP TWO: DATA COLLECTION

The coach needs information about the present state of the organization and what it wants the coach to achieve. He or she needs information about the clients they will be coaching and what behaviour their clients need to change to meet their performance goals.

Working with the organization, the coach defines the scope of the programme, the number of clients, the number of sessions and the time schedule. How to measure the impact of the coaching must also be agreed. Coaches will also need to consult with many different stakeholders regarding their clients – peers, direct reports, executive teams and sometimes customers, depending on the scope of the coaching. The individual clients, their teams and organizational factors are all taken into account.

Data are collected by interviews, focus groups, direct observation and surveys. Psychometric tests may also be used. There is already a lot of psychological research into personality models and these may be used in the assessment of individual clients.

Data are useless unless they are put into a context and have a purpose; then they become useful information. The purpose of collecting these data is to assess the individual and team behavioural strengths and weaknesses as they relate to the required competences needed to achieve personal, team or corporate goals. A competence is a specific skill, defined for the business context, that is required to achieve individual and corporate goals as defined by the business. The assessment should suggest the best way to bring out the clients' strengths, as well as address their weaknesses. It should also suggest measurements to provide feedback to determine the success of the coaching.

There are four important relationships that need care in the business coaching process.

1 *The individual client and the coach.* This is the most visible and obvious relationship, and it is vital that they work effectively together.
2 *The coach and the Human Resources department,* or whichever department of the business contracted the coach. The coach needs fully to understand the organizational context of the coaching.
3 *The client and the Human Resources department.* Clients need to know the reason they are being coached and what is expected of them; HR need to be convinced that clients can take the best advantage of the coaching.
4 *The client and their line manager.* The line manager must understand and support the client during the coaching. They may also be involved in helping to decide the objectives for the coaching programme.

These first steps are an important preparation for any business intervention in coaching, consultancy and training.

SINGLE- AND MULTIPLE-LOOP QUESTIONING

Behavioural coaching has a model of questioning used in data collection. Single-loop questions are those that raise and explore issues without going into depth about the reasons why they are occurring. Double-loop questions explore why problems have arisen and the factors that influence them.

Triple-loop questions explore the organizational assumptions and values that may have contributed to the problem. These are more systemic questions, relating individual behaviour to the business system and the business results.

These questions form a similar model to the single- and double-loop coaching in the NLP coaching model.

STEP THREE: ACTION PLANNING

Once the coach knows the behaviour to be changed, the question is how to change it. The behaviour needs to be specific and observable. It may be new, or an improvement on an existing behaviour. The new behaviour together with the associated results becomes the goal and then an action plan is made to achieve it. This action plan often takes the form of a personal development plan (PDP) – a written record of tasks done and results achieved. It provides material for both coach and client to reflect on, and is also part of the evidence for the effectiveness of the coaching. Whatever form of action plan coach and client agree on, it needs to be specific, shared and written down.

An important part of the planning phase is to check if there are any organizational factors that maintain behaviour that needs to be changed. These might be difficult supervisors, poor relationships, ineffective procedures, lack of leadership or poor corporate communication systems. The coach might point these out as part of their report, although in that case she would be wearing a consultant's 'hat'. Finally, behaviour needs to be reinforced if it is to be maintained. What are the rewards of the new behaviour? What will the client get as a result that they will value?

STEP FOUR: BEHAVIOURAL CHANGE

Now coaches can begin the coaching with their clients. There are many techniques that behavioural coaches use to manage and change behaviour.

⇨ Modelling is when clients observe and copy someone who has achieved the desired behaviour.
⇨ Clients are made aware of the stimuli (anchors) that bring out any undesired behaviour so they can remove them, or at least be aware of them sufficiently that they lose their power.
⇨ Practice with feedback and role-playing can be useful. Clients monitor their own performance and notice their own progress. In the end, clients have to be independent of the coach and maintain the new behaviour. Any lasting change requires persistence, practice and repetition if old habits are to change and be replaced by new ones.
⇨ Behavioural coaches also use *prompts* – reminders to stop a particular behaviour and to replace it with another. Examples might include a new

screen saver on the computer, Post-it notes or pictures on the desk. These are called 'anchors' in NLP coaching and 'structures' in coactive coaching.

⇨ And, of course – *questions*. For example: 'What are you going to do differently?' is a behavioural question rather than an insight-oriented cognitive question, like 'Why do you think you did that?' or a question about emotions, like 'How do you feel about that?'

THE DEVELOPMENTAL PIPELINE

Behavioural coaches also use the idea of a developmental pipeline [4]. This means the necessary and sufficient conditions for behavioural change. There are five elements and they all relate to the clients and their internal thoughts and response to the coaching.

The first element is *insight*. This is the degree to which clients understand what areas need to be developed, what needs to change and how their present behaviour is not working for them.

The second is *motivation*. How important is the change? How does it relate to their values? This will determine the time and energy that clients are willing to give to make the change.

The third element is the *existing level of competence*. Do the clients have the specific skills needed to make the change and to move to a higher performance level? If they do not, then those competences need to be developed and practised.

The fourth is *practice opportunities*. Clients need not only the motivation, but also the opportunity to practise the skill and to use that skill. This may involve a training programme.

Accountability is the fifth element. Will clients receive feedback about progress and their change in behaviour? Who are they accountable to? What are the personal consequences for change? Is there a reward that they value? Are there any negative consequences for not changing?

These five elements are all necessary, and the coach can use this model to see where clients are limited. For example, a client may have high insight, high competence but low motivation, so the coach needs to work with the client's values. They may also need to work with the business organization to make sure that clients are rewarded with something they value. Other clients may have good insight but not know what to do, so they need to work on competence. By using this model to focus on the areas the client needs to develop to make the change, the coach can avoid wasting time and make sure the coaching is suited to each of their clients.

THE GAPS GRID

Another useful tool in behavioural coaching is the GAPS grid; it helps to build insight and motivation, collecting information about the client's present state. 'GAPS' stands for **G**oals and Values, **A**bilities, **P**erceptions and **S**tandards (or **S**uccess factors).

The top left area of the grid is how clients see themselves and the skills they have and they need. The upper right area is for goals and values. Both these are from the client's perspective.

The bottom left area is how other important people see the client (for example, peers, customers, or their managers). The standards are in the bottom right area – what matters to others and how they will measure success. There are some possible questions to ask in each area of the grid.

	Where the client is	Where they are going
	Abilities	**Goals and values**
The client's view	What skills does the client have? What resources does the client have? What skills and resources does the client need? What are the client's strengths? What are the client's weaknesses? What is their present behaviour? What needs changing?	What are the client's goals? What is important to the client? What motivates the client? What demotivates them? What inspires the client? How do they view taking risks?

Other perspectives	How do other people see the client? In what areas do they think the client is strong? In what areas do they think the client is weak? To what do they attribute the client's success up until now? What future do they see for the client?	What impact does the client's behaviour have on others? How will their success be measured? What standards do they have to meet? What are the expectations of the client's managers?

The GAPS grid is particularly useful when the client's insight and motivation are questionable. Coach and client work together to fill in all the areas. The right-hand boxes are important. The goals and values will make it clear what is important to clients, what motivates them and what level of performance they want. The standards area will make it clear what is expected. Often the coach will need to help clients find answers in the lower-right box. The left-hand columns will define the present state and give other perspectives on what needs to happen in the coaching.

STEP FIVE: FEEDBACK AND MEASUREMENT

The coach needs to collect feedback throughout the process to make sure the coaching is on track. What is happening as a result of the coaching?

Clients need to monitor their progress with the help of their personal development plan. The feedback needs to be specific and in terms of the measurement criteria agreed at the beginning of the program. The clients' peers and managers also play a part in measuring through their reports.

STEP SIX: EVALUATION

Has the coaching programme been a success? Has it delivered what was agreed in the first step? You cannot evaluate unless you have measured. The behavioural result for the individual or team needs to be linked back to the performance of the organization. These are some examples of questions that need to be answered at this stage:

⇨ Did the clients change their behaviour?

⇨ Was there a change in team behaviour as a result?

⇨ How do the clients feel about the change?

⇨ Have the clients maintained the change?

⇨ Has the change in behaviour resulted in the desired high performance from the clients?

⇨ Has the change in behaviour resulted in the desired business goals?

Measurement and evaluation can be done on different levels:

⇨ Subjective feeling of the client

⇨ Increase in knowledge and skill

⇨ Behavioural changes

⇨ Business results

The latter two are the most important in behavioural coaching. A return on investment (ROI) or a return on expectations (ROE) calculation may also be done. There are more details about these measurements in Part Three.

BEHAVIOURAL COACHING AND MOTIVATION

Behavioural coaching has some assumptions: first, that change occurs by influencing behaviour, and behaviour can be shaped; and second, people will take action if there is something important at stake for them, as they perceive it. The coach's role is as a motivator, adviser and a giver of feedback. Clients will change if they are motivated to do so. Motivation is needed to change behaviour, and motivation is invisible. The word 'motivation' means movement and means the reason (motive) why you move. Motivation is an abstract idea but the feeling is real. It is a willingness to do something or make a change – for a reason. Behavioural coaching explores the incentives that make people want to change. How do they work?

The incentive can come from the outside. In a business setting, this usually means someone telling you to do something and is the basis of so-called theory X. (Theory X proposes that most people do not want to work and need some prodding from the outside.)

The incentive can also be internal. The energy to act comes from inside you, because you want to and you feel it is important. This is the basis of so-called theory Y. (Theory Y proposes that people are naturally motivated and will work by themselves if left to themselves.)

Both theories are right but incomplete. Psychology research does not endorse one at the expense of the other. It depends on the context and on the person. One individual may mostly respond to outside motivation, another mostly to internal motivation, but it also depends on what they are doing. Positive internal motivation comes from clients' values, what are important to them, for example recognition, challenge or career prospects. Coaches need to know how their clients respond to outside incentives, and know what values provide the internal incentives.

Often behavioural coaches need to coach clients to ask for those things that are important to them. When people are not getting what they want, they will become demotivated. However, if management do not know what they want, then employees cannot be expected to give it to them.

Surveys report that for managers, one of the highest incen-tives is recognition of their achievement. It is most motivating if this recognition comes from someone they respect. Greater responsibility and more money are also incentives. Money on its own has no value, but it buys things of value, not just computers and flat-screen TVs, but more important things like security and freedom. Money on its own will not buy creativity or ensure high performance [5].

From a behavioural point of view, behaviour that is rewarded tends to be repeated. Behaviour that has bad results tends not to be repeated, provided that the person sees the link between the behaviour and the consequences. The reward needs to be perceived as such by the client. For example, the 'reward' for finishing a difficult project on time is often an even harder project with a tighter deadline. This is not a reward from the clients' point of view [6].

Motivation drives behaviour, so although behavioural coaching focuses on behaviour, it needs to take into account the whole person. Emotions and thinking lead to action, and action in turn modifies thinking and emotions. People are not stimulus/response machines. They respond to incentives that they value.

To summarize, coaches generate awareness in their clients of a need to change; they build motivation and commitment to get the desired goals. The client and coach build an action plan and the coach gives feedback as the client gets the results.

Many business interventions do not last for long; the clients cannot maintain the changes in an unsupportive environment, even when they want to. To change their behaviour, and get better results, clients need to embed their new insights in practice so that they develop new habits. Without clear practical steps and practice to help them do this, old habits will soon reassert themselves. Learning will only last if the underlying emotional commitment is there – 'Do I really want to change?' And this is a key question for the client in any model of coaching.

CASE STUDY

Behavioural coaching would take a different approach to Brian as a client, focusing more on his performance at work. There would be consultations between Brian and his manager, the Human Resources department that arranged the coaching, and the coach. Brian would be able to clarify his expectations regarding the coaching, and he and his coach would agree what behaviour Brian needed to change and what the results would be. Brian would probably concentrate on changing his moods, and working with his team in a more productive way. Brian would need to decide whether to confide in the coach regarding his doubts about staying with the company. The coach would not try to persuade him to stay, but would try to make sure that if he did stay, he was clear that this was the right thing to do.

The coach would ask different types of questions. For example, what are the problems and issues that Brian faces in his work? Why have these problems arisen? How does Brian feel about his work? Are there organizational assumptions behind Brian's problems? Do his employers expect too much from him? Why has he been passed over for promotion? Was he given clear feedback in the past about his performance? How are teams put together here? Does the way teams are made up lead to conflict?

The coach would work with Brian to help him with his team, to help him to ask his managers for help and support when he needs it. Brian finds it difficult to ask for help, and then soldiers on under pressure until he loses his temper. This is a pattern that he and the coach would seek to stop.

What incentives does Brian have in his work? What does he value? Why is he in this job? Together the coach would explore with Brian what motivates him to do his work and what he needs to feel good about it. Does he want a promotion? What does it mean to him? More recognition? A pay rise? At the moment it is clear that Brian lacks motivation.

Brian has a great deal of insight into his situation, but he needs to learn communications skills and he needs opportunities to practise them. His coach would help him by showing him the kind of skills he needs to manage his team and help him by role-playing and giving feedback. Together they would identify any triggers for unresourceful moods and eliminate them. Brian would work on his PDP and a GAPS grid to understand what is expected of him and what is important to him.

The coaching would help Brian to work better and help him clarify whether he should stay or leave his present job.

REFERENCES

1 Zeus, P. & Skiffington, S. (2000) *The Complete Guide to Coaching at Work*
2 Zeus, P. & Skiffington, S. (2002) *The Coaching at Work Tool Kit*
3 Skiffington, S. & Zeus, P. (2003) *Behavioral Coaching*
4 Hicks, M. & Peterson, D. (1999) The Development Pipeline: How People Really Learn, *Knowledge Management Review* 9
5 Kohn, A. (1993) *Punished by Rewards*
6 Fournies, F. (2000) *Coaching for Improved Work Performance*

6 ONTOLOGICAL COACHING

'Fishing nets are for catching fish. But when the fish are caught, the nets are forgotten. Traps are for catching hares, but when the hares are caught, the traps are forgotten. Words are for putting across ideas, and when the ideas are understood, the words are forgotten. How I long to listen to a storyteller who has forgotten all the words.'

Chuang Tzu

Ontological coaching begins from principles, not behaviour. Ontology is the study of being; the nature and quality of existence – not something we think about every day, but something we live every day. Ontological coaching takes these unexamined ideas and brings them to the forefront of coaching practice.

Ontological coaching focuses on what it calls the client's 'way of being', not on behaviour. This 'way of being' is defined as 'the dynamic interaction of language, emotions and physiology' [1]. It drives behaviour, generating what we feel, say and do. Shifting a client's way of being is the goal of ontological coaching. Unlike NLP or the integral approach, ontological coaching was specifically developed as a coaching model, and has its own coaching terminology.

Fernando Flores was the first to use the term 'ontological coaching' and was the main originator of the ideas. Flores was a minister in the government of Chile under President Salvador Allende when it was overthrown by a military coup headed by General Pinochet in 1973. He was imprisoned until Amnesty International negotiated his release, along with that of other political prisoners. Flores moved to the United States, where he worked as a consultant and developed his thinking about organizations [2] and the key ideas in ontological coaching. He elaborates on these in the interview that follows this chapter. Flores' views on systems and the structure and function of language were profoundly influenced by the Chilean biologist Humberto Maturana [3]. Flores collaborated in the 1980s with two other Chileans, Julio Olalla (a government lawyer who also worked with President Allende and was exiled under Pinochet) and Rafael Echeverria [4]. Echeverria and Olalla formed their own company in 1990. Ontological coaching is strongly represented in Spain and the Spanish-speaking countries of South America, especially Argentina and Chile.

The basic steps of ontological coaching are:

1   Establish the coaching relationship.
2   Identify the client's concern to be addressed and the extent of the breakdown in their life.
3   Explore the language, moods, emotions and physiology that the client is using to create their way of being.
4   Help clients change those things that are preventing them from dealing with the breakdown in a useful and productive way.

THE COACHING RELATIONSHIP

In ontological coaching, the client is held as a 'legitimate other'. What does this mean? It means the coach listens out for what really matters to their clients, not necessarily what they want to achieve. The coach accepts clients as they are and on their own terms. They create a shared understanding through different types of conversation.

LISTENING

Listening is central to ontological coaching. Hearing is purely aural – the sound waves hit your eardrum. Listening adds meaning to the sounds. Listening means paying attention to the person behind the words.

Language is constructed between at least two people and is a combination of speaking and listening. Spoken language does not exist if there is not someone listening. Do your words count if no one else can hear them? Yes, because there is always someone listening – yourself. Our internal dialogues have a speaker and listener, and the private conversations that go on inside our head shape how we observe and listen to others.

Listening is not passive but is an active process that makes language real and makes sense of what is said. The meaning that we interpret depends on who is speaking, and the context in which they are speaking. (When someone shouts 'Fire!' on stage in a theatre, the audience doesn't suddenly evacuate the building.)

Like NLP, ontological coaching does not consider words as the innocent carriers of a fixed meaning. What meaning they have for the speaker may be (and very likely is) different from that for the listener. In the ontological sense we are always listening, because we are always making interpretations of our own. When we communicate with another person we match interpretations, we co-ordinate the meaning each one of us makes of what is said.

Ontological coaches are encouraged to ask themselves three questions while listening:

1   How am I listening; what meaning am I making of what is being said?
2   Why am I listening like this; what concerns do I have?
3   What are the concerns of my clients that they are speaking this way?

THE CLIENTS' BREAKDOWN AND CONCERN

The word 'concern' means 'with attention'. In ontological coaching, a 'concern' is what is important; in other coaching models it is called a 'value'. The meaning and fulfilment in our lives come from taking care of our concerns, and they merit extra attention when we have a problem.

In ontological coaching, clients consult a coach because of a *breakdown*, and it is the client who defines the breakdown, not the coach. A breakdown in ontological coaching is an interruption in the flow of living, and this description comes from the writings of Martin Heidegger [5], the German philosopher who died in 1976. For Heidegger, most of our life is 'transparent'. This means that you do not notice it, like a transparent glass pane; you see right through it without realizing it is there. An example is physical health. We do not notice we are healthy until illness strikes. When life is transparent, we are acting habitually. We build habits of behaviour, habits of attention and habits of thinking. When these habits work well, everything is fine. When we meet a situation which we cannot deal with, then life becomes less transparent and we experience a 'breakdown'. The habits are not adequate to deal with the situation.

Breakdowns make us question habits of thinking as well as habits of doing. A breakdown does not have to be bad. For example, a new partner, a promotion at work, or being profoundly influenced by a book – any of these can be a breakdown if they bring our habits of living into question. A breakdown can also be negative: a separation, a quarrel or the loss of a job. And it can be neutral, but still demand some action like having to take a decision and not knowing the best course of action.

What we normally do is to repair the breakdown, as quickly as possible so we can have a transparent life again, but sometimes this is not possible. Some people can take a disaster in their stride, for others a small disturbance in their routine is enough to disturb them (and everyone else around them). Breakdowns are a call for action, and also a call for help. When a breakdown happens, the client suffers; they do not know what to do and they ask for help. In ontological coaching, the breakdown needs to be discussed so it can be thought about and repaired.

LANGUAGE

In ontological coaching, language is far more than the words we say to each other. Language is a technology by which we can get things done. Language is both speaking *and* listening, and the means by which we co-ordinate actions between ourselves and others. Using language is an essential part of being human. When we speak, we make our decisions public and take responsibility for them. Ontological coaching takes language very seriously, like NLP but in a different way. While NLP pays particular attention to the words said, ontological coaching sees language as action – creating commitments for the future. Ontological coaching helps clients see how they are unwittingly using language to create and maintain limits and problems. It shows them how they can use language to construct a better 'reality'. In doing so, it explores and resolves some parts of their way of being that is hindering effective action.

Ontological coaching defines six different basic 'linguistic acts'. Fernando Flores developed these from the work of John Searle [6], Professor of Philosophy at the University of Berkeley, California. These basic linguistic acts are the words, together with the body language and the emotion that goes with them. How well we use these linguistic acts determines how well we take care of our concerns and deal with the breakdowns in our lives.

A *declaration* is one linguistic act; it is a statement of fact that has authority and general agreement, and, as such, determines the future. For example, a judge passes sentence in court – guilty or innocent. This is a declaration. A priest pronounces two people married – a declaration. A football referee holds up the red card – another declaration. Any statement that has authority in context is valid (the referee's wife will not pay attention to the red card at home, as that is not the domain where the referee has authority – as a referee). The authority and the validity of the declaration exist in the listening of the people who accept it. Otherwise it is an opinion, no better or worse than any other.

Declarations are powerful and they need authority to have effects on others. However, everyone can make declarations about themselves. Stating a personal goal is a declaration. Stating a goal publicly, for example 'I will give up smoking from today', makes it exist in the listening of others. However, we do not always follow through on our personal declarations. Often they are merely hopes. An ontological coach helps people become the authority in their own lives and therefore helps them make and keep their declarations about themselves.

Assertions are factual statements about our observations. They can be true assertions – we call these facts. Facts need social agreement to be true; when people agree about assertions, they take action together. An example of an assertion would be 'I will meet you at the station to catch the nine o'clock train'. Assertions can be mistaken, yet still acted on: for example, the train may leave at ten o'clock, so my friend and I will have to wait on the platform for an hour. Many times, although people have conflicting information, they still believe assertions to be true. 'Pending assertions' are predictions yet to be decided or acted upon.

Assessments are judgments and evaluations. The judgment of good or bad comes from us, not from what we observe. 'I am an honest person' is an assessment about oneself; 'John is an honest person' is an assessment about John. It seems as if John is the subject of this statement, but this is the mirage of language. An assessment is a statement about the assessor; it comes from their own standards. 'I am more honest than John' is an assessment about both of us. Any comparison, qualities or attributes that are not generally agreed as facts are an assessment. The criteria for making the assessment are inside the person who is making that assessment, not in the wider social reality.

We make assessments all the time about others and ourselves. Where do we get our self-assessments? Well, first we get them from authority figures when we are children and we get them from important experiences in our life. Then we may think that negative self-assessments are true assertions. But negative self-assessments poison the soul, while positive self-assessments give self-esteem and self-confidence.

An ontological coach can help their clients by exploring negative self-assessments. One way they do this is by 'grounding'. This means exploring how and why the client is making an assessment. Imagine, for example, a client is planning to start an exercise regime. He tells the coach about how he failed in the past through lack of perseverance. Finally he says with a sigh, 'I just do not have enough discipline.' This is a negative self-assessment. To ground this, an ontological coach would explore with the following five questions:

First, 'What is the purpose of this assessment?' Another similar question would be 'How does this opinion help you accomplish what is important in your life?' The question is about the future, while assessments have been made from information in the past. The assessment may actually be doing something positive, at least from the client's point of view, but that is not the point of the question.

Second, 'What specific areas are you referring to?' This is a question that challenges the generalization. The negative assessment makes a very general judgment that leaves behind the initial context (the exercise regime) and embraces the whole of the client's life. It is important to make this clear.

Third, 'According to what standards?' A judgment must be the result of applying a standard, but the standard is not in the assessment. Is it something a parent said? What constitutes discipline for the client and how does he decide that he lacks it? Is discipline an all or nothing quality?

Fourth, 'Are there any true assertions that support this assessment?' These must be factual statements, not more assessments. 'Because I am so lazy' is just another assessment. 'Because last week I wanted to go to the gym, but ended up watching TV instead' is an assertion, but now we are on the level of behaviour, and we can move to the last question, 'What true assertions are there against that assessment?'

There may be plenty of true assertions when the client showed discipline through specific actions. These are easy to find once you have the criteria from the third question.

Grounding assessments involves being rigorous and accountable for your opinions and is a useful procedure for any important assessment regardless of whether it is positive or negative. It has some similarities with the ABCDE process in positive psychology coaching.

A *request* is another basic language pattern. A request asks someone to perform a future action. When you make a request, you make a commitment to have something done by someone else. When there is sufficient authority behind the request and the person feels they have no choice but to comply, then the request becomes a declaration.

Many people do not make good requests, or are afraid to make requests. They hint ('Wow, this room is dirty!'), or they ask no one in particular ('I wish someone would clean up in here!'). There are other sloppy ways of making a request, like not saying exactly what should be done, when it should be done, and to what standard. These are recipes for disappointment and resentment. When you make a request, you should also check the person has understood and not assume that they have. Some clients expect people to read their mind and carry out their unspoken requests. ('If you really appreciated me, you would know I hate to sit in an untidy room.') An ontological coach will help clients to make clear, simple and effective requests, and by doing so, clients will feel listened to and appreciated instead of blaming others for their misfortunes.

Equally important for clients is the ability to deal with requests made by others. There are five ways to deal with a request.

1 You can accept, and this creates a promise.
2 You can decline.
3 You can make a counter-offer about when or how the action is to be done.
4 You can make a slippery promise ('I'll try'), which usually means 'No' but you are afraid of saying 'No' outright.
5 Finally, you can lie and say you will do it and have no intention of doing so, so your internal language will not match your external words. Then you are not sincere and therefore cannot be trusted.

A request and a declaration of acceptance is a *promise*, another basic linguistic act. A promise is a commitment to take a future action, and presupposes that the person is reliable, and capable of carrying out the promise. If you make a request and the other person accepts, then they will carry out the action, and the promise involves you both.

An offer is a conditional promise, conditional on a declaration of acceptance by the other person. ('I'll only do it if you pay me.') If you make an offer and it is accepted, then you will do the action, but the promise involves both of you.

Summary of basic linguistic acts in ontological coaching	
Declaration	A statement by an authority that determines future action.
Assertion	A factual statement about the past from observation. What makes it factual is the shared agreement between people.
Assessment	A judgment or evaluation that comes from a person's way of interpreting the world.
Request	Asking another person to do something.
Offer	Saying you will do something for someone else with conditions.
Promise	A mutual commitment to action. Promises consist of a request and acceptance, or an offer and acceptance.

CONVERSATIONS

A 'conversation' has a specific meaning in ontological coaching. A conversation is not trivial; the word comes from the Latin root '*con*', meaning 'with', and '*versare*', meaning 'to turn'. So, a conversation can be thought of as a verbal dance. A conversation with another person impacts our moods, emotions and physiology as we speak, listen and observe. Conversations are ways of co-ordinating actions with others, making sense of events, creating the future and improving relationships. Ontological coaching distinguishes several different types of conversation.

The first type is a conversation of stories and personal assessments. This is used to understand events and to 'talk' them through with a (hopefully) sympathetic listener. Second, conversations for clarity articulate and share understandings and learning from an event. There are conversations for possible actions to create and explore future scenarios; other conversations concern relationships and accomplishment. Sometimes, however, we do not know what to say, and here we can have a conversation about possible conversations.

Much of the skill of ontological coaching, especially in organizations, involves calculating what sort of conversation you need to have and with whom. Lack of clarity or poor decision making means that the required type of conversation has not happened.

Ontological coaching proposes that we create our own personal *stories* that define who we are and how we act, so the ontological coach will help clients monitor the stories they tell themselves in their internal dialogue. We are also born into impersonal *narratives* that embed us in our culture and community and shape the ways we use language and the ideas we have. There is the Christian narrative, the Islamic narrative, the cultural narrative of different countries, stories that are bigger than we are; they were there when we were born and will still be there when we are gone. Not only through introspection, but also through history do we come to know ourselves. In the words of Heidegger, 'Stories are buildings that house man.'

Our relationships and networks with others predefine how we are to a greater extent than we think. Ontological coaching supports the post-modern ideas of the importance of culture and shared meanings in defining our individuality. Our language and community provide the air that we breathe and which we do not notice. We are defined by our relationship to others.

How coaching relates to post-modern thinking will be explored in more detail in Part Three of this book.

MOODS AND EMOTIONS

Ontological coaches not only explore their clients' language, but also deal with moods, emotions and posture. Emotions are energy; the very word 'emotion' comes from the same root as 'motor' and 'motion', and emotions move you. Conversation does not take place in an emotional vacuum. The words we use and the conversations we take part in come from our concerns, so emotions are always represented in the conversations we have.

Moods are pervasive, emotional 'tones' like the key of a piece of music, or the light in a picture. They are dispositions to certain types of action and they support our self-esteem. There are moods that people maintain in order to be superior to others, like cynicism that tries to pass for sophistication, and moods that put a person as inferior to others, like resentment and frustration.

Ontological coaching distinguishes six basic moods. Resentment, resignation and anxiety are three negative moods, although they may provoke some very positive actions. What they have in common is a contraction of the person's energy inwards. The corresponding positive moods are peace, optimism and wonder, which push the emotion outwards and connect with the world. An ontological coach may encourage the client to keep an emotional diary, to track the changing moods and to see what kind of mood predominates.

Physiology is important in ontological coaching. Our moods, emotions and habits, both physical and mental, are 'embodied'; they write their message on our face and posture. People who are habitually angry (and so have a prevailing mood of resentment) will show this in their facial expressions, because the muscles are so used to contracting in a certain way that the expression becomes habit. When parents say, 'Don't make that face; if the wind changes you will be stuck like that', they make this point (albeit melodramatically). Your emotions reflect in your face moment by moment, and if there are too many moments of one emotion over time, then they will etch there for good. A person in constant anxiety will express that in their voice tone, their posture and their way of being with people.

Therefore, an ontological coach will often adjust the client's body (with permission, of course) so that the posture is in line with the changes that the client wants to make in words and emotion. The client's way of being will not change without mind, body and emotions changing together in a sustainable way. Ontological coaches argue that if problematic emotions and moods are still carried in the body, it will be hard for cognitive insight alone to make the changes. They will help clients be more aware of their posture and expressions and show how these reflect their moods and thinking.

A BETTER OBSERVER

What else does ontological coaching do? It helps the client become a better *observer*. The term comes from Humberto Maturana's ideas on cognition. Our inner structure of the senses determines how we see things and therefore how we respond to what we think is 'reality'. For example, the structure of the human eye makes the world appear in a certain way. Each eye captures one view from a different angle and the two separate images go to the brain for processing. The brain makes them into one picture, and the combined image is more than the sum of its parts. It gives stereoscopic vision – a heightened perception of depth. Good vision in one eye only does not allow you to have full stereoscopic vision, so the world appears different, although it is the inner structure of vision that is different.

The eye of the housefly gives a multifaceted image. What is the world really like? How many dimensions does it have? We do not know, except that it has the possibility to appear in an infinite number of ways, depending on who is looking. What we see depends on how we see, and how we see depends on who we are and our assumptions. 'What a loaf of bread looks like depends on how hungry you are.' To observe is to interpret, and we see things not as they are but as we are. This basic constructivist idea pervades ontological coaching. We cannot change what we do not observe. Ontological coaching therefore aims to create a more powerful observer, one able to question his or her own ideas [7].

First-order learning is when we observe our behaviour and how this impacts our outcomes:

Observation   ⟶   behaviour   ⟶   goals

Second-order learning is when we become observers of how we are observing:

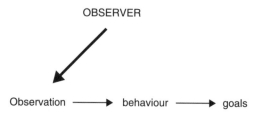

OBSERVER

Observation ⟶ behaviour ⟶ goals

This gives us the power to question our observations and therefore our habits. This is not a developmental model – the new observer is not a different level of being; it is the same person with more powerful distinctions.

WHAT DOES AN ONTOLOGICAL COACH DO?

Ontological coaches help clients to deal with their breakdown. They help them to change their way of being by working on moods, emotions, physiology and language, thus helping the clients move ahead with their lives. They help them realize their concerns and help them observe their linguistic acts and decide what conversations they need to have. Coaches are the facilitators of learning; they serve their clients by being attentive and responsive to their needs, interests and concerns. A coaching conversation is a path that leads to new possibilities for the clients' way of being.

CASE STUDY

An ontological coach would first establish the breakdown in Brian's life and work. What is troubling him? What are his concerns? What are his most important values and how does he feel these have been compromised by what is happening in his life at the moment? Then the coach would focus on changing those things that are preventing Brian from dealing with the breakdown in a productive and positive way.

Brian and his coach would explore Brian's language – in particular, the assessments he is making about himself and others, such as his work colleagues, his wife and family. Brian is likely to be making a number of negative assessments about himself and his colleagues, so the coach would help him to ground these. What is their purpose? Perhaps they are making him feel better in the short term, but overall they are making him feel like a victim. What is the exact area they cover? The fact that Brian is having difficulties with one person does not mean his social relationships have broken down. According to what standards is he judging himself and others? What true assertions are there that support or contradict his negative assessments? What parts of his work are going well?

The coach might also explore with Brian what sort of conversations he is having with his boss, his colleagues and his wife. Perhaps he needs to have a conversation about possible conversations with his boss about his dissatisfaction with work. Brian probably needs to learn how to make requests, so he can get what he wants and have his concerns met. The coach would help him to set clear goals in the form of positive declarations about the future. Coach and client would create a promise between them that Brian would be committed to working towards his goals.

What moods and physiology does Brian have that are part of his way of being? What is his prevailing mood? It sounds as though it is resentment and anxiety. An ontological coach would encourage him to keep a diary to track his emotions, to notice when they surface and what triggers them. The coach would also make Brian aware of his posture and expressions and how they embody his way of being and what messages they give to others. They might work together to improve his posture and be more aware of his body language. This would reinforce the change in his thinking and mood.

Finally, the coach would explore with Brian the Korean cultural narrative he is living. What does it mean to be a Korean? How was he brought up? What sort of expectations does he have? How does this part of his story fit into his wider life story? This might give him greater insight into his history so that he feels a sense of completeness.

REFERENCES

1   Sieler, A. (2003) *Coaching to the Human Soul*

2   Flores, F. & Solomon, R. (2001) *Building Trust*

3   Maturana, H. & Varela, F. (1987) *The Tree of Knowledge: The Biological Roots of Human Understanding*

4   Echeverria, R. (2003) *Ontologia Del Lenguaje*

5   Heidegger, M. (1962) *Being and Time*

6   Searle, J. (1969) *Speech Acts: An Essay in the Philosophy of Language*

7   Flaherty, J. (1999) *Coaching: Evoking Excellence in Others*

INTERVIEW WITH FERNANDO FLORES

January 2007

Can you tell us a little about your background and how you became interested in coaching?

Let me start with my background. I took my first degree in Chile, where I studied industrial engineering. Once I'd graduated, my career took off and I eventually landed a job at the Ministry of Economic Affairs and Finance in the Chilean government. That job ended when the General Pinochet overthrew the government in a military coup.

I was in a military prison for three years. Finally I was released and I went to teach in California, where I was Associate Researcher in Computer Science at Stanford.

While I was in prison, I became increasingly familiar with cognitive issues that interested me. Francisco Varela trained me in the cognitive sciences, and I began to have what I call my personal fight with Cartesian ontology. To cut a long story short, in 1978 I started my interdisciplinary studies in Berkeley, at the University of California. I studied philosophy, which was difficult because my background was engineering. But people were very kind to me and I finished the course in record time.

As I was the father of five children, I needed to find work urgently. Around then, I believe I invented a new way of understanding communications, and this was very, very important for both companies and management. I'm sure this was when I had a breakthrough that has since been recognized by many in that field, but at the time I needed to earn a living.

What year was this?

I'd say 1978, around June. I remember very clearly one day I was talking about football with some friends. We agreed on the pleasure and knowledge a player has. Now imagine a journalist, making comments before the game and after the game; he has no effect on who wins the game. The coach is the guy who is able to observe and reflect on the game, before and after, but the central aim of the coach is to make the player stick to the game during the action, not afterwards.

So, when you have a coaching conversation, you realize that something has been bothering you, but the difference here is that you are not so much looking to past experience, more to potential possibilities; not informational knowledge, but sheer commitment.

People began to tell me that they had had very good experiences as a result of trying these ideas, so I began to expand this theory and afterwards I came up with the notion that people are very troubled because they confuse assessment and assertion.

Can you explain those?

'I am Fernando Flores from Chile' – that's an assertion. It is clear and can be true or false. But suppose I said to you, 'I am a very good coach'; that is an assessment. It also has an assertion component (that I am a coach), but saying I am a *good* coach is an assessment. The kind of commitment I offer to you with this assessment is very different from the kind of commitment that I am making when I say I am Fernando Flores.

A good coach in what domain? I am certainly not a good basketball coach. Also, how do I know that I am a good coach? The only way to decide is to take action and to define the standard to which you want that action to be for 'good coach' to make sense.

Let me define 'talking nonsense' in an ontological way. What you need to do when you are a coach is to teach people to listen to their own nonsense. You see, lies are very easy to spot. And when you are a liar, you know that you are lying, but when you are talking nonsense, you are not aware that you are doing so. But other people can see it. How do you realize that you are talking nonsense? Especially since in our culture it has become a habit.

The difference is that a liar knows that he is deceiving you, but the person talking nonsense does not. The same can happen with promises. If you are an honest person, your intentions and your promise go together. When you are a liar, your promise has an intention to deceive; you know that you are not going to complete the promise. But when you are talking nonsense, you have the basic intentions, and you have goodwill – that is what makes it dangerous.

Coaching involves teaching people how to be honest; this can be a moral pressure. A good coach needs to be very patient and compassionate and have the time for their client to develop the skill. That is very liberating for people.

You need to be a listener, but not just listen generally; you need to listen to the intentions behind what the client is saying. That is the phenomenon of blindness. A coach will reveal to the individual the consequence of social blindness. Let me give you a cultural example. For a Latin guy, time is not the same as for others. The Americans are very impatient; they want to get to the point, because they believe that life is about doing things. But there are moments when you should wait. There may be something you need to hear.

We think ontological coaching is interesting because it pays particular attention to the emotions and also to the body, the physiology. Would you give us your thoughts on this?

There is a difference between ontological coaching and ontological design.

It is not a question about the individual alone. It is also about the architecture of the media, of the environment in question, and that is very important when you ask about mood, for example.

Take the environment of a church. It has a certain mood. If you want the opposite, imagine a bar or a nightclub. The place shapes and modifies mood, and I believe architects and musicians know a lot about mood and how to shape it with what they do.

Then you can make an emotional shift in the situation, which will affect the body. You can see it very clearly in mammals; dogs, for example – the way they move their ears, the way they stand alert. When danger passes, then they go back to a relaxed position. Little kids do the same. I call this an operation mood. But a mood is emotional and intentional in the sense of the way you are oriented. Joy is something you have when you encounter something that you have been looking for that was missing. Good coaches have a natural capacity to be sensitive to mood, and they need to unlearn any culture that doesn't allow them to do that.

My work can apply to whole corporations, and refine the business process. This makes my methodology unique and that is why I have been able to coach large organizations.

We are interested in the effects of culture on coaching. Do you think that it is important that people understand how to coach in different cultures, or coach cross-culturally?

My impression is that most of the people that I have been talking to about coaching don't understand it well and don't have very good communication skills. They repeat a formula that they can learn from someone. Coaches worry about trust and self-confidence.

In my opinion, trust is the capacity that you have for being sincere, so people will be open with you and offer commitment that they wouldn't offer to others. Most of the time, people accumulate negative experiences about trust, and in that way many possibilities disappear.

And self-confidence is the same. We accumulate a bunch of negative assessments about ourselves and many times we don't have the force or the courage to deal with the situation that needs to be dealt with. Because what damages your self-confidence and trust frequently has to do with instances from the past that you have never examined carefully. That's the trouble with living by rigid rules.

What do you think is the future of coaching?

I believe that coaching is arousing great interest, especially with what is happening on the Internet. We need to explore the potential and limits of online coaching. And I am keen to explore how the network might be useful for intercultural communications. Being a senator, I have had many chances to consider coaching, and I hope I will continue in this vein.

Fernando Flores PhD developed the basis of ontological coaching in the 1980s working in applications of philosophy, in software design, management and human development. He is a Doctor in Philosophy in Interdisciplinary Studies at the University of California in Berkeley, and founder of several companies in the United States and in Chile. The author of numerous books and papers, he became a government minister at the age of 29. Since 2002 he has been a senator in the Chilean government.

7 AN INTEGRATED MODEL

'There is nothing more practical than a good theory.'

Kurt Lewin

'A theory is primarily a form of insight, a way of looking at the world and not a form of knowledge of how the world is.'

David Boehm

At the beginning of Part Two, we left our protagonist Nasrudin puzzled by the different stories he had heard in his courtroom. This story is not finished. His legal adviser, being versed in Aristotelian logic, made a final comeback.

'You cannot leave it like this, Your Excellency,' he hisses. 'Only one of them can be telling the truth!'

'The problem is not truth,' answers Nasrudin. 'The problem is trust.'

The words 'truth' and 'trust' derive from the same root, as you might expect. We trust what we think is true. This brings us to the heart of coaching – the trust that is built between coach and client and between coach, client and the methodology.

This chapter reveals the core model we have distilled from other models, which we believe to be the heart of coaching and that we use in our trainings and in our practice. This is not about best practice, which is always limited to its time. What we have are the necessary and sufficient elements that allow coaching to work, and which pluck the core methodology from the chaotic flux of coaching in practice. We have tested them for years in many different countries and we believe they stand the test of practice.

What elements must come into such a core methodology? We need the four perspectives from the integral model below.

Coaching quadrants

	Interior	Exterior
Individual	The goals, mental habits and values of the coach and client. The subjective expectations of coach, client and other stakeholders.	The behaviours of coach and client. Body language and spoken language. The psychogeography of the coaching session.
Collective	The relationship between coach and client as experienced by them. The shared expectations and synergy that results.	The external systems that support the sessions, the business framework, logistics, economic system, etc.

First, there is the upper-left area, the subjective area. What goes on inside the client's head? What is going on inside the coach's head? How does the coach need to think? What sort of beliefs, values and goals work for coach and client?

In the upper right, we have the external behaviour of coach and client in the relationship and the changes that result.

How does that affect their performance?

In the lower left area are the systems and structures.

How is coaching delivered? What sort of systems and practices are needed for it to be successfully introduced into a company? What has to happen? What people need to be consulted? What framing needs to be done and how are expectations to be managed?

Finally, there is the lower right area of relationship.

What sort of relationship needs to be built between coach and client? How is the relationship built and what happens within it?

All four areas need to be considered for successful coaching.

A methodology has a set of distinctions. Every profession has distinctions that enable practitioners to understand each other, to view the world in a certain way and to take action based on that worldview. Coaching is a profession in the making, and we believe that our suggestions will be a start in constructing a set of distinctions suitable for the profession. We believe that coaching will become a profession because the discipline and methodology are the same as the name and the practice. This is generally true for professions, for example, law and psychology.

BASIC COACHING PROCESS

Coaching is a methodology of change. There are three basic steps that are present in all the models.

Core Coaching Processes
1 Supporting the client and guiding their attention.
2 Giving meaning and reflecting the client's material in a way that goes beyond the client's thinking.
3 Helping the client to take action.

The first process is supporting clients and guiding their attention. This is done through the coaches' questions and the quality of attention they pay their clients. Coaches see what their clients do, what they say, what they do not say, and what they can and cannot take responsibility for.

The second is giving meaning and reflection. This fits what the clients say (language) and do (behaviour and body language) into a coaching 'model' that coaches have in their mind. From that model, the coaches give feedback and reflect back to the client a different and, hopefully, helpful perspective on their issue. The coaching model that is in the coach's mind needs to be rich enough to encompass the myriad material the client presents. The richer the model, the better the coaching.

The third is helping the clients to take action. The action they take will be different from what they have been doing or intend to do. What they did before was based on habits and perpetuated those habits. The new actions give different feedback and lead to change.

All coaching models also ask three basic questions implicitly or explicitly. Underlying these questions is an idea of what it means to be a human being and what coach and client believe is possible for them in the relationship.

⇨ Where does the coach intervene to *start* the change process?
⇨ What should coach and client pay attention to?
⇨ What results do coach and client want and how will it be measured?

THE STARTING POINT

People have many dimensions – cognitive, emotional, physiological and spiritual – and the coach needs to keep them all in mind to decide where to begin and where to intervene. All dimensions are connected, and a change in one will bring changes in the others, but the changes need to be in the direction the client wants and they need to be sustainable. Each coaching method may vary in its preferred starting point, because each method of coaching sees different elements of the client and the context as more relevant than others.

Most coaching begins at the cognitive level, asking clients to think differently about the issue. Thinking differently leads to different behaviour, different emotions and different language. Generally speaking, coaches do not *begin* at the emotional level and they do not try to bring out emotions, especially not negative emotions, related to the problem. They do pay attention to emotions, however. They rarely start at the physiological level, which is left for professionals who look at posture and body language. However, ontological coaches sometimes work with their clients' posture and expressions. Not surprisingly, behavioural coaches often start at the level of behaviour. NLP coaches and ontological coaches are most likely to pay more attention to the client's language patterns.

There is no dispute between cognitive coaching and behavioural coaching. They go together, as a change in thinking leads to a change in behaviour and vice versa. These two approaches differ in where they start and what they pay more attention to, not in the result. Behavioural coaching emphasizes the right quadrants of the Integral model, whereas cognitive coaching stresses the left ones. Behavioural and cognitive coaching take different perspectives, and a balanced view will include both.

Coaching is a helping profession concerned with human learning and development. It is the identification and realization of possibilities for both coach and client. The client wants to change, but the process touches and involves the coach, too. The change happens through the type of relationship that is created between them.

A comprehensive treatment of how coaching works needs to consider both coach and client and the relationship between them. This means:

⇨ **The subjective world of the coach.**
⇨ **The subjective world of the client.**
⇨ **The relationship between coach and client (where the two subjective worlds meet).**
⇨ **The coach's behaviour and language.**
⇨ **The client's behaviour and language.**
⇨ **The external means and systems of delivery for the coaching.**

(We will assume coach and client share the same cultural background for now and will deal with cross-cultural coaching in Part Three.)

Different coaching models will put emphasis on different parts of the process. The relationship and balance between these elements determine how the methodology is used in practice. We will begin with the coach before considering the relationship and finally the client.

1 THE COACH

Coaches are the co-creators of the coaching relationship with their clients, so they cannot be completely objective. They are inside the system; however, they have their own ideas about coaching and the nature of the client's issue. Coaches cannot not bring their own ideas to the coaching relationship. They are not perfect mirrors only reflecting the client's ideas;

not only is this not possible, it is not even desirable. There has to be a difference between the coach's and the client's perspective on the situation or there is no progress.

ASKING QUESTIONS

What does the coach do? Mostly, ask questions. The coach has the questions, and the client answers. In no model of coaching does the coach provide the answers or attempt to solve the problem. The quality of the questions will influence the quality of the answers, the relationship and the results. These ideas generate hypotheses about the client and the issue the client brings. The questions test the hypotheses. These hypotheses are *not* the solutions to the problem. They are hypotheses about how the client is thinking, what possible blind spots they might have and the perspectives they are taking.

Knowing how to ask questions is the first core skill of coaching. Questions support clients, guide their attention and test the coach's hypotheses about the situation. All the models of coaching agree on this, and NLP coaching and ontological coaching deal with the linguistic aspect of questions in depth. Questions are the coach's main intervention. But what is special about questions?

Questions do a number of things that are essential to the coaching process.

First, questions are irresistible. Whether clients agree or disagree, answer 'yes' or 'no', they have to think. A question is a searchlight that the coach shines into the dark places of their clients' mind. When clients come to a coach, they do not have the answer. It does not make sense to say that the client has all the answers, but we can say that answers are created in the relationship; neither coach nor client had them before.

There is a Zen story about a man who is looking frantically under a streetlamp at night. A passer-by stops to see what he is doing.

'What are you looking for?' he asks.

'My keys,' replies the man.

'Let me help you,' says the Good Samaritan, and together they hunt round in the lamplight.

'I can't see them anywhere,' he says after about five minutes, 'Where exactly did you drop them?'

'Oh, I lost them over there,' replies the man, pointing to an area about 20 metres away.

'But wait a minute,' says the helpful stranger, 'If you lost them over there, why are you looking for them over here?'

'Because it is dark over there,' replies the man, 'I can't see. Over here there is a light, so this is where I am looking.'

This is what clients do; they look for answers in the places they know. Coaches' questions act as lights so clients can look in places they could not see before. If we continue with the metaphor, a coach does not produce a key from his pocket and give it to the client. Nor does he offer to break into the client's house.

Questions give the client new perspectives and they open up possibilities. Questions also change emotions. A question about good experiences will evoke positive emotions. A question about bad experiences will evoke negative emotions. Questions also help clients to think in different directions and take different perspectives.

Asking a question is behaviour; it is visible and audible. What attitude must coaches have for their questions to be most effective and most helpful?

The coach
asks questions from an attitude of respect, commitment
and not knowing.

First, a question must be non-judgmental. Coaches must not judge their clients; the clients are usually judging themselves already. Coaches' ability to quiet their mind, to still inner conversations and to stay focused on their clients is part of the self-management process in coactive coaching.

Second, coaches must respect their clients, at least in the domain in which they are coaching them. They need not admire their clients, they need not agree with their clients, but they need to respect their clients as people.

Third, coaches must be committed to their clients. There is a lot written about the importance of the client's commitment to the coaching process, but coaches must also be committed. If coaches are not committed, or have doubts about their clients' ability, the clients will pick this up and the relationship will suffer. The coaches' commitment will make their questions honest and not manipulative. Coaches should never ask a question to which they already know the answer, or one where they have a vested interest in a specific answer. And coaches should never ask a question which is constructed in such a way as to push their clients down a particular path. Coaches may be tempted to ask a question whose purpose is to guide the client to an answer that the coach thinks is a solution and so fool the client into thinking they themselves came up with it unaided. This does not work, and the clients will feel manipulated. The answer, however interesting, will not be the client's. When coaches have an idea they think could be helpful, it is much better if they tell their clients outright rather than try to manipulate the clients into saying it. Clients do not want to be ventriloquists' dummies.

When coaches are honest, this evokes honesty in their clients. Clients want to please their coach, impress their coach, make their coach think well of them. So, they may be tempted to twist their answers a little to make them appear in a good light. When coaches already respect their clients and when coaches are honest, this will be less of a problem for their clients. Clients tend to model the qualities they experience in their coach. Coaches need to give what they want to receive. Any quality that a coach wants the client to demonstrate, the coach needs to demonstrate first. A client learns by example as well as by understanding and action.

Lastly, coaches need to ask questions from an attitude of curiosity and 'not knowing'. The coach does not have the answers and does not know better than the client. Clients are the experts in their own lives, and coaches do not know where the keys to the situation are hidden.

All questions contain some assumptions, and it is important that the coach's questions contain assumptions about the client's motivation, resources and eventual success.

CLIENTS' QUESTIONS – THE 'MU' RESPONSE

What of the questions clients ask themselves? They may be in the wrong direction and based on limiting assumptions about the situation.

Sometimes a coach will respond to the client's question or problem with a comment about the assumptions the client is making. There is Zen story that illustrates this.

A Zen disciple is sweeping the yard in the monastery when the master comes out to see what he is doing. Fearing being hit with the stick, the disciple decides to get in first with a question. There is a mangy dog in the yard, skulking in the shadows, and gnawing at scraps that have been thrown from the kitchen into the dust.

'Master,' says the disciple, 'does that dog have Buddha nature?'

The Master looks at him and replies, 'Mu'.

What does 'Mu' mean? It means, 'I unask your question.' It means that the master does not accept the assumptions behind the question and therefore does not say yes or no. He deconstructs the question. This is what coaches often need to do. Clients come with questions, problems and issues, wondering what to do. They are asking the wrong questions. The coach responds, 'Mu'.

A coach's attitude of respect, commitment and not knowing will generate the best questions and allow the client to find the best answers. This attitude comes from a coach's beliefs about people, a model of what it means to be human.

THE COACH'S BELIEFS

What sort of beliefs do coaches need to demonstrate in their actions?

> **Beliefs of a coach**
> 1 An optimistic view of human nature.
> 2 We construct our reality – what we construct we can also deconstruct.
> 3 Choice is better than no choice and there are always more choices.
> 4 Their coaching skill and methodology works.

First, coaches should have an optimistic view of human nature, based on humanistic psychology. They need to believe that their clients are not completely stuck, that they want to escape and make the most of themselves, and they are willing and able to do so. Coaches do not take on people who are mentally ill, so their clients are usually committed and want to be the best they can be. There will be obstacles, but they are not insurmountable. To get the best from individuals, you need to believe the best is there. This is true for every type of client from the most senior business executive to the most naïve client.

Coaches must also apply the same principle to themselves, believing that they can always do better, that they have not reached their limit, and that they are travelling with the client – maybe a little bit further along, but on the same road.

Second, coaches need to believe that we all construct our own reality and then *maintain* it. Everyone is unique, and in order to help someone change their world, you do not give them a better world; you help them to create a better one for themselves. Clients have constructed their situation, so they can deconstruct it.

Third, coaches need to assume that having a choice is better than not having a choice. Clients have run out of choices, or the choices they have do not seem to lead to anything they want. The coaches' job is to help their clients construct more and better choices.

Lastly, coaches must believe in their own coaching skill and methodology, whatever that may be. If coaches are doubtful, how can their clients trust them? The coaches' own self-belief may be as important as the particular methodology they use.

2 THE COACHING RELATIONSHIP

The work is done through the relationship created between the coach and the client. All coaching models stress the importance of this relationship, and it has two aspects – the outer (right-hand quadrants in the integral model) and inner (left-hand quadrants).

The outer qualities – support systems

What are the practical arrangements?

How are the expectations managed?

How do coach and client behave in the meeting?

These external factors are important and correspond to the lower right quadrant of the integral model. The most skilful coaches will not be able to use their skill if the logistics are not managed properly. Behavioural coaching pays the most attention to the detailed co-ordination of the coaching operations, managing expectations, setting up measurement systems and matching coach to client in business coaching. The external systems and communications must work between coach, client and other stakeholders such as the Human Resources department to facilitate the best possible relationship.

In life coaching, the coach and client also need to agree the practical details that will support the relationship: when and for how long the coaching will take place, the means, the cost and the place. These matters are about the outer system that supports the coaching relationship.

The support systems of the coaching relationship

The outside system of communication and co-ordination needs to be in place.

The practical issues of the time, place, costs and duration need to be clearly established.

The environment needs to be suitable.

The psychogeography needs to be appropriate.

The other outer aspect of the relationship is the context and behaviour of coach and client *in the session*. The room needs to be comfortable, and the session should be uninterrupted. NLP coaching pays a lot of attention to this aspect – establishing rapport through eye contact, body posture and voice matching. The psychogeography of the room (the position of coach and client) is also important. The distance between the coach and the client needs to be appropriate for the culture. (They will sit closer in Latin cultures than they would in Britain or the United States, for example.)

Coach and client will usually sit at between 90° and 120° to each other. This will allow them to talk and maintain all the eye contact they want, without being opposite each other (a psychogeography of 'opposition'). Both will be able to draw or write or gesture easily.

THE INNER QUALITIES

What are the inner qualities of the coaching relationship?

This corresponds to the lower left quadrant of the integral model.

The inner qualities of the coaching relationship

1 Rapport.

2 Listening.

3 Commitment.

First, there must be rapport – a relationship where both people are open to be influenced by the other. NLP coaching has many tools to help coaches to foster rapport through matching. The relationship will also be enhanced by the coach's qualities of respect, listening and a non-judgmental approach.

To take a term from ontological coaching, the coach's *way of being* helps to make the relationship. Good coaches have *presence*. They are there for the client in a non-judgmental and open way. They do not have an agenda for the client to follow. This is what makes the relationship both special and effective. There are many coaching tools, but they are used inside this relationship; they are not a substitute for it.

Listening establishes the relationship, and is an essential skill in all the coaching models, emphasized in both ontological coaching and coactive coaching. The coach's listening helps the client articulate their issue in the clearest way. The client needs to listen too, but the coach's listening has an open quality that gives the client space to tell their story. When someone does not listen (as happens at cocktail parties when the person you are talking to is looking around to see if there is someone else more interesting to talk to), you doubt yourself and it is hard to maintain the conversation. Only once listening is established can ontological coaching focus on the types of conversation that can occur between coach and client.

Listening allows the coach's intuition to be engaged, and this is an important part of coactive coaching. Intuition is the ability to have helpful ideas without the logical justification that usually accompanies them. These ideas come from unconscious processing of all the information that coaches have been picking up while they are listening. No listening – no information to process and so no intuition.

When coaches are listening, they will automatically and naturally match some of their clients' body language . This is a fundamental human ability, first documented by researcher William Condon [1] in the 1960s.

Body language and voice tone always go with certain emotions so if coaches are matching their clients naturally, they will be matching tiny muscle movements of the face and these will give coaches a whisper of what their clients are feeling. Coaches need to be relaxed, or else muscle tension in their face (if they are 'trying hard' to understand) will stop the natural matching, and therefore the intuitions.

Coaches will not be able to listen if their heads are full of their own internal dialogue, partly because this will obstruct intuitive messages. So, keeping an internal 'stillness' is an important coaching skill that helps coaches maintain an attitude of 'not knowing'. This contributes to their presence.

Commitment is another element common to all models. The word 'commitment' means a state or quality of being dedicated to a cause, or a pledge. Both coach and client are committed to the relationship, because that is where the changes happen for both. Both coach and client have many other commitments in their lives, and the coaching has to fit into those – another aspect of the outer management of the relationship.

HOW COACHING WORKS

What happens in this relationship?

How do the changes happen?

We think coaching works by developing three crucial skills for the client. These three are what lead to change and achievement for the client.

⇨ **The ability to take new perspectives**

⇨ **The ability to make new distinctions**

⇨ **The ability to *stop* identifying with some limited aspect of themselves. They can be objective about something they were formerly subject to.**

The coach develops these elements by:

⇨ **Questions**

⇨ **Direct statements and interpretations**

⇨ **Demonstrating (modelling) the element for the client overtly or covertly**

The elements in coaching that lead to change for the client

1 Taking new perspectives.

2 Making distinctions.

3 Ceasing to identify with limited aspects of themselves.

---

1 TAKING NEW PERSPECTIVES

A perspective is a point of view. The word means to 'look through', and what you see depends what you are looking through. When you look through a dirty window, what you see is dirt, not what is on the other side. Coaches will always have a different perspective on their clients' issues because they are not involved, so they can give a different interpretation. Clients are looking for an answer and not finding it. They need to look in another place – or perhaps in the same place from another direction. By giving another perspective, coaches give their clients an opportunity to look at their experience from another angle, to see another possibility or choice that they did not see before.

A good metaphor for perspectives is the visual blind spot. There is a spot in the retina of both your eyes where the optic nerve goes to the brain and so there are no light-sensitive cells. When an image falls on this part of the eye, it will be invisible to you.

Try this experiment. Look at the black dot below with both eyes from about six inches away. Now close your right eye and look directly at the dot with your left eye. *Keep staring straight ahead* and slowly move the page to your left. At one point, the dot will disappear, because the image is falling on the blind spot in your left eye.

The blind spot

One viewpoint makes the dot disappear, and shifting your viewpoint makes the dot appear. A coach cannot tell a client, 'You've got a blind spot!' The client will reply, 'Where is it, then?' A client will only know they have a blind spot when they shift viewpoint. Then they will not need telling.

For example, in integral coaching, the four quadrants are perspectives, so are states and stages, lines and levels. NLP coaching has a clear model of perspectives. You can look at anything from the first position (your own point of view – how it affects you), second position (the point of view of another person) and third position (the systemic position that includes you both). The inner game gave a different way of watching the ball as a metaphor to help clients be objective and non-judgmental. Positive psychology coaching has optimism and pessimism. The GAPS grid gives four important perspectives in the behavioural model. In a wider frame, the different coaching models are perspectives, and so we propose that a coach may *change between coaching models* to help their client. Culture is also a perspective, and being bound to one culture may obscure other helpful perspectives.

Clients may reject or not use some perspectives. This does not matter. A new perspective can be very helpful, and it allows the client to learn the skill of switching perspectives – a skill more useful than any one perspective.

It is not enough for clients to appreciate the new perspective intellectually. They must 'put it on' and they must act on it, as if it is true, even though they may not completely believe it. It is the difference between knowing you have a blind spot, and actually *seeing* what you did not see before.

2 MAKING DISTINCTIONS

A distinction is a concept 'cut off' from others. When you make a distinction you make a foreground and a background. Coaching gives clients helpful distinctions – and it develops their skill in making distinctions, a skill more valuable than any distinction. The client may make new distinctions or more subtle and finer distinctions in the concepts they have.

We construct our world by making distinctions. By making more and richer distinctions, our world becomes a larger, richer and more detailed place. A new word creates a new distinction (provided it is not just a new word for the same thing as an old word). Coaches help clients to make distinctions about their experience and reconstruct their world. The ability to make new distinctions is a cognitive skill that coaches can demonstrate in their coaching for their clients to learn.

You can only pay attention to something that you have made a distinction about; otherwise it is invisible, merged with the background. Clients are usually fixated with the problem in the foreground. Coaches encourage them to look more carefully.

Here are some examples. Learning a new language creates many new distinctions, as we will explore in a later section on cross-cultural coaching. A perspective is a distinction. Only when you have it as a concept can you use it. For some people, all bottles of fermented grapes are 'wine'. They sort by personal likes and dislikes. A wine-tasting course will help them to make a distinction between different types of wine, with different names and different tastes. Making distinctions in music means being able to hear nuances of tone, key and structure that add to your enjoyment. Education involves making distinctions in a field (determined by the teacher). Coaching helps to make distinctions in your own experience.

Once you make a distinction, you can see it, understand it, talk about it and analyse it. The different coaching models make different distinctions. For example, NLP coaching makes distinctions about different types of eye movements showing different types of thinking. Our eyes are not under the influence of gravity; they do not flop down to the bottom of our eyes when we are not using them. They move around, and we take that for granted. Once you have noticed people's eye movements, you can see a pattern.

Ontological coaching makes distinctions between various speech acts and different types of conversation. Positive psychology coaching makes a distinction between pleasure and gratification as well as the core character strengths.

A profession creates its own distinctions. To be able to practise coaching, you need to master several distinctions, and these create a specialist vocabulary. The intention of this vocabulary is to make it easier for practitioners to understand each other and communicate clearly about complex concepts. When professional distinctions become unwieldy and serve to confuse rather than enlighten, they become jargon.

A coaching vocabulary creates distinctions for coaches that they use to form hypotheses about their clients' experience. These distinctions also help clients to create a different model of their own experience (often through giving them another perspective). For example, instead of feeling and acting like a 'victim', they can start to be proactive.

Distinctions in coaching

⇨ Those used by coaches in their coaching method (specialist vocabulary).
⇨ Those used by the coach to understand the client ('to make a model of the client').
⇨ Those the coach uses to understand the client's issue.
⇨ Those the client is using to understand their issue (which are not helping).
⇨ Those the client develops about their experience as a result of the coaching.

---

3 CEASING TO IDENTIFY WITH LIMITED ASPECTS

We all make a fundamental distinction between what is 'me' and what is 'not me'. As we mature, we lose our absolute egocentricity, the world becomes bigger, and we realize our place in the world. We do this by separating ourselves, by seeing what is 'me' and what is 'not me'. When you identify with something, you are subject to it: it *is* you. You cannot see it, just as you cannot see your own eye. Anything you separate from, you can be objective about; you can analyse it and evaluate it. It becomes part of your world. The most important skill is for clients to be able to reflect on their own thinking. Until they can do that, they cannot make a distinction between thinking and belief. We are all subject to our cultural conditioning, but this is not a problem unless we want to live and work in another culture. As the saying goes, 'You need to know two cultures before you can know your own.'

A simple example is when we are subject to an emotional state. When someone is angry, the emotion consumes them. They do not think, 'Oh! I am angry. Do I want to be angry? I don't like it. I wonder what I can do about it?' If they could think that, they would not be subject to their anger at that moment. They would have put a distance between it and themselves, they would have made it an object that they could observe, think about and make choices about. We are under the spell of anything we are subject to, so it is very difficult to separate from it without the help of another person. You do not 'have' it. You are 'had' by it.

This has important implications for coaching. Coaches cannot reflect on any cognitive habit that they themselves are subject to. Therefore, they cannot help clients change any idea that they themselves are subject to. They will simply agree with it at an unconscious level and focus their attention on other things that the client says. Coaches' ideas and level of development limit their ability to see certain things. The richness of the model that coaches build of their clients reflects the richness of their own thinking. And the richness of the model they build reflects the new perspectives and distinctions they are able to give the client.

All models of coaching help clients separate from the limiting ideas and habits of thinking that created or maintained the breakdown or problem in their life. These are called 'limiting ideas' in behavioural coaching, 'limiting beliefs' in NLP coaching, and 'limited ways of being' in ontological coaching. They all point to the same thing – an idea that the client is subject to and which handicaps him or her. Pointing out these ideas, or helping the client see them, is a major part of coaching. Rational, logical argument alone does not work. You cannot argue a client out of their belief. Many beliefs have an emotional element and they help the client deal with the world.

What can coaches do? First, they draw attention to the limiting idea. This allows the clients (if they wish) to look at it from the outside. Then they can explore all the ramifications and consequences of acting on that idea. Finally, they may together agree a task for their clients to do that will help them test the limits of the idea and to get feedback on it.

Here is an example from one of our training sessions. We were talking about goals and goal setting being an important part of coaching. One of the participants said, 'I have always thought you get what you are given.' This was such an interesting statement that we started to explore it with him. He started to look at it more critically. It had the positive aspect that it allowed others to be generous, and it fostered gratitude, but as he talked about it more, he saw that this idea was restricting his life. The full idea was actually, 'You get *only* what you are given.' If this was true for him, goal setting was a waste of time because it would not achieve anything. He

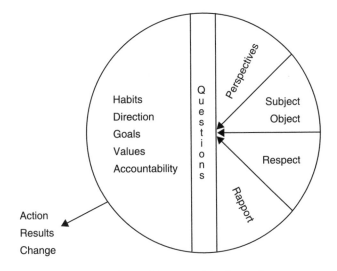

Model of coaching: coach's viewpoint

started to realize how this idea had stopped him setting goals, and made him passive even when he did not like what happened. It even seemed to have influenced his choice of career (he worked for a government welfare agency that helped people who needed money or social payments). He came to see over the next few days that he had been subject to this idea, and after due reflection he decided that he did not want to be any more; it did not fit with the sort of person he wanted to become.

3 THE CLIENT

What does the client bring to the coaching relationship? They bring themselves and their issue. They bring a desire to change, and want better results in some area of their lives. The key word here is 'want'. Clients want something. They bring their wants, their needs and their desire for new directions. They also bring their values and their habits of behaviour and of thinking. They bring their physical way of being, body language and expressions. They bring their emotions and moods, which may be derived from their issues, or may contribute to them. They bring their way of being and characteristic postures and body language. An ontological coach might help clients adjust their posture, but no other main coaching model intervenes directly to adjust a client's physiology. All coaching models, however, treat clients as a whole, and therefore the changes that take place in the cognitive and emotional areas will affect and ultimately change the clients' physiology.

The client

Clients bring:
- ⇨ Their goals and desired direction
- ⇨ Their values
- ⇨ Their habits of thinking and behaviour

GOAL AND DIRECTION

Clients want something that they do not have. Perhaps they need to make a decision or start a new job – there has to be some issue, breakdown, disturbance, ambiguity or imbalance in their life that they want to resolve. It may be provoked by a problem in the present or they may want to work on their vision and life planning. Helping clients clarify exactly what they want is an important part of coaching.

Goals are an important element in all the coaching models, and clarifying the goal is a major part of the coach's work. In behavioural coaching, the goals are likely to be performance levels or managerial skills that are linked to corporate goals. NLP coaching has a sophisticated model for thinking about goals. Ontological coaching uses conversations for possible actions to clarify goals; the GROW model has 'G' for goal at the front. There are long-term and short-term goals, abstract and concrete, specific and general, learning and process goals, even competing and conflicting goals. There are many types of goals, and the distinctions in the various goal-setting models can be very useful for clients.

However, coaching is not simply about achieving goals. Coaches do not simply take what their clients want and help them to achieve it. Sometimes the goal they bring to a coaching session is not really a goal, but their solution to another problem. Coaches help clients evaluate the goal, to see how it fits in with the other goals they have in their life and how it aligns with their values. They help them take different perspectives and make new distinctions. In this process, the original goal may change; sometimes there is a goal behind the goal. They may discover other and different ways to achieve what they want. Problems can be dissolved and resolved as well as solved.

A goal is a particular type of distinction backed up with ideas and values around individual achievement. For some clients, thinking in terms of goals may seem limiting. They need a better distinction to help them think about their life. Not all cultures think in terms of goals. Even clients from North America or Europe, where there is a strong ethic of individual achievement, may not be goal oriented. We prefer to make the distinction of setting a direction. Setting a direction may include a goal, but it need not. In football, a goal is putting the ball in the net. To continue the metaphor, many clients want to score goals and they want the coach to help them put the ball in the net – a specific ball and a specific net. Other clients may not be sure where the net is, or the net may change place for them as they run towards it. So, instead of trying to put the ball in the net, they decide which way to run, and the coach helps the client run in the direction they want, as fast as they want. As they run, they may find many other things they want to do with the ball rather than put it in the goal, or they may discover other, different goals. Alternatively, they may decide they do not want to play football at all. What game they do want to play is a much wider question. Coaches help clients choose and evaluate their direction in life and find a game worth playing.

VALUES

All coaching models agree that clients bring values – what is important to them – to the coaching relationship. In ontological coaching these are called 'concerns'. How clients think about them can be analysed in NLP coaching in terms of submodalities. In behavioural coaching they are the key to intrinsic motivation. Of all the possible goals people could have or directions they could go in, they choose some above others. How do they make this choice? They choose what is important to them, what makes them excited. Values bring energy to direction; otherwise there is no reason to run anywhere.

Values cannot be seen, heard or touched; they are mostly expressed in abstract words like 'love', 'honour', 'respect', 'health', 'friendship', 'honesty' and 'integrity'. Yet these most abstract of words are what move people, what bring the colour to their cheeks. People fight for their values.

Behavioural coaching concerns itself with motivation for behaviour, and values clearly are what motivate people; they provide the fuel for the journey in the direction the client wants. We make a distinction between three types of values giving three types of motivation.

Extrinsic motivation is experienced by individuals as coming from outside themselves and does not necessarily align with their values. It may be positive, like a reward, or it may be negative, like a punishment or a threat. Without this outside push, the person might not do anything. Coaches never push their clients with rewards or punishments, although many clients may look to the outside for motivation, or try to construct what the coach says into a sort of reward. (Praise by the coach is often seen as a reward.)

The second type of motivation comes from *introjected values*. Introjected values are other people's values taken in and experienced as your own. You can tell introjected values, because clients will feel obliged to behave in a particular way, and often feel guilty if they do not. Introjected values show up as obligations, and the clients' language will reflect this. ('I should do this', or 'I shouldn't do this'.) Introjected values stand halfway between extrinsic motivation and intrinsic motivation. We will deal more with introjected values in Part Three.

Intrinsic motivation is the third type of motivation. It comes from your own authentic values and is rewarded at the very least with the satisfaction of fulfilling those values. Coaches work as much as possible with intrinsic values. They do not push or reward their clients and do not encourage clients to please them, but always help them to connect with their authentic values. Clients need to be at a certain level of personal development to have authentic values.

Three types of value give three types of motivation

1 *Extrinsic* – experienced by clients as originating outside the self.
2 *Introjected* – external values that have been taken inside by clients and experienced as their own, and are accompanied by feelings of obligation.
3 *Intrinsic* – the clients' own authentic values that are freely chosen.

A coach works in four ways with values:

1 They help put clients in touch with their authentic values.
2 They help clients align their direction and goals with these values and find the values behind the goals.
3 They help clients see their introjected values, if this is appropriate. Coach and client can then turn 'shoulds' into 'wants'.
4 They help clients develop a coherent set of integrated values that truly spring from the clients' own personal development. Coaches cannot help clients do this unless they themselves have an authentic and coherent set of values that spring from their own personality. We shall explore this issue more in Part Three.

Self-concordance theory [2] refers to how far goals are aligned with a person's values. When the motivation is external, clients experience the push as coming from the outside, consequently there is little self-determination. When the motivation is intrinsic, clients experience the cause as coming from inside themselves and self-determination is high.

High self-determination

$\uparrow$

Intrinsic motivation
Comes from your own authentic values
('I do it because I truly want to and it is worthwhile.')

Introjected motivation
Values come from the outside but are experienced as your own
('I do it because I should.')

External motivation
Value seen as coming from the outside
('I do it because someone makes me do it.')

No self-determination

HABITS

The last part of the trilogy that clients bring to coaching is their habits. What is a habit? A habit is some automatic, repetitive action or way of thinking that we have learned by paying attention and now happens 'by itself' without thought. We decide on some thought or action, and practise it over and over until it goes underground and we forget about it. This is how all habits are formed. There is always some value behind a habit, as it comes from a repeated action, and we only repeat actions that seem valuable. However, times change and what was once a useful habit can become limiting.

We spend a lot of time and practice setting up habits precisely so that we do not have to think, to release our attention for other things that are more interesting. The habit drops into the background, where it merges with life. This is the blessing and the curse of habits – they are thoughtless. When life is going well, our habits are working well, we feel in control, we have adapted to the life we lead. However, when we want to change, or life demands our attention and there is a breakdown in the ontological coaching sense, habits need to be revised. But habits resist change because we have already put a great deal of thought and even physical effort into making the neural pathways, cutting the groove so that we naturally fall into the habitual path of least resistance.

When we say 'habit', we are talking not only about actions (such as driving a car, scratching your head, smoking cigarettes), but also about thinking, particularly those assumptions we take for granted, that have been reinforced by our experience, and now limit the experiences that we allow ourselves. Behavioural coaching deals directly with habits of action; cognitive coaching deals with thinking habits, and a change in thinking habits will result in changed actions.

Gulliver's Travels by Jonathan Swift [3], written in 1726, has a great metaphor about how habits work. Gulliver is a sailor whose ship is wrecked in a storm. He clings to a piece of driftwood and is eventually washed up, exhausted and alone, on the beach of a desert island, where he falls asleep. When he wakes, he finds he cannot move. He looks around and sees that he is tied down by thousands of tiny ropes, any one of which he could snap easily, but the combined number of them keep him helpless. He cannot get any purchase to move and exert his strength. He has been tied down by very small people called Lilliputians; they are naturally concerned about the giant who has been washed up on their shore and the havoc he could wreak if he broke free.

These ropes are like habits; they tie us down. Some are strong and some are weak. The strength of the habit is proportional to the time and practice put into forming it, and thus also the value it has for us. It is the combined weight of habits, the inertia of life that keeps the client in place. Coaches help clients to snap a rope/habit here, another one there, in strategic positions, until the whole structure is weak enough for the clients to pull themselves free with their own strength.

Habits are a special example of the subject–object distinction. We are subject to habits because we have no choice when we are not aware of them. The coach's first job is to make the client aware of the habit. We saw this in the inner game, with the individual becoming aware of a habit of playing a tennis stroke in the wrong way. The same principle applies in a habit like blaming yourself (or pessimistic attribution in positive psychology coaching, or making ungrounded negative assessments in ontological coaching). In the GROW model, habits come under 'R' for reality.

Ontological coaching has many self-awareness exercises. Basically, coaches set structures to 'wake up' their clients at certain times so they are aware of how they are acting and thinking. Then they record their observations in a personal coaching record. Behavioural coaching does the same with behavioural habits and encourages clients to keep a personal development plan (PDP). You cannot plan unless you are aware of what you are doing. NLP coaching calls habits of thinking 'beliefs'.

Once clients are aware of the habit, they can reflect on it without judging themselves as bad or stupid. Non-judgmental awareness is important in every coaching model. Finally, the client and coach decide how to deal with the limiting habits. Habits cannot be destroyed, but they can be deconstructed, taken to pieces and replaced by something that works better. All habits have good reason to be built in the first place, and clients need to remember this. Sometimes the habit is obsolete; it was formed when the client's life was different, but it lives on as a vestige of an earlier time. For example, many habits are built to keep us safe, especially in childhood, when we are weaker and more vulnerable. Sometimes the reason for the habit still exists, in which case the client and coach need to replace the existing limiting habit with one that does not limit the client but honours the same intention.

For example, one client had a habit of thinking that she summarized like this: 'Work is a sacrifice and always causes problems.' This was a habit of thinking she was subject to, and so it was like a belief; she did not question it. She experienced it as true in her own work. Her father had worked hard all his life with passion, but always with problems; the family admired him but at the same time wished he were at home more. He sacrificed his time for his family, so the belief honoured her father, and her father was a very important person in her life. Once she was aware of the thought, the client intellectually agreed that it was a limiting one and might not be true, but all the jobs she had found so far had bored her.

She wanted to find a job she could do with passion, but despaired that it even existed. She did not want this old thinking habit, so with the help of her coach she decided to change it to 'I can work in a profession where I am satisfied and can help people.' The 'helping people' phrase directly replaced the 'sacrifice' part. Before, 'helping people' had meant the same as 'sacrifice', so the coach had helped her to make a distinction between the two. Part of her action plan was to begin researching possible jobs; the belief had blocked her from doing this previously. Why search for something you do not think exists?

It is also interesting to see that the first phrase of her original limiting belief ('Work is. . .') is a passive generalization. It applies to all work. She, the client, was not represented in the sentence. It seemed to be a sentence about work, but of course it is about her. The new belief started with her

('*I* can work. . .') and was proactive. She is actively seeking her own experience instead of being subject to a habit.

Many models of coaching distinguish between coaching that changes habits of thinking (transformational – a change in the system) and coaching that changes behaviour (transactional – a change of the system). Behavioural coaching uses single- and multiple-loop questions, while NLP coaching talks of simple and generative coaching. Ontological coaching speaks of deep questions that challenge ideas and more shallow questions that challenge behaviour.

Here is a way of looking at the two different types of coaching. In the transactional type, the client starts with a problem and coaching leads him to action; the feedback from this action helps him to solve the problem. An example would be a manager who needs to learn delegation skills. He learns the skills with the help of a behavioural coach, he practises and the change makes a positive difference to his performance and that of his team.

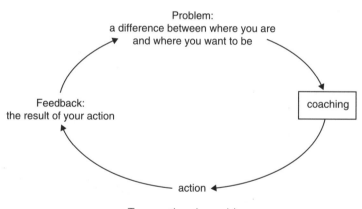

Transactional coaching

The manager continues to practise until he builds a new behaviour that achieves his goal and the problem is solved. Some coaching follows this pattern.

Now imagine that during the initial conversation with the coach, the manager says something like 'Of course, I don't delegate. I can't trust anyone around here; if I give it to my people they just screw up. I know it's a problem but *if you want something done well, you have to do it yourself*.'

This is a habit of thinking. As long as the manager thinks this, he is unlikely to delegate anything important. He may know all the rules of good delegation but he will not do it, because he does not believe it works. Here the coach and client need to work on this belief, not to disprove it, but to see how much truth there is in it – and, of course, to find out how much the manager's attitude is contributing to the bad results he is getting. A change in the belief would be generative change; the manager would be able to solve other problems besides the delegation problem.

Many business people assume (habitual thinking) that because people know how to do something, they will do it. If they do not do it well, they need to learn how to do it better. But this is not always so. Habitual thinking can block skills. Transformational coaching not only solves problems, but also stops the thinking that gave rise to and maintains the problem. It also helps the person solve not just one problem, but a class of problems.

Sustainable change means changing habits. The creation and reinforcement of new habits of behaviour is something a behavioural coach pays a good deal of attention to. All models of coaching recognize habits, make clients aware of habits and help them to change them if they are part of the problem. Most coaching is transformational.

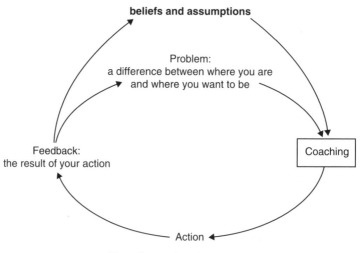

Transformational coaching

CHANGE

Change is the result of the work in the coaching relationship. The one word 'change' covers three ideas:

⇨ The starting state

⇨ The end state

⇨ The process between the two

The Two Types of Change

1 Learning – change in time (horizontal change)

2 Development – change through time (vertical change)

Learning adds to what you *have*. Development changes who you *are*.

There are two main types of change – learning and development. Learning leads to horizontal change – change *in* time. It happens moment by moment and builds into greater expertise in both thinking and behaviour. Learning adds to what you have.

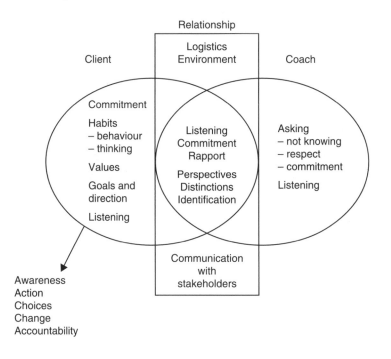

Developmental shifts lead to vertical change – change *across* time. Developmental shifts are more sudden and lead to a radical new way of looking at the world, or a new way of being, in ontological terms. Our stage of development influences the way we learn and how we organize our learning. We all go through developmental shifts; the world appears different, but it is we who have changed.

Horizontal change is like getting more furniture, or more expensive furniture, in your apartment. Vertical change is moving to a new and bigger apartment on the floor above. You may bring some furniture with you, but some you will leave behind because it will not fit any more. Your tastes have changed and your view has expanded. Integral coaching talks about the difference between states and stages – states are horizontal, stages are vertical. Ontological coaching talks about shifts in the clients' way of being.

Coaching can lead to both horizontal changes and vertical changes. As we shall argue later, we believe that one of the important and overlooked functions of coaching is to prompt and guide developmental changes. In Part Three, we will see how to add a developmental aspect to our model of coaching.

ACCOUNTABILITY AND RESPONSIBILITY

The client is accountable for the goal in all coaching models. Accountability is often confused with responsibility and seen as a burden and an obligation. Responsibility is something that comes from the outside. We talk about 'taking' responsibility. Responsibility is something a person can accept (or not).

Accountability is something that comes from the inside. A person can say, 'I am accountable.' Coaching fosters accountability and commitment. These form the basis of a promise as defined in ontological coaching. Clients are accountable for their goals. Coach and client are responsible for the relationship and the process.

ACTION

All coaching models agree that clients need to take action. Insight is probably necessary but not sufficient for change. (Behavioural coaching would argue that behavioural change is what counts and insight is not necessary). Habits are made by action and changed by different actions which may be outside the clients' comfort zone. The clients will need the coach's support to act differently and they need to understand and feel that their new actions are congruent with their values and new direction. These actions give clients a wider range of feedback, they make them more aware, they shake the habits and start breaking the mental ropes that bind them. They lead to feedback and reflection with the coach, which, in turn, lead to more action steps. Small action steps are one of the results of any coaching process.

TRANSITION

Change does not happen all at once; it takes time. Horizontal change can take place continuously and regularly. Vertical change or developmental shifts tend to happen discontinuously. Transition is the part when clients are on their journey, and they are off balance, having left the safety of what they knew but not yet having reached the place they are aiming for. There is a full model of transition in our book *Coaching with NLP* [4]. Most transitions in coaching are initiated by clients, rather than forced on them by outside circumstances. (Then the coaching may be more about adapting to change.) Clients usually pass through three main stages of transition – consideration, preparation and action.

The three stages of transition

1 Consideration.
2 Preparation.
3 Action.

CONSIDERATION

Consideration is the first stage – thinking about making the change, but not doing anything about it. The clients may be ambivalent and afraid of losing something important. At this stage, coaches help their clients explore the value behind the fear and the ambivalence they feel. They help them balance the pros and cons of moving forward. The coaches will be asking what has to be true for the clients for them to make this change, if indeed they really want to make it.

PREPARATION

In the preparation phase, the clients have dealt with the fear and are ready to move. Coaches help the clients commit to an action plan and also help them motivate themselves by linking the change to their values. The more the coach and client honour the small changes, the more they support the main change. Life is a series of small decisions that combine to make big changes – a series of small actions, each bringing you closer, step by step, to the main one.

ACTION

Now the clients are committed and taking action, though sometimes they relapse. Coaches will always try to prevent relapse, but if it happens it is best treated as a natural part of the process of change. Behavioural coaching has many tools to firmly embed the new learning and to prevent relapse. NLP coaching and coactive coaching have structures to remind the client.

Throughout the period of change, clients will experience more choice, and they will feel that the coaching is helping them.

More choice in their thinking.

More choice in their emotions, more emotional intelligence and an end to being subject to emotions and thoughts rather than being their owner.

More choice in their behaviour, so a greater feeling of being at the centre of their life instead of a minor character in someone else's story. More choice means more freedom. Behaviour, thinking, emotion and the way they talk about issues will change. They will have worked through the specific issue they had brought to the coach, and they will have insight into how their way of thinking helped to create it and therefore how to avoid such issues in future.

Finally, the change can be measured, but only if this has been decided in advance and measured at the start. You measure the distance between two points – start and finish. For example, if the developmental level of the client has not been measured at the beginning of the coaching, then any change will be invisible. If the level of performance has not been measured at the beginning, there is nothing to compare the final level with. But this does not mean to say nothing has happened. In this sense, there is a paradox that while you measure what you get, you also get what you measure. We will consider measuring the change in the next section.

REFERENCES

1   Condon, W. (1982) 'Cultural Microrhythms' in Davis (ed.), *Interactional Rhythms: Periodicity in Communicative Behavior*

2   Sheldon K. & Elliot, A. (1998) *Not All Personal Goals Are Personal, Personality and Social Psychology Bulletin* 24 (5)

3   O'Connor, J. and Lages, A. (2004) *Coaching with NLP*

4   Swift, J. (1988) *Gulliver's Travels,* edited by Paul Turner

PART THREE

1 MEASURING THE RESULTS OF COACHING

'In theory, there should not be much difference between theory and practice – in practice there often is.'

Anonymous

How do we decide if coaching is successful?

As coaching becomes part of leadership development and organizational initiatives, subjective evaluations and anecdotal evidence are not adequate measures of coaching effectiveness. When an external coach is employed in a business, the employer is not the client. The employer is the business and the client is the individual manager. There are many more stakeholders and the coach needs to satisfy them all. How can we measure the impact of coaching?

The same question applies to life coaching, although it is simpler; the client is also the coach's employer. He pays for the coaching directly; he decides how he will evaluate the coaching, and what he will measure.

We need to develop new thinking to measure the results of coaching. There is a great temptation to use existing models, especially the medical model. However, a medical model diagnoses illnesses that fit with existing descriptions. While a panel of doctors might well agree on a diagnosis, a panel of coaches would be very unlikely to agree on exactly what to do with a client. This is because the medical model treats the illness and symptoms (and this is appropriate for medical illness), whereas coaching treats the client.

The scientific mentality likes tangible, linear measurements that can be seen and easily quantified, such as behavioural changes and increased profits. However, this is only one way of measuring the results of coaching. Revisiting the integral model of four quadrants, we can measure the effects of coaching in four ways:

1   The individual client's subjective internal evaluation (the upper left quadrant of internal experience).
2   The changes in individual behaviour (the upper right quadrant of visible actions).
3   The change in company culture and morale (the lower left quadrant of the internal group experience).
4   The increased efficient and effective functioning of the business system (the lower right quadrant of visible systems).

COACHING AS ART AND SCIENCE

Coaching is an art as well as a science – an art because it deals with human beings, a science because it has a structure, a methodology and a set of principles. The science of coaching needs to be grounded in empirical research. Research will never explain the artistic side, just as the waveform on an oscilloscope will not explain or measure the pleasure the listener will get from the music it represents. It belongs to another domain. Randomized trials of artistic appreciation will not explain why people will pay millions of dollars for a Van Gogh. Subjective artistry always has a counterpart in the external scientific world, but can never be reduced to it.

The science of coaching practice, education and research is becoming increasingly evidence based. Evidence-based coaching has been defined by Dianne Stober and Anthony Grant as 'intelligent and conscientious use of best current knowledge integrated with practitioner expertise in making decisions about how to deliver coaching to individual coaching clients and in designing and teaching coach training programs' [1]. This is a good definition, because it brings in all the important elements. The knowledge is current, so always updated; coaches need to keep abreast with current developments in their field and related fields. Practitioner expertise is also crucial, and it is determined by success and feedback. The coach himself or herself is taken into account. The individual client matters. Coaching does not exist in a vacuum without a real coach and a real client. Coaching is not magic that works in exactly the same way on every client. Despite the many computer analogies that have sprung up, human beings are not computers. Best available knowledge – and we would add skill to this – will take into account controlled and tested studies. Correlated observations from many different sources, case histories, anecdotes and studies should all be taken into account and results measured in many different ways to get a multiple perspective. If coaching teaches multiple perspectives, then it is fair that the same rules apply to measuring the results.

Coaching is an art too, so we should look to the artistic world for models of how they measure results and decide about different approaches. How does the art world, or the world of film and theatre, decide what is good and what is not? Mainly through the opinion of experts. An art critic goes to an exhibition and writes a review; he or she looks at the art with a trained eye and critiques on the basis of established criteria. The critic is educated. He has read, he has studied and probably been active in the profession himself. A respected critic not only leads but also shapes and follows public opinion.

The critic's opinions influence public opinion, but will never substitute for it. If the majority of the paying public decide that an art exhibition is nonsense, they will not pay to see it and the exhibition will lose money. Critics may rail against the uncultured masses, but feedback from paying customers counts. And many a film has been a success despite unfavourable reviews.

People who have studied coaching have an important part to play in evaluating coaching. We should pay attention to experienced coaches, who have studied, who have gained knowledge and skill, and developed themselves. Not everyone's opinion has equal weight. So, in our evidence-based approach there will always be people whose opinions carry more weight because of who they are and what they have done.

LIFE COACHING EVALUATION

Life-coaching clients want changes; they want results, but how will these be measured? What do the clients want to achieve from the coaching? Specifically,

⇨ **What do they want to do differently?**
⇨ **What do they want to do more of?**
⇨ **What do they want to do less of?**

It is useful for the client to explore these questions at the start, thinking about what they want and how they will measure the results. All clients will evaluate the coaching subjectively: how they like it, how much progress they think they are making, whether it meets their expectations and so on. Clients' expectations need to be educated. They may not have a complete picture of what will happen in the coaching. They may think that the coach is a magician of change and they only need to sit back and enjoy.

How will results be measured? During the coaching, the coach and client need to track progress with agreed measures. Life coaching is more open-ended than business coaching, which usually lasts for a fixed period (on average four months). Life coaching may extend for many more months and deal with much more abstract issues such as quality of life, quality of relationship, developmental level and many others. Coach and client together need to make sure that they measure the progress, even if only on a simple scale of client satisfaction. Life coaching clients will evaluate how they like the coaching, the skills and learning they get, and the results in different areas of their life.

BUSINESS COACHING EVALUATION

In the United Kingdom, it has been estimated that 95% of organizations have or are using coaching [2], and the value of the business coaching industry in the United States is estimated at around $1 billion and growing. Companies are willing to invest up to $100,000 a year on coaching for CEOs and top managers. What do they get for their investment? How can we measure the effects of coaching, and how can this be turned into a figure that gives a return on investment (ROI)? How do we judge the value of coaching? As coaching grows in importance and influence, there is more and more demand for evidence-based approaches to show coaching is having the impact it promises.

So what do we measure and how do we measure it? *You get what you measure*, because if something is not measured it is invisible. You need to decide in advance what to measure, because you are measuring change, and 'change' contains a start, an end and the distance between. If a carpenter gets the measurements wrong before he starts work, the shelves he is making will not fit. If coach and client do not decide on the starting point, then the change will be impossible to prove. At the moment, few businesses are measuring the results of coaching. According to a report on coaching services in 2006 [3], 35% of coaching in business is unmonitored, and just 9% of organizations have a formal process to evaluate effectiveness and return on investment (ROI), measured in that most ubiquitous and unarguable measure of all – money. However, most evaluation remains anecdotal.

How is business coaching evaluated? By taking different perspectives, using a similar model to that developed by Kirkpatrick [4], which has been extensively used in evaluating the results of training. Kirkpatrick distinguished four possible levels of evaluation, each building on the previous one: individual reaction, learning, transfer of learning and business results. Coaching is different from training, so we will change the model slightly and use these categories: subjective reaction, learning, behaviour, business results and ROI.

Evaluating the results of coaching

1 Subjective reactions – the experience of the client.
2 Learning – the changes in knowledge and skills.
3 Behaviour – the actions of the client as a result of their learning.
4 Business results – what the business achieves as a result of the individual changes.
5 ROI – return on investment: the financial benefit of the coaching less the cost, divided by the cost.

---

1 SUBJECTIVE REACTIONS

The subjective reaction of the client belongs in the upper-left quadrant of the integral model – internal individual awareness. Only the client can measure this, and it can be done easily from a questionnaire before and after the coaching.

⇨ **What are the inner changes they experienced?**
⇨ **Did they enjoy the process?**
⇨ **Did they achieve the clarity, direction and improvement that they wanted?**
⇨ **What were their goals?**
⇨ **Did they achieve them in the way they wanted and expected?**

All measurement starts with this subjective reaction. For example, clients might want to improve their ability to get on with others at work. They can rate their satisfaction on a scale of 1 to 10 before the coaching and after the coaching. If the number rises in line with their expectations, or above their expectations, then the coaching has been a success.

In a recent survey [5], a large majority of people reported increased self-awareness (68%), better goal setting (62%) and a more balanced life (61%) as a result of coaching. This is a valid measurement and the one most used in life coaching. Everything can be measured on a simple scale of 1 to 10 – this is the basis of the 'happy sheets' that are used to evaluate training all over the world. An organization wants its people to feel happy and satisfied, but from its point of view that is not enough. The satisfaction needs to be translated into something more tangible. To justify the investment, this subjective reaction has to result in different behaviour and then in different business results. Clients may rate the coaching highly, but not change their behaviour. From the organizational viewpoint, this is a failure. Regardless of how highly clients rated the coaching, the business wants to see changes in their knowledge, skills and behaviour.

2 LEARNING

The second perspective is the learning the clients make and the resulting increase in their knowledge and skill. Clients can measure this subjectively (how much they think they have learned), and it can also be measured objectively. Coaching does not teach clients directly, but clients will learn more about themselves, their work, their goals and values. Coaching may also be used to consolidate and get the most from previous training.

The more complex the learning, the harder it is to evaluate. Knowledge and skills can be evaluated by tests taken by clients before and after the coaching. Learning can be measured by formal and informal testing, self-assessment and team assessment. An individual's increase in learning may express itself in better results for their team. Many organizations train, foster and measure their core competences. The competences themselves are abstract qualities; they need behavioural markers to measure any changes and this is the next level of measurement.

One further point about learning and competences. Coaching may increase the client's ability to learn. After the coaching they may be able to learn more, and more quickly. We can say it has increased the client's capability, which they can then apply to specific competences. The results will only show up in the long term, but as organizations do not routinely measure the employee's capacity to learn, any evidence for an increase in capability will remain subjective and anecdotal.

3 BEHAVIOUR

New learning and skill hopefully will result in behavioural change; this belongs in the upper right quadrant of the integral model, and is directly observable. Are the new skills, knowledge and attitudes being used in the everyday environment? Learning, knowledge and attitudes are invisible, but behaviour is visible and therefore the easiest to measure and the most convincing evidence.

Behavioural changes can be evaluated in many ways – 360° feedback, through observation of others and through tests. For example, a client wants better communication skills and to be less argumentative and more positive with their team. Before the coaching, the coach and client would need to agree categories of behaviour such as attacking, defending, disagreeing etc that the client wants to change, eliminate or reduce. The client would also list some behaviours that he or she wants to do more of, such as supporting, agreeing etc. All these would be measured before the coaching by self-assessment and feedback from peers and managers. Then they would be measured after the coaching in the same way, and the differences noted.

Measuring behaviour is not as straightforward as managers sometimes imagine. The same behaviour can come from different thinking, different values and different emotions. It cannot be isolated from the person who does it.

Second, the same behaviour can come from different developmental levels, so a person may have changed in their thinking and values, but their behaviour may stay the same. Third, behaviour is always related to context. Behaviour may change because the person is in a different context. For example, an argumentative executive may have coaching, and in the course of the coaching he finishes a large project, and so feels less stressed. Perhaps a team member he did not get along with is transferred. As a result, his behaviour changes measurably, with less attacking and fewer arguments, but coaching alone does not account for the change. Fourth, development occurs in stages, so there may be little or no change during the period of coaching, then a big jump some weeks or months later.

Entwined with this is the time factor. How long after the coaching do you measure? A week? A month? A year? A comprehensive follow-up and evaluation should last at least three months, but it is hard to isolate other influences during that time. How do you distinguish the effects of coaching from all the myriad influences that the client is exposed to?

Similarly, if we reverse the last point, suppose behavioural changes do occur immediately, but then fade and are not sustained? Is the presence of the coach required for the client to maintain the change? Has the client become dependent on coaching? Is the behaviour linked with a change in attitude? Is it linked with the development of the individual? Finally, when sustainable changes do occur, how can you be sure they are a result of the coaching?

4 BUSINESS RESULTS

The fourth measurement is the impact of the behavioural changes on business results. These belong in the lower-left quadrant of the integral model (external systems). Examples are:

⇨ Improved retention of clients.

⇨ Improved retention of client's reports.

⇨ Better results from the team – improvement in speed and/or quality of the team projects.

⇨ Improved morale resulting in better work or more work.

⇨ Fewer days lost to sickness.

⇨ More new ideas with business applications (e.g. patents filed).

⇨ Fewer customer complaints.

These results are often routinely measured, and in these circumstances, any difference can be seen before and after coaching. Coaches are used in organizations mainly to increase performance, for leadership development, developing competences or accomplishing specific goals [5].

Results depend on changes in behaviour, and changes in behaviour depend on changes in learning, skills, context and stages of development. Coaching will help clients with their personal development, regardless of the business results, so there can be a tension between achieving business results and personal mental growth. Coaches will often need to show that the results are organizationally desirable as well as personally beneficial for clients. For the organization, these will be one and the same; for clients they may be different. Results that come from clients moving up in their stage of development could form part of the ROI, but are even harder to quantify.

There will always be intangible benefits in a coaching programme that are not easy to measure. Examples include improvement in morale, leadership and communication skills, and in various measures of emotional intelligence, conflict resolution and job satisfaction; attracting good people to join because the employer is seen to be investing and caring about its workforce; and improvement in time management skills and client relationships. These may all be present but are not always appreciated or measured.

5 RETURN ON INVESTMENT (ROI)

The fifth and final measurement is the ROI. The business has invested time and money in coaching, so what overall return is it getting for this? Quantifying all the factors is far from easy, and all of the following need to be agreed:

⇨ The goals of the programme.

⇨ The method of evaluation that will be used.

⇨ What will be measured – how, when, for whom and how often.

⇨ Relevant information that must be collected before the coaching begins.

⇨ Relevant information that is collected during the programme.

⇨ Relevant information that is collected after the programme.

⇨ The coaching programme itself.

⇨ The effects of the coaching.

⇨ Intangible benefits.

Then, measurements are converted into monetary terms so that ROI can be calculated. The ROI is calculated by a simple formula:

$$\frac{\textit{Financial gain from coaching minus cost of coaching}}{\textit{The cost of coaching}}$$

Starting with the bottom line of the equation, the cost of the coaching might include (but not be limited to):

⇨ The coach's time

⇨ The client's time (work lost during coaching sessions)

⇨ The direct costs in fees, travel, accommodation etc for the coach

⇨ Administration costs

⇨ Other costs due to disruption of normal business

The business results go on the top of the equation, so the financial gains might include (but not be limited to):

⇨ Improved retention of customers

⇨ Improved retention of client's reports

⇨ Measurable gains from improved teamwork

⇨ More efficient work from client and team (less time spent doing a task)

⇨ More effective work from client and team (better solutions to business problems)

⇨ Fewer days lost to sickness

⇨ More innovative work

⇨ Fewer customer complaints

Converting these into a financial figure is daunting and in iterative fashion will take time and effort and have a cost itself that needs to be factored in. Small wonder that ROIs are only done on large coaching projects. There is a useful and growing literature such as *The ROI of Human Capital* [6], which can help measure the human element in business.

There is also a simple measure developed by the Consortium for Coaching in Organizations (ICCO) [7].

First, estimate the value of making the change in increased productivity or savings made. For example, let's say this comes to $200,000.

Second, estimate how much of this is attributable to coaching. For example, 60%. Multiply the previous value by this percentage. To continue our example, this comes to $120,000.

Third, estimate how confident you are in your estimates so far. Let's say 75%.

Multiply the last figure by this percentage. This gives $90,000.

This is the *adjusted coaching benefit*.

Fourth, subtract the cost of the coaching. If this comes to $30,000 the *net coaching benefit* is $60,000.

Finally, to calculate the ROI, divide the net coaching benefit ($60,000) by the cost of the coaching ($30,000).

This example gives an ROI of 200% (sixty thousand divided by thirty thousand).

There have been several studies on the ROI of coaching. A study between 1996 and 2000 by Manchester Consulting Inc. showed an ROI of 600% for an executive coaching programme. An evaluation study by Metrix Global LLC [8] showed 529% for a coaching programme for leadership development, while a coaching programme at Sun Microsystems showed an estimated ROI of 100%, mostly through staff retention.

A return on expectations (ROE) [9] is more common and easier to manage. It does not need to be so highly quantified, but keeps the important element of measuring the impact of the coaching vis-à-vis prior expectations.

ROI is difficult to calculate accurately and ignores many of the important aspects of coaching. It takes into account only behavioural changes and the business results. It is not a *developmental* model. Because coaching is about developing the individual, and development takes place in stages, perhaps a broader measure is needed over a longer timeframe that takes these factors into account. Laske [10] has proposed a measure called coaching return on investment (CROI) to take into account developmental shifts. As coaching grows and becomes an accepted, even essential, part of business, so methods to measure effectiveness will also be better developed. We will discuss this further in our final chapter, which looks at the future of coaching.

REFERENCES

1 Stober, D. and Grant, A. (2006) *Evidence Based Coaching Handbook*
2 Sherpa Coaching Survey, Cincinnati Ohio, available at www.sherpa coaching.com/survey.html
3 Jarvis, J. (2004) *Coaching and Buying Coaching Services – A CIPD Guide*
4 Kirkpatrick, D.L. (1994) *Evaluating Training Programs: The Four Levels*
5 Auerbach, J. (2005) *Seeing the Light: What Organizations Need to Know About Executive Coaching*
6 Fitz-enz, J. (2000) *The ROI of Human Capital*
7 www.coachingconsortium.org
8 Anderson, M. (2001) *Executive Briefing: Case Study on the Return on Investment of Executive Coaching*
9 Skiffington, S. and Zeus, P. (2003) *Behavioural Coaching*
10 Laske, O. Can Evidence Based Coaching Increase ROI?, *International Journal of Evidence Based Coaching and Mentoring*, 2(2)

REFLECTIONS ON COACHING PSYCHOLOGY

by Anthony M. Grant

The notion of writing a short piece about my reflections on coaching psychology strikes me as being amusingly ironic. Reflection is obviously a central and vital part of the coaching process, yet in our busy, busy world we rarely stop to examine where we are, how we got there and what lessons we can bring from the past into the present, as we work towards the future. So I welcome this opportunity to reflect, both on how I came to be involved in coaching psychology, and on the journey and development of the coaching industry. I hope this reflection stimulates thought and debate, is perhaps somewhat provocative, and in this way contributes to the development of coaching.

I came to coaching, as many of us do, by a rather circuitous route. From the early 1960s to the present day, my parents have studied and sometimes taught the philosophies of Gurdjieff and Ouspensky, and practised meditation and applied philosophy. Thus, I grew up exposed to a wide range of philosophical, religious and spiritual practices and frameworks. While I found the teachings of Zen Buddhism and writings of Tolstoy, Colin Wilson and the like mesmerizing, I could not seem to engage meaningfully with the formal education system. In my classes at school, I always seemed to be near or at the bottom of the class, and I came to think of myself as stupid and unteachable.

Eventually my teachers and I decided that we should part company and I left school shortly before my 15th birthday with no qualifications. I spent the next few years immersed in pursuing a hedonistic lifestyle, somewhere along the way becoming a carpenter, and in my late 20s I became involved in a number of personal development and peer-support groups, both as a member and as a mentor to others.

I moved from the UK to Sydney, Australia in 1988 and I found the open, egalitarian nature of Australian society an amazing revelation. In contrast to the UK, class and occupation did not seem to matter. I was as good as who I was as a person, regardless of what I did for a job or how I spoke.

I continued my involvement with personal development groups and I really wanted to be involved professionally in some sort of development work with others. However, I was extremely wary of many of the people who ran the groups and courses I attended. Very few, if any, seemed to really know what they were doing. Almost to a person, they seemed to have a very limited knowledge base and were unable to answer questions about the underpinning theories. There was little, if any, supporting empirical evidence. When asked searching questions, at best they shrugged them off, at worst they mocked or belittled the questioner.

I knew that I wanted to do work with others in a developmental way, but I had seen enough dodgy personal development 'gurus' to know that I did not want to be someone who only had a seven- or 14-day 'Master Certification', a degree-mill self-directed learning PhD in 'hypnosis' or 'religion', or be presenting myself as 'self-educated'. If I was going to work in this area, I wanted to know what I was doing.

The Australian university system was far more accessible than the UK's, with pathways for mature-age students who had no prior qualifications, and in 1993 at the age of 39, along with 1,500 other first-year undergraduates, I began my bachelor's degree, majoring in psychology at the University of Sydney. I chose psychology as it (naïvely) seemed obvious to me that a psychology degree should be about the science of human development and well-being. I quickly found out that psychology as then taught was often more about brain structure than behaviour, and frequently more about rats than people. Nevertheless, I ploughed on, found much of the degree an interesting and rigorous training in applied critical thinking, and finally graduated, much to my surprise, with a first-class honours degree and the University Medal. From bottom of the school to top of the university – possibly a testimony to the efficacy of self-coaching!

In 1997 no universities taught coaching. About the only coach training programmes available were American tele-classes, and looking at the material being taught I could see that this was not what I was looking for. Much of the coaching material at that time appeared to be atheoretical recycled personal development courses, and few of the people teaching had any kind of academic qualification.

I enrolled in a combined Master of Clinical Psychology and PhD programme. My thesis title was 'Towards a psychology of coaching: The impact of coaching on metacognition, mental health and goal attainment'. At that time there were only 14 PhDs and 78 academic articles on the topic of coaching in the PsycINFO database. I was very fortunate in having Dr John Franklin as my PhD supervisor. He encouraged me to follow my interests even though my topic was not 'clinical' psychology.

Towards the end of my thesis, I started to think about what I should call myself. I did not want to call myself a clinical psychologist – I wanted to work with non-clinical clients, and I was not a counselling psychologist. I thought, 'I'm a coach, and I'm a psychologist', so I should call myself as a 'coaching psychologist'. I liked the sound of that! At that time, as far as I could discover, there was no psychological sub-discipline called 'Coaching Psychology'. To be sure, some psychologists were practising executive and life coaches, but the idea of a dedicated sub-discipline of coaching psychology was new and exciting.

In 2000, with the invaluable support of Professors Beryl Hesketh and Ian Curthoys, I was fortunate enough to be able to found the Coaching Psychology Unit in the School of Psychology at the University of Sydney – the first such unit in the world – and I began to design the first postgraduate degree programme in coaching psychology. I was soon joined by my good friend and colleague Dr Michael Cavanagh and so we began the process of teaching, researching and practising coaching psychology.

Since then, I have been lucky enough to have had 20 reviewed academic papers and five books on coaching published, and at the time of writing I have been involved in running seven coaching outcome studies. At the last count, there are now 15 universities worldwide that offer genuine postgraduate degrees in coaching or coaching psychology. I believe that the involvement of universities in coaching is vital. Although many people may see universities as the clichéd ivory tower, they are still revered and important social institutions central to the sanctioning of knowledge as being perceived as valuable. More importantly, they provide a platform for the sharing and peer evaluation of ideas and research, and the development of commonly held knowledge, and this approach stands in stark contrast to the secrecy often surrounding proprietary commercial coaching systems.

A key factor in the derailment of the human potential movement in the 1960s and 1970s was a reluctance to engage with the academic community. For example, if it were not for the anti-science sentiments shown by the founders of NLP, today we could have seen the original NLP making a useful contribution to the applied psychology curriculum taught at universities – after all, the core of NLP is an often elegant application of cognitive behavioural science and linguistics. Instead, we have seen some sections of the NLP community drift further and further away from solid foundations towards increasingly esoteric learnings and sometimes outright bizarre ideologies.

Fortunately for the development of coaching psychology, such moves seem to have been avoided. Coaching is beginning to be accepted in mainstream professional societies. For example, there are now special interest groups in Coaching Psychology in both the Australian and the British Psychological Societies. In 2000 there were no coach-specific academic journals. It was quite hard to get coaching research published. Now there are three peer-reviewed coaching journals. The *Journal of Consulting Psychology* has had two special editions devoted to executive coaching. The publication rate for academic coaching articles has skyrocketed. According to the database PsycINFO, there have been more academic articles published between 2000 and 2007 than were published from 1935 to 2000!

Partly as a result of the increased academic interest in coaching, we have seen the bar raised substantially in the coaching industry. Both coaching clients and people looking for coach training are demanding that coaching have a solid evidence-based approach. We have seen coaching go from being a fad to being an accepted methodology for creating individual and systematic change.

But coaching is still a long way from being a real profession. There are still no barriers to entry. Anyone can call themselves a coach. More disturbingly, anyone can set themselves up as a trainer of coaches – even those with no qualifications or training at all. Many coach-training schools do a very good job. However, there are issues and difficult questions that have, as yet, not been addressed.

For example, our research indicates that between 25% and 52% of life coaching clients may have clinically significant mental health issues. Clearly there is a concern here, and as yet this issue has not been openly discussed in coaching circles. Many are satisfied to resort to the claim that coaching is not therapy. And of course this is true. Coaching is not therapy. But the fact remains that many coaching clients are seeing coaching as a socially acceptable form of therapy. So, the coaching industry has a clear duty of care here. We need to ensure that coach training covers the essentials of mental health, so coaches can recognize and refer appropriately.

We also need to ensure that the coaching industry does not fall into the trap of making wide and unsubstantiated claims about its effectiveness. Coaching is not a panacea for the problems of contemporary organizations. There is no research to show, and no reason to believe, that coaching will create the life of your wildest dreams. The industry abounds with pseudo-qualifications and self-appointed, yet unqualified, 'global thought leaders'. Our 2006 research into the self-presentation of Australian life coaching training organizations showed that although many made quite flamboyant claims, only a few made really outrageous claims. We need to watch out for the hype, watch out for the pseudo-science and build a solid foundation for the emerging profession of coaching.

I believe that coaching and coaching psychology have a bright future. Coaching truly can be a very effective methodology for creating change. But we need solid, relevant information on coaching that spans the whole range of interests, from the straightforward and practical books sought by beginning practitioners, to the often complex theory-based academic texts. Regardless of the depth of your coaching experience, I hope you enjoy this book and find that it contributes to the broad development of your coaching practice and the development of the coaching industry as a whole.

Dr Anthony M Grant is a coaching psychologist and the founder and Director of the Coaching Psychology Unit in the School of Psychology, University of Sydney. He is both a coaching practitioner and an academic, and is widely recognized as the key founding figure of contemporary coaching psychology and evidence-based coaching. Contact Anthony at: anthonyg@psych.usyd.edu.au

2 DEVELOPMENTAL COACHING

'Things do not change – we change.'

Henry David Thoreau

Our quest is an adventure story, and like all good adventure stories, it follows a pattern. There must be a final challenge, a final hurdle to navigate to bring everyone safely home. In fact we have two remaining challenges: How does coaching deal with adult development? We will deal with this here. And how do we take cross-cultural issues into account in coaching? We will deal with this in the next chapter.

DEVELOPMENTAL STAGES

Coaching is a helping profession whose material is human learning and development. But what does development mean? Think back on your life for a moment. What can you do now that you could not do ten or fifteen years ago? (Ignore your physical prowess.) How are your relationships different? How is your thinking different? What problems can you solve now that you could not solve then? What problems do you see now that you did not consider then? How has your view about what is true changed?

When you look at the trajectory of your life you will see that not only have you learned more and built on your knowledge, but also you have developed different ways of seeing yourself and the world. Your thinking has grown deeper, with new distinctions and new perspectives, and you are no longer subject to ideas that used to limit you, so you act differently. Some things that were problems are no longer, and new, different sorts of problem have taken their place.

You have both learned and developed. Learning is horizontal change, adding to what you have, or becoming better at what you can do already. Learning is linear and proceeds at a fairly steady pace. It is adding and upgrading the furnishings in your mental apartment.

Development is vertical change; it means you can learn more and learn in different ways. It is like moving apartment to a higher level where you have a wider view. You may bring some of your furniture with you, and you may leave some behind. You may refurnish completely. Development does not proceed at a steady pace; it moves in jumps, discontinuously, like going up steps. You stay on one step until you make the move, then you are on a different level. This is also what makes development very hard to measure in coaching, because it may happen weeks or months after the coaching finishes. Development unfolds and allows you to climb ever higher as you expand your mental horizons and go ever deeper into your heart and emotional centre.

The differences between learning and development	
Learning What you have.	**Development** What you are.
1 Horizontal progress.	1 Vertical progress.
2 Linear progress.	2 Discontinuous progress.
3 Adds to what you have.	3 Adds to what you are.
4 Adding furniture and redecorating your mental apartment.	4 Moving apartment to a higher floor with a wider view.
5 Continuous.	5 Discontinuous.
6 Happens steadily.	6 Usually takes some time between stages.

Adults can develop throughout their life but they may need help. They can construct their world in increasingly complex and systematic ways. In this chapter we want to consider adult developmental stages, chart them and then explore the implications for coaching.

STAGES OF THINKING

Jean Piaget was the first person to propose a model of mental growth in stages [1] by studying children's thinking. Children's reasoning is not a wrong kind of adult thinking, but a particular type of thinking that is appropriate for their age and mental development, and which they must first grow into before they can grow out of.

Piaget described development as a sequence of increasingly complex stages of making meaning. He claimed that development goes in only one direction. You can't go back to the previous stage (unless you are psychotic), and the stages are hierarchical, each built on the last. You cannot skip stages. These rules hold for all human development.

Children's thinking goes through four stages, according to Piaget, and these stages are generally accepted in developmental psychology. The first is the sensorimotor stage. In this stage, children are co-ordinating their reflexes. They make little differentiation between themselves and the world, including other people. They *are* the world. This stage lasts until children are about two years old.

Piaget's main stages of development in children

Stage	Approximate age in years	Characteristics
Sensori-motor	0–2	Co-ordinating responses. No differentiation between the self and world.
Pre-operational	2–7	Egocentric, self is separate from the world. Magical thinking – thinking causes events.
Concrete operational	7–12	Things can be manipulated. No abstract reasoning, but they can consider their own and another viewpoint.
Formal reasoning	12 upwards	Can think abstractly and theoretically and manipulate concepts.

The second stage is the pre-operational stage; children are aware of themselves as separate from the world. They are egocentric, at the centre of their world, although the world has grown. It seems a huge, frightening place and they are trying to find ways to control it and make sense of it. This is the phase of magical thinking, where children think they can cause changes in the real world just by thinking about it, because they do not yet have a good theory of cause and effect. They imagine they have a lot of power. They are Superman or Superwoman.

Then a miracle occurs and they move into the next stage, that of concrete operational thinking. This is when children learn to take the role of the other person, to 'put themselves in the other person's shoes'. This means they realize that others have a different perspective from theirs (a tremendous intellectual feat), and they are able mentally to construct other perspective.

As we continue to mature, we learn to think abstractly and manipulate ideas as well as things. This is the formal reasoning stage and the last stage Piaget considered. We learn to connect thoughts and feelings, to see sequences of action and their consequences. Gradually egocentricity diminishes. The world grows bigger as we grow smaller. As the astronaut John Glenn remarked, 'A life spent centering only on itself will in the end occupy a very, very small universe.'

Formal reasoning is analytical and modernistic; it analyses problems into variables in order to solve them. It is the modern, scientific mindset. People at this stage think of themselves as separate and responsible. They make rational decisions and believe they have control over their lives. If adult thinking stayed at this stage, the world would be boring indeed.

As we grow older, however, our thinking develops beyond this. We can think more systematically, see many sides of an issue and understand how things mutually affect each other. We see the importance of context and how a right action in one context can be wrong in another. Truth becomes uncertain. We start to make abstractions about abstractions. We also start to see that nothing is independent of anything else. Language plays a major role in this development of thinking.

The different and more complex types of thinking and understanding that develop as we become older have been mapped by many researchers, the most prominent being King and Kitchener [2], Wilber [3] and Basseches [4].

Mental growth is the continuous acquiring and organizing of ever subtler distinctions and ordering them into layered systems of meaning.

Let's take a simple example – numbers.

At the first stage (sensorimotor), a baby has no concept of numbers, just sensations of one or many things that may be comfortable or uncomfortable. Give a baby a book on calculus and he might try to eat it.

At the second stage of pre-operational thinking, the child is aware of manipulating objects, perhaps building bricks, and perhaps will attach labels to them ('one', 'two', etc). These bricks follow their wishes and what they think magically happens – usually.

In the third stage of concrete operational thinking, children are aware of numbers of concrete objects and of different people's opinions about them, but they are only starting to learn a system of numbers and the possible relationships between them.

At the stage of formal reasoning, people can manipulate numbers, see how they change, and appreciate the rules of mathematics. Give them a book on calculus and they might read it.

It is clear from these examples that *what* you learn and what you can learn *from*, as well as *how* you learn, depends on your developmental stage. We can see these developmental stages as babies grow; clearly they have a different *sort of consciousness* compared to a mature adult. However, then we assume that just because physical growth stops, so too do mental, emotional and social development. They do not.

Coaches cannot deny, although they often ignore, developmental differences. Clearly we are not all the same ('We are all really the same' really translates to 'You are all like me'). What makes us assume that development stops with adulthood? Adulthood is a slippery concept anyway. When exactly are we adult? Fully formed biologically? Chronological age (years on this planet) has no exact correspondence with psychological age. We all know people 'wise beyond their years', just as we know people whose thinking seemed to freeze in their 20s and never develop.

STAGES OF DEVELOPMENT

Mental and emotional growth continue throughout life in all cultures. We develop new ways of thinking and feeling; how do we know? The same action may come from very different motives, so actions alone will not tell us. Different stages will produce different behaviour, but do not mistake the behaviour for the structure of the mind that created it.

How can we 'see' these stages? We know through changes in the way the person uses language. Language reflects thinking directly. Language is a tool for constructing the world; it reflects how we construct the world as well as describing it. Over 30 years of research have shown that adults' emotions and thinking go through a number of developmental stages. At each of these stages, individuals have very different views of the world and define themselves, other people and the world differently. There is a great deal of evidence for adult developmental stages, each with their own characteristics. The fact that stages are hierarchical, sequential and built on the previous stage makes developmental coaching different from coaching with Myers–Briggs-type indicators, or DiSC, or the Enneagram, for example. These three last are examples of static psychometric descriptions that give the coach an idea of the present state of the client; they can be intellectually understood by coach and client and used accordingly. They are transparent. Developmental stages are different. They come from the way we construct the world from our experience, our culture and our language.

Clare Graves [5], who created the model of spiral dynamics, used extensively in social and individual development [6], put it like this: 'Each successive stage, wave or level of existence is a state through which people pass on their way to other states of being. When the human being is centralized in one state of existence (centre of gravity), he or she has a psychology particular to that state. His or her feelings, motivations, ethics and values, biochemistry, degree of neurological activation, learning systems, belief systems, concepts of mental health, ideas as to what mental illness is and how it is to be treated, conception of and preferences for management, education, economics and political theory and practice are all appropriate to that state.'

Developmental stages are part of the integral model, and Ken Wilber [3] has written about them in detail. Carol Gilligan [7] has charted three or four stages of social, emotional and moral development for women. The most useful and best-researched model for us to apply to coaching is the one elaborated by Robert Kegan [8].

Kegan identifies a number of stages that adults may pass through, once they have reached the formal reasoning stage. They are not cut and dried stages, as people are usually drifting between two stages, showing some characteristics of both. They are like centres of gravity (to use William James' phrase) [9]. Centre of gravity is a good metaphor because it is the place where you come back to even after you have lost balance. Most people have a centre of gravity at or between stages, and, depending on stress, circumstances and other factors, may drift up or down from their centre of gravity. Otto Laske [10], who has written much on developmental coaching, has divided the gaps between stages into further distinctions to facilitate understanding where a person is, and has applied the model to coaching.

Each stage is natural, and in order to go the next one, you have to pass through the stage before. You cannot jump stages. There is nothing wrong with any stage, and while you are in it, it seems the best and obvious place to be. No stage is a wrong or inferior version of the next stage, just a different place to live and a different way to construct the world. However, each stage does build on the last and each stage constructs an increasingly rich and varied world.

STAGE TWO – THE INDIVIDUALIST

The first stage in Kegan's model is Stage Two – the *individualist* stage. People in this stage see others as instruments for their use. Self and other are opposites. There is a win–lose mentality and, of course, the person at that stage wants to win. Life is a game where they need to win with the best weapons. Individualists have a low level of self-insight; everything is obvious, their needs override other people's needs, because they are who they are and the law of the jungle operates. An individualist in a business organization will single-mindedly pursue their own career, not caring very much about who they step on as they go. They can be charming, but they will use people. They have one perspective – their own. They are subject to their own ego. In other words, they have no ability to step outside themselves and see their limitations. Research indicates that about 10% of the adult population is at this stage. Everyone goes through this stage in adolescence. This is why coaching is not used for children, because coaching implies a relationship, an ability to understand the other and their perspective. A person at Stage Two is not yet able to do this. At this stage, my world and the world of others are different and cannot be reconciled, and mine must prevail.

It is unusual to meet adults at this stage; most grow out of it in their teens. Individualists will consider other people's opinions, but only in so far as they affect their own well-being. They cannot imagine others' thoughts and feelings. Thus, a teenager might phone home because they think they will be in trouble if they do not, and not because they can enter into their sleepless, worried parents' state of mind. They follow community rules if it suits them, or if they think they will be caught and punished if they do not.

Stage Two
The individualist

⇨ Separate from others.
⇨ Ultimate concern is that they will lose the help and support of other people.
⇨ Guided by their own self-interest.
⇨ Know people in terms of how helpful they are.
⇨ Have their own perspective.
⇨ Play a win–lose game (zero-sum game).
⇨ Cannot empathise with other people's feelings about them; they cannot 'walk in other people's shoes'.
⇨ Subject to their own small ego.

STAGE THREE – COMMUNITY MEMBER

Stage Three is the conventional social stage. Here, people can easily take another's perspective; the problem is that they are lost in it. They cannot clearly distinguish between their own wants and values and the internalized wants and values of others. They have learned to subordinate their needs to those of the group. Research indicates that 55% of adults are at this stage. They have internalized group values and are defined by social expectations. They feel subject to many obligations and may feel guilty when they do not meet them. In work, they rely on best practices. They are subject to their way of being, which is based on community values. They cannot step outside the introjected values that they have taken in from the community and culture in which they live. Ontological coaching proposes that we spend most of our time under the authority (declarations) of others.

Stage Three
Community member

⇨ Other people's viewpoints are internalized.

⇨ Defined by social expectations.

⇨ Hold to community values.

⇨ Feel obligations and have possible guilt feelings for not following them.

⇨ Ultimate concern is that they will lose other people's regard.

⇨ Guided by group interests.

⇨ Their perspective is composed of internalized other perspectives.

⇨ Play a win–win game (non-zero-sum game).

⇨ Can easily imagine other people's experience and 'walk in other people's shoes'.

⇨ Can take many different perspectives.

⇨ Rely on best practice.

STAGE FOUR – SELF-AUTHORING

The next stage, Stage Four, is known as 'self-authoring'. An author is a creator, so people at this stage create themselves in the way they want to be. They are a long way beyond the individualist because they understand other people's viewpoints. Stage Four individuals have a high degree of self-insight and define themselves by their own values. Integrity is the key value for them; they need to be 'true to themselves'. They value their own individual experience and are well aware of their own value and uniqueness. Their values are self-determined and they strive for integrity; they have to act from their own values; their greatest fear is not being true to themselves and therefore they will withstand group pressure and take risks that Stage Three individuals will not. They want to be the best that they can be. They need to distance themselves from others and to go it alone. They respect others and will not interfere with their values and goals. They are identified with their own values.

Individuals at Stage Four can be professional. Professionals are people who are able to work for others, yet consider themselves bound by a higher standard of behaviour. They stand by a code of values and ethics that they will not violate. They balance the demands of their employer with the demands of their values. Professionals need a detached approach that does not reflect their own personality. Lawyers or doctors are professionals. We say they do not act professionally if they bend the rules in favour of their clients.

Self-authoring people are subject to their own system of values. They cannot reflect on their own value system; it is simply true for them. They cannot step outside their own integrity and practice to see how others define them, so they may appear rigid. Stage Three introjects their values. Stage Four decides them for themselves and lives by them. Research indicates that 20–25% of the adult population is in this stage (in the United States, where most of the research has been done).

Stage Four
Self-authoring

⇨ Defined by their own values.
⇨ Strive for integrity.
⇨ Define their own path and separate from other people.
⇨ Ultimate concern is that they will lose their integrity.
⇨ Guided by their values.
⇨ They have their own individual perspective and take other people's perspective into account. They make a rigorous distinction between their own and others' experience.
⇨ Can be professional.
⇨ Respect others and are reluctant to advise or interfere with them.
⇨ Define the rules of the game for a win–win or no deal (non-zero-sum game).
⇨ Can easily imagine other people's experience and 'walk in other people's shoes'.
⇨ Create best practice, but may not follow it.

Here is an example to illustrate the difference between a Stage Three and a Stage Four reaction. It is a well-known principle of good communication to give negative feedback with 'I' statements. 'I feel this. . .' or 'I think that this was wrong. . .' instead of 'you' statements. (For example, 'You make me feel. . .' or 'You did this wrong. . .') 'I' statements are about myself, not about the other person, so there is less chance that the other person will feel attacked and become defensive. I am not making the other person a cause of my feelings, but am essentially saying, 'I cause myself to feel this way in response to what you do. . .' and hope that the other person will be concerned enough to change whatever they are doing.

At Stage Three, when someone experiences something wrong and makes 'I' statements, they cannot set things right for themselves. The person and their construction of the relationship have been damaged and need to be put right. The other person has to change what they are doing, and then the breach is healed. Even the 'I' statement is a demand for something to be put right and an expectation that the *other person* will change as a result.

The person at Stage Three who hears 'I' statements as feedback will still feel an obligation to put right what is wrong in order to keep the relationship. They will feel defensive. They are constructing an experience of being attacked, and do not like it. They will still feel responsible for the other person's feelings. They will still feel a demand on them as if the person had used a 'you' statement. So, even when a person is making 'I' statements as feedback, the response and feeling of the person at Stage Three to whom they are addressed will not be as intended, however well the feedback is crafted. 'Good communication skills' (of which 'I' statements form part) make a demand – not just on the person who uses them, but also on the person who receives them. That demand is to be at Stage Four. The way we hear something is a function of our stage of development, regardless of how it is intended to be heard.

Now, suppose the 'I statement' feedback is being made by someone at Stage Four. That person feels that something has gone amiss in *their view* of how the relationship should be, or how the situation should be. They understand this from the point of view of their own self and value system. However much the person is committed to the relationship, they exist outside the relationship in an important way. They will evaluate the response to their feedback but there is no demand on the other person to put it right.

A person at Stage Four on the receiving end of 'I' statement feedback can hear it for what it is (a statement about the other person), and not take responsibility for what is the other person's responsibility. They will decide to change – or not – based on their own values.

STAGE FIVE – SELF-AWARE

The last stage that Kegan identifies is Stage Five, or the *self-aware* stage. At this stage, people have overcome the identification with their own idiosyncratic value set. They have a very high level of self-insight and very little need to control. They see themselves defined by others just as they define others, and they see their own ego as a filter with which they have viewed life. A Stage Five individual can enter into the flow of life. They are aware of the limitations of their own history, culture and frame of reference. They develop others, sometimes at a cost to themselves. Their focus is more on all of humanity rather than their individual self. They are like Stage Three in that they are in communion with others, but different in so far as they are not subject to and dependent on others' values, opinions and expectations. Research suggests about 10% of the adult population are at Stage Five. Stage Five individuals are no longer subject to their own value system; they are committed to deconstructing their own values and benefiting from others; they show humility in the face of the amazingly complex world (which includes themselves) and take multiple perspectives and contextual awareness as given.

Stage Five
Self-aware

⇨ Aware of their own personal history and values and its effect.
⇨ Defined by relationships with others and with self.
⇨ Values in flow.
⇨ Risk themselves by opening themselves to relationships.
⇨ No need for control.
⇨ Not attached to any particular aspect of themselves; 'going with the flow'.
⇨ Take multiple perspectives on multiple perspectives.
⇨ Play an infinite game, the purpose of which is to continue to play.

These stages take time to traverse. It makes sense that people at Stage Four and Five will tend to be in their 40s, or older, as it normally takes some years to completely pass through a stage. Age is an indication of possible development, but not a guarantee. There is no certainty that as you get older, you will automatically progress through all stages. It is possible to grow old in Stage Two. Although the distribution of the stages tends to follow chronological age, it is not tied exactly to it.

The socialization process on teenagers is a social forcing mechanism for people to move from Stage Two to Stage Three. Society wants Stage Three members, and part of a parent's duty (not usually expressed in these terms) is to move their children from Stage Two to Stage Three. Schools play their part, too. Moral educators also aim to move people from Stage Two to Stage Three, as Stage Two individuals do not fit well into communal society.

However, once you have reached Stage Three and become established, there is no further social mechanism to move you forward. You are on your own. This is why most people stay on Stage Three. We shall argue later that coaching has developed as a social mechanism to move people from Stage Three to Stage Four, and perhaps beyond.

POST-CONVENTIONAL DEVELOPMENT

Many writers and researchers and spiritual explorers have wandered through and wondered about further stages, known as post-conventional or post-autonomous stages. Stage Five is usually defined as the first post-conventional stage.

Social emotional development means the loss of egocentricity; throughout the stages there is a gradual loss of self and gradual expansion of the world. What you were subject to becomes an object, something you can reflect on. The most salient aspect of post–conventional development is the increasing ability of the person to see through the meaning-making process itself as a limitation. From Stage Five onwards, there is an increasing awareness of the self as a constraint and a bottleneck of experience, a keen awareness of the paradoxes of a self wanting to get rid of a self. (Should you be intolerant of your own intolerance? How can you go beyond desire by wanting to stop wanting?) You cannot lose yourself unless you have a self to lose. There is also an increasing awareness of how language shapes reality and makes distinctions that are not there, but are necessary for social living and communication. This is the world of the spiritual explorers, and our quest does not yet go to this wonderful land. The main researchers in this area are Susanne Cook-Greuter [11], William Torbert [12], Herb Koplowitz [13], Ken Wilber and Jane Loevinger [14].

IMPLICATIONS FOR COACHING

How do these stages of development impact coaching? There are considerable implications, which have been researched mainly by Otto Laske [10].

COACHES' SELF-DEVELOPMENT

Coaching looks, feels and is perceived differently at different stages. Coaches build a model of their clients: what it is like to be that person. They also have a model of the world – what the world is like, and therefore how their client fits in. Coaches ask themselves, 'What can my client do?' and 'What should my client do?' The developmental stage of coaches puts a limit on the answers they can give. In other words, the stage that a coach has reached determines how far he or she can help a particular client. This is a most important point.

Everyone is subject to his or her own developmental stage. One of the key elements of coaching is helping the client to stop identifying, to take what they were subject to and reflect on it instead of living it. Coaches cannot point out something to their clients unless they can reflect on it themselves. Coaches cannot make clients free of anything that enslaves the coaches themselves. So, coaches are very unlikely to be able to help any client who is trying to reach a stage above the coach. From an ontological point of view we can say that clients cannot be aware of their own way of being. It is for the coaches to objectify it for them, but only a coach who has seen that level in themselves and are separating themselves from it can do this. Unless coaches have an idea of developmental stages, they will use their methods without awareness – they will be subject to their coaching methodology. This means that it is an ethical obligation for coaches to know their own developmental level. This is a crucial part of their own self-management and self-development.

There are undiscussed demands on coaches that need to surface. People at Stage Two cannot be coaches; indeed, they are very unlikely to be attracted to such a profession (unless they believe it will make them a lot of money). They will treat their clients as means for their own benefit and not be able to relate to them.

Coaches at Stage Three can coach well when their clients are also at Stage Three. They can help clients to change their behaviour, teach clients and have good coaching results. However, it is unlikely that this will lead to any developmental movement. Coaches at Stage Three cannot effectively coach clients at Stage Four. They may achieve some changes in behaviour, but they may well have the feeling that they do not understand their clients, or that their clients are 'loners' in some way. And so they may delay their clients' development through Stage Four. Stage Three coaches will use best practices, but will be 'in over their head', in Robert Kegan's phrase, when they try to coach anyone at a higher level.

Søren Kierkegaard, the Danish philosopher and one of the inspirations of ontological coaching, wrote over 150 years ago, 'In order to help another effectively, I must understand what he understands. If I do not know that, my greater understanding will be of no help to him. . . instruction begins when you put yourself in his place so that you may understand what he understands and in the way he understands it.' [15] You cannot put yourself in another person's place if you do not know where they are. You cannot walk in another person's shoes if they do not wear shoes.

A Stage Four coach will be able to coach clients at Stage Three very well, provided they do not stretch them too far from their centre of gravity. They will be professional, understand their own position and how it is different from that of their clients. They will be able to stand back completely from the conventions and expectations of their clients in an appropriate way. They will not interfere, but will help their clients make the changes that they want to make. Equally, Stage Four coaches will be able to help Stage Four clients, but may not be able to help them make any developmental movement.

Many top executives are at Stage Four or very close; it is almost requisite in order to deal with people at that level and to have the range of vision required. It is highly unlikely that a coach below the level of Stage Four can help an executive very much, beyond some behavioural changes.

The 'presence' of the coach in the relationship with the executive needs to come from Stage Four. We suspect that if executive coaching does not work, it is because coach and client are at different developmental stages. A Stage Five coach will be able to coach clients at Stage Three or Four, but there is a danger that they might stretch them too far from their centre of gravity. It is more difficult for people at Stage Five to act as coaches. To what extent can they stay professional and detached from their clients and not interfere, while at the same time being transparent equals with their clients? This is not easy, and the Stage Five coach will be in conflict. Many give up coaching as a methodology.

Why are developmental shifts so important? Because they lead to a different and wider world-view. At higher levels of development, people construct their world and understand differently; they are able to think more systemically, make finer distinctions, and see the world as a bigger place, because they are not so identified with parts of their own ego. They become more like a leader. Developmental coaching is coaching for leadership.

Also, the stage of social development determines the way people think and therefore their ability to make distinctions and their ability to take multiple perspectives. Both these are key coaching indicators in the coaching relationship. The stage of the coach vis-à-vis the client could be one of the most important predictors of the success of coaching.

STANDARDS AND ETHICS OF COACHING

The developmental stage of the coach also influences how they understand and interpret professional standards and ethics of coaching. Active listening, respect for the client and professional standards all mean something slightly different at different levels, although this is tacitly understood rather than specified. Many coaching skills and ways of looking presuppose a Stage Four coach.

SELF-CONCORDANCE

Self-concordance theory [16], which we looked at in Part 2, Chapter 7, distinguishes between extrinsic values, those that are experienced as outside one's self, and introjected values, those that are taken in and experienced as one's own. Both are different from intrinsic values that are authentically one's own. Extrinsic values and motivation can work at any stage; however, introjected values are characteristic of Stage Three. Many coaching clients come to coaching pressured by 'shoulds' and obligations, and perhaps feeling guilty for not living up to expectations. This can be the beginning of a journey to Stage Four, but only if coaches can understand what is going on developmentally, which means that they themselves need to have gone beyond the introjected values of others.

Sometimes the client is caught between two obligations, and this is the basis of many difficult decisions. They are in a double bind. Damned if they do, damned if they don't, and they have to do something. The only way out of a double bind is to go to another level that makes the double bind an object to reflect on. In this case, Stage Four can determine what they really want authentically, and although they may feel sad at losing something, they will not feel guilt. They will stand between the values and make a decision. They can convert their 'shoulds' into 'wants'.

Stage Four coaches can help their clients develop a coherent set of integrated values that truly spring from their clients' own personality. Stage Three coaches cannot.

WHAT CAN COACHING DO?

Coaching helps people change horizontally and vertically. Mostly it helps them to develop their thinking, their learning and their capacity for learning. It may also help their development.

Coaching is a social mechanism that has evolved to move people from Stage Three to Stage Four and perhaps, given the right coach, from Stage Four to Stage Five. This fits with the presuppositions of the roots of the coaching movement, the optimistic view of human nature, the natural movement to self-actualize. (These developmental levels are in many ways steps on the road to what Maslow called 'self-actualization'.) Developmental coaching takes self-actualization seriously. Coaches presuppose that many things are possible for their clients. It is not a question of pushing clients to achieve, but of clearing the obstructions that are preventing clients from achieving and developing all they can. You do not know your limits, so you construct them. What has been constructed can be deconstructed.

REFERENCES

1 Piaget, J. (1952) *The Origins of Intelligence in Children*

2 King, P. & Kitchener, K. (1994) *Developing Reflective Judgment*

3 Wilber, K. (1995) *Sex, Ecology, Spirituality*

4 Basseches, M. (1984) *Dialectical Thinking and Adult Development*

5 Graves, C. (1981) The Emergent, Cyclical Double Helix Model of the Adult Human Biosocial System, handout for presentation to the World Future Society, Boston, Mass., May 20, 1981 (compiled for Dr Graves by Christopher Cowan)

6 Beck, D. and Cowan, C. (1996) *Spiral Dynamics*

7 Gilligan, C. (1982) *In a Different Voice*

8 Kegan, R. (1994) *In over Our Heads*

9 James, W. (1902) *The Varieties of Religious Experience*

10 Laske, O. (2005) *Measuring Hidden Dimensions*

11 Cook-Greuter, S. (2005) Post Autonomous Ego Development, Dissertation presented to the Faculty of the Harvard University Graduate School of Education, available from cookgsu@comcast.net

12 Torbert, W. (1991) *The Power of Balance: Transforming Self, Society, and Scientific Inquiry*

13 Koplowitz, H. (1990) *Unitary Consciousness and the Highest Development of Mind*

14 Loevinger, J. (1987) *Paradigms of Personality*

15 Kierkegaard, S. (1959) *Journals,* translated by A. Dru

16 Sheldon, K. and Elliot, A (1998) Not All Personal Goals Are Personal, *Personality and Social Psychology Bulletin* 24 (5)

3 POST-MODERN COACHING

Coaching grew from humanistic psychology, which was a reaction to the modernist way of seeing the world. Modernism has certain assumptions.

Modernists are archetypal scientists who use logic and experiment to solve clearly defined problems; they apply formal reasoning to everything. They believe in a stable, rational self, 'in here', that can know itself through introspection and the world through reason. To a modernist, everything can be analysed by reason. From this view, reality is 'out there' waiting to be discovered, like an unknown continent. Thus, 'reality' is an objective and knowable world and the truth exists independently of the observer. Science is neutral and objective and can provide universal truths, and these truths lead to progress. Language is rational and transparent; in other words, there is a definite connection between a word and the object it signifies. Pure behaviourism was the psychology of modernism.

Modernism – assumptions

Problems can be clearly defined.

The self is stable and rational and can know itself through introspection.

Reality is out there, objective and knowable, and independent of the observer.

Words and language point to definite objects and ideas.

The world is defined only from the top right quadrant in the integral model.

Modernism has been incredibly successful, but was forced to admit defeat when confronted with quantum physics, cross-cultural studies and comparative linguistics. It was dethroned in mathematics by Kurt Gödel's incompleteness theorem, which says, essentially, that you can never explain a closed system without importing something from the outside that cannot itself be proved by that system. Reality is not a closed system and it is more slippery than we know or perhaps than we can know. Words do not have definite and fixed meanings. Ten people looking at the same situation will give ten different views. Everything cannot be known by looking at it only from the outside. Modernism is essentially dead as a comprehensive world-view.

Coaching is built on constructivist approaches, as we saw in Part Two. Humanistic psychology and coaching celebrate the human, artistic part of the world. Humanistic psychology looked at people from the inside, their thoughts, goals, values and way of being. However, we cannot say that everything can be known from the inside. That would be to say the world only exists in the top-left quadrant in the integral model and would simply be the reverse of modernism, and equally mistaken.

Post-modernism goes beyond modernism and takes a different perspective – that of relationship. Our personality, way of acting, and all our knowledge are made from our relationships, our intersubjective networks and, particularly, our immersion in language. Post-modernism views the world primarily from the bottom left–hand quadrant in the integral model. We are part of a web of relationships and cannot stand outside, even though it feels as if we are separate. We take in culture, language, thinking and knowledge through our relationships. We do not stand alone. It seems as if we have a whole, complete and detached consciousness that is all ours, but this is an illusion. We cannot know ourselves through introspection alone, because these ties that bind us to our community are invisible when we look inside. Introspection alone does not see history, but only the present.

Our bodies seem separate from the rest of the world, yet they are completely replaced every few years by different molecules. Matter flows through our bodies all the time. There is not a single molecule in your body now that was there five years ago. Our solid body is organized by a pattern. Our self is also a pattern that seems stable but is being constantly renewed, like a river. The river stays the same, it seems to be one thing, but it is constantly flowing. Our thinking and knowledge are grounded in language. Without language we cannot relate to the rest of humanity. Language is more than a description of what is there; it is also a construction of what we see, and that construction is shared by our fellows. We are prisoners of our language, and while it gives us much space, if we venture far enough we will come up against the walls.

Constructivism demolished the objective world that was supposed to be 'out there' by showing that we do not passively take in some given objective reality, but are creators of the world we experience. Then post-modernism demolished the objective world 'in here' by showing that it is really a web of language, culture and social relationships. We do not *have* relationships; in a sense we *are* relationships. We need history as well as introspection to understand ourselves. However, this does not mean that everything is relative and there is nothing to grasp. It does not mean that any viewpoint is as good as another (which is a paradoxical claim anyway, because that would be claiming that this extreme relativistic viewpoint was better than any other).

Coaching needs a post-modern perspective. The client's problem does not exist simply inside the client's head, while the coach attempts to untangle the knots. Coaches need ways to help clients see that they did not create the problems on their own and they cannot solve them on their own. Their situation and their experience are based on being brought up in a human community and being an integral part of an intersubjective network. Language plays a large part in the way we construct problems when we mistake our words for an adequate representation of our ideas and therefore for an adequate representation of the world. Languages are social constructs. Many forms of coaching (ontological coaching and NLP in particular) help clients untangle the language as a way of untangling their problem. The way we think about a problem may itself be part of the problem.

What can coaching learn from post-modernism?

Post-modernism has four main ideas:

1   **The world is not given, but constructed by our perceptions, experience and language, and the world 'in here' is constructed by our relationships. This means that knowledge is not universal, but situational and provisional.**
2   **The meaning of any action depends on the context in which it takes place.**
3   **There are always many points of view you can choose from, so your choice is crucial. The privileged view has power. Perspective is power.**
4   **Our consciousness is made from social networks that are invisible to us when we introspect.**

What does the above mean for coaching? Coaching helps people make meaning of their lives, because modernist certainties like science and religious faith have been eroded. Coaches help their clients construct the world in a more positive and empowering way. They can help clients to move from Stage Three, which is other-dependent, to Stage Four, which is self-authoring, where they decide to snap many of the 'ropes' that have 'tied them to sand' over the years. These ropes are in part made of other people's expectations. As self-authoring people, they have taken the first step to free themselves from the confines of a particular language and a particular society.

Post-modernism also helps us see the importance of the coaching relationship. It is created between coach and client and defines them both. It is where the work is done. Coaches must be sure of their own values and stance, without imposing it on their clients. This means coaches need to be at Stage Four, or close to it. It also means that clients do not have all the answers or the resources they need, but these answers and resources are constructed from their relationship with their coaches and their relationships with others.

GENDER IN COACHING

Post-modern thinking deals with relationships. What are the distinctions that we need to make about the relationship between coach and client? The obvious one is gender. There are many studies showing that men and women think in different ways, with different emphases. One of the findings of evolutionary biology is how men and women think differently, notice different things and have different priorities.

In general, men are more analytical, more concerned with responsibility, rights and obligations. Women appreciate relationship; the two genders have different ways of knowing and making meaning. There is no obvious divide; there are extremes in every culture – for example, the 'macho' man in Latin countries.

For the best results, should you find a coach of your own gender? This is a question that all clients need to answer for themselves. The coaching profession tends to have a slight predominance of women worldwide. No one has suggested (and we have never seen any suggestion) that men cannot coach women well, or that women cannot coach men well.

Coaches need to take into account and be aware of their gender-specific ways of dealing with problems, so they can set them aside as much as possible in dealing with their clients. The issue of gender in coaching is another fascinating detour that is largely unexplored, and we could not do it justice without writing another book. We hope that in this book, by having two authors, a man and a woman, we have threaded our way successfully through the pitfalls of gender bias.

CROSS-CULTURAL COACHING

How coaching works across cultures is a subject that has not been well explored.

Post-modernism tells us that we are prisoners of our culture and our own language, but we do not see the bars. We are born into, and raised inside, a culture – an invisible intersubjective network. We take it on. We think it the best or even the only way to deal with the world instead of one of many possible ways. We are subject to our cultural conditioning, and our culture puts boundaries on our thinking. Different cultures make different distinctions, especially through language. As the saying goes, you cannot know your own culture until you know another. This means that you see your own culture objectively only when you contrast it with another. To make the contrast, you need to see both clearly, which means putting aside cultural biases and appreciating other cultures in their own terms.

We, the authors, both know this, as we have both lived in other cultures. Andrea lived in Argentina for two years. Joseph lived in England most of his life, and moving to Brazil was a big cultural shift. At first, he did not really know how to behave, and sometimes Brazilians would take his English reserve for rudeness. It was only after two years or so that he was able to see how English culture is different and how strange it appears to Brazilians.

Here is our proposal. Many coaching models are culturally conditioned. They may work well in one culture, but are not easily exported to another. This is not a problem for coaches so long as they coach within their own culture, but with international companies calling on coaches for international programmes, more and more coaches are crossing geographical, and therefore cultural, barriers. At the time of writing, there is only one book on cross-cultural coaching [1] that we know of, but there will undoubtedly be more. Culture can be seen in behaviour, but underneath these behaviours, like a subterranean stream, is a set of values and ideas that bubble up into specific actions like hot springs. There are many implications for coaching – here are what we consider to be the most important ones.

Culture involves shared expectations, and therefore becomes part of the demands and obligations at developmental level Three. This means coaches at Stage Three will not be able to coach effectively cross-culturally. Cultures differ in many respects – how they approach relationships, how they think about power and responsibility and how they see the relationship between individuals and groups. There are also differences in how people deal with emotions, privacy, time management and status. There are several excellent books on cultural differences that are interesting for coaches who are planning to coach clients from a different culture [2] [3] [4].

LANGUAGE

Language is part of culture – even countries that speak the same language speak it differently. For example, the inhabitants of England, Ireland, Scotland and the United States all speak forms of English, but their cultures are very different. Brazilian Portuguese is very different from Portuguese from Portugal. Speaking a language is a way of seeing the world. Different language, different world.

Here are some relevant examples for coaches. We are struck by the fact that Portuguese has two verbs for the English verb 'to be'. '*Ser*' means 'to be' in a permanent sense: 'I am a person', 'I am an author', 'we live here', 'you are this nationality'. Then there is the verb '*estar*', which means 'to be' in a time-bound and limited sense: 'I am tired,' 'you are hungry', 'they are living here at the moment'. This means that the Portuguese can make distinctions that English-speakers cannot and are far less likely to confuse behaviour with identity through using the same verb. 'You are angry' and 'you are an adult', for example – one is a state of mind, the other is an identity. We use the same verb in English, but it has a different meaning. So, the Brazilians and the Portuguese have a more fluid sense of time; nothing is defined as absolutely as it is in English.

When clients speak of values in a coaching session, it is very important that they use their own language. Words only have emotional force when they are your native language, because those words are linked to experiences and emotions. A translation is an empty concept. Some words do not have an adequate translation. '*Saudade*' is a Portuguese word often translated as 'nostalgia', but it is more than this. '*Duende*' is a complex mixture of passion and darkness in Spanish. English has two words, 'freedom' and 'liberty', where Portuguese has only one, '*liberdade*'. Yet there are fine distinctions between Freedom and Liberty in English that are lost in the single-word translation. So, there are linguistic traps when coaching in another language or using a translator, or coaching a native speaker of another language.

Not all clients want to be 'master of their destiny'; not all cultures want to conquer the world in the spirit of the modernist western thinking. This is also reflected in the language. In the UK and Europe, people 'take' decisions. In the United States, they 'make' decisions, while in Germany they 'cut' decisions. In Tibet and India, they say, 'the decision took me'. This is why a specific goal achievement orientation is a culturally conditioned part of coaching and therefore we prefer to think about clients finding their direction.

Without a perspective on our own culture, we will judge people from a different culture, often in a negative way. For example, people from the US and the UK have no trouble separating the domains of work and personal life. A manager may critique your work quite strongly, and then you can both go out happily for a beer together at the end of the day. The criticism does not leak out of its work context. Things are different in Brazilian culture. Brazilians take things personally and do not keep such clear-cut boundaries. A manager making the same criticism of a Brazilian worker would be seen as rude and disrespectful. Of course, Brazilian managers give feedback, but it is delivered more obliquely and at greater length. This can leave American managers drumming their fingers in impatience, but Brazilians will understand – the criticism will have an effect, something the US manager may not understand.

Time management is another issue. In most Latin countries (with the exception of Chile), time is elastic. A meeting scheduled to start at 10.00am will often not get going until 10.20 at the earliest. In Germany, if a meeting is scheduled to start at 10.00, then it starts at 10.00, and if you are late, this is taken as lack of respect. In many Latin countries, if you show up on time this is not respectful. The attitude there is that you need to give other people a chance to arrive.

A third example of cultural difference involves social distance. Brazilians feel comfortable being physically closer to you than do English people: for them, social space is smaller. So, when a Brazilian tries to talk with an English person, the Brazilian is constantly moving closer (which is interpreted by the Englishman as invasion of personal space and disrespectful), and the English person is constantly moving away, trying to make the distance more comfortable. The Brazilian then thinks that the English are aloof and 'distant'. Neither is right or wrong. It is about cultural expectation. Coaches need to understand this when dealing with the psychogeography of the coaching session.

CROSS-CULTURAL MISUNDERSTANDING

We have an example that illustrates well the pitfalls in cross-cultural coaching. We were supervising a session between a Spanish coach and an Argentinian client. We were in Barcelona, and the Argentinian client had lived there for a year. The client wanted to improve his skill of active listening.

The coach asked a good question: 'What does active listening mean for you?'

The client answered, 'Focus on the other person, avoiding internal dialogue and outside distractions when being with people'. He wanted to focus visually on the person; this was the most important thing for him in active listening. He also mentioned tranquillity as a value. He said he wanted internal tranquillity.

Where did he want to apply this skill of active listening? With clients, certainly (he worked as a coach), but also in all areas of his life. He particularly wanted to do better in his relationship with his Spanish girlfriend. The coach and client continued to explore the issue and it became clear that the client wanted to focus visually on the person he was talking to. He gave an example of being with his girlfriend in a restaurant where he kept looking around and his girlfriend accused him of not paying attention to her. He said he is easily distracted, he tries to be focused, but he finds he has a habit of looking around when he is with people. The coach continued to probe in two directions; first, what resources did the client have to be focused, and secondly, at what times in the past had he been able to stay focused and what hindered him from focusing? The client made a joke that maybe he should buy a set of blinkers like those that horses wear to keep him focused on the person in front of him. He really wanted to pay attention to his girlfriend; she was the most important person for him right now, and they were quarrelling because of this issue. She said he was interested in other women; he denied this.

The session continued and at the end the client felt better about the issue. We had an intuition about the situation, based on the fact that the client was Argentinian from a poor neighbourhood of Buenos Aires. We asked him whether there were any places where he focused, as we had noticed he was completely focused on the coach during the session. He said yes, but he tended to get distracted when in public, particularly places like restaurants or walking on the street.

We put forward an idea to see what he thought. Poor areas of Buenos Aires are dangerous; it is an essential survival skill to scan the environment in public places for robbers. Children pick up this skill early and it becomes natural and instinctive. He automatically scanned the environment in public places. This was necessary in Buenos Aires (and indeed any large South American city), but not necessary in Barcelona, which is altogether safer (except in the area called Ramblas). What he experienced as a lack of discipline and a problem was actually a useful habit, but not needed in his new context. When he realized this, he was able to make a choice about scanning (and also reassure his girlfriend), without the use of blinkers.

Knowledge of cultural differences allowed us to make that jump of intuition. We might have been wrong, though in fact we were right. The coach in this situation accepted at face value his client's idea that it was a bad habit to scan the environment and he should stop it. Knowing other cultures helps coaches not to jump to conclusions based on what is right in their culture, and not to take at face value the judgments that clients make on some of their own habits.

The next and final chapter will bring our quest to a close with a look at the future of coaching.

REFERENCES

1 Rossinski, P. (2003) *Coaching across Cultures*
2 Trompenaars, F. (1997) *Riding the Waves of Culture*
3 Hofstede, G. (1997) *Cultures and Organizations*
4 Hall, E. and Hall, M. (1990) *Understanding Cultural Differences*

PART FOUR

THE FUTURE

'We should all be concerned about the future because we will have to spend the rest of our lives there.'

Charles Kettering

Our quest is almost finished. We began this book with coaching at the edge of chaos, a metaphor for a situation unstable enough for change and learning, and stable enough not to fly apart. A tightrope, indeed. We hope that coaching can navigate this high wire for several years yet, and continue to grow and learn in a creative way. To walk a tightrope you need to have dynamic balance – slightly losing your balance in both directions and then always regaining it. Too far either way and you lose balance and fall. The alternative is to be frozen on the sidelines, and then the crowds will eventually wander off to a better show.

The trends that helped coaching to grow have accelerated in the last five years. We have to deal with circumstances we cannot control, and adapt to shorter and shorter time spans. Acts that would have been seen as magic decades ago are now everyday miracles. We laugh at the mindset that believed that juggling was impossible without help from supernatural powers, and who will be laughing in a hundred years or so about our limited mindsets? The future comes earlier and earlier every year and we have no blueprints or prints of any other colour to deal with it. Evolution happens a lot faster in the mental sphere than in the biological one. Coaching is both an expression of this and perhaps a partial answer. Perhaps (if we can personalize evolution for a moment) mental evolution is providing us with something that we need in order to adapt to these times.

So, like a good coach, we finish this book with a series of questions and not answers.

WHAT DOES THE FUTURE HOLD?

'The best way to predict the future is to create it.'

Peter Drucker

With this backdrop, what is the future of coaching? We do not know, nor does anyone else. We hope it will go from strength to strength as a powerful way for helping people to change and grow, and, through them, their businesses – and through their businesses the whole of humanity will also change and grow. We all benefit. While we were wondering how to write this section, we discussed our dreams and nightmares together, and we decided to record them here and let them speak for themselves.

A NIGHTMARE

We were in a junkyard, concrete slabs pushing from the ground like drunken gravestones, leaning over at crazy angles. There was a triangle in the middle with a sharp edge pointing upwards with a small model of a cathedral on top, balanced precariously, swaying in the wind. Suddenly the gusts came more strongly, the cathedral started to tip, the dust kicked up in mini-tornadoes and litter blew across the broken concrete. The wind sped across the yard, and right in front of us a huge ball of amber light formed, sending out blue lightning flashes all around as if trying to anchor itself into the earth. The lightning crackled and fizzed like water dropped on a hot plate. It was too bright to see; we looked at each other. There was a peal of thunder and the light blinked out, leaving a man crouching on all fours. He looked as though he was balanced on starting blocks, ready to sprint towards us. He straightened out slowly, like a cat. We jumped back, but we saw he had a friendly smile on his face. He was wearing sunglasses and a brown suit, with black lace-up shoes, and his black hair was slicked down so tight to his skull, it was hard to say where his head ended and his hair began. Not a hair was out of place even in the wind.

He walked towards us.

'When am I?' he asked.

'Don't you mean where?' we asked.

'I know what I mean. What year is this?'

'This is October 2007,' we replied. 'Who are you?'

'I am corporate class coach E37. We must act quickly, we have way too much time.'

'When are you from?' we asked.

'Another when,' he said. Somehow this was not surprising.

We sat down together on an old sofa with several of the springs sticking out.

'Tell us about coaching in your time,' we asked.

'Ah, I hoped you would ask that. We know how to coach,' he said. 'We know the winning formula. ROI in hundreds of per cent. Clients fulfilling their calculated potential to within a few percentage points. Dominant coaching spreading throughout the world. We have a disciplined process. Coaches just follow the method and the clients just don't know what hit them. The World Coaching Board of Governors makes sure there is strict quality control. Coaching is a serious business. We have conferences every month and every registered coach has to attend at least three a year.'

'What happens if they don't'?' we asked.

'They lose their registration and ID card,' said our friend from the future. 'And you don't work without being registered and up to date. No one employs a non-registered coach, because they know that if they did, they would be blacklisted. There are 17 grades of coach, and when a client request comes in, we assign the appropriate grade of coach, with a supervisor one grade higher.'

'Are there coaches all over the world?' we asked.

'Goodness me, yes! A client can get the right coach from anywhere in the world. Virtual sessions, no problem. Coaches are taught to make allowances for different cultures by special software. At the end of the coaching, the coach writes a report for their mentor coach that is stored online.'

'Does anything ever go wrong with the system?'

'If there are any glitches, like occasionally someone tries to engage a non-registered coach, the CP (that's the coaching police) soon move in and sort it out. Some people just don't have their own good at heart. Good intentions are no substitute for a real honest to goodness change.' The coach laughed. 'We have three approved training schools in the world; they are all oversubscribed and we only take the best. Entrants need to go through a battery of psychological and physical tests; they also have to play backgammon to a high standard.'

'Why backgammon?' we asked.

'Why not? Don't you care about all the other stuff? People always question the backgammon, I just don't understand it. They get seduced by trivialities. Coaching is too powerful to leave to just anybody.'

'Why are you here?' we asked.

'I am from the Skynetwork of coaches,' he replied. "I have come to see how coaching was done back in the bad old days and to give you a task, should you choose to accept it. I have to be careful, though, not to change the temporal fluxxxx . . . ' he broke off and his face started to melt. 'Oh Hell,' he said, 'I just have, by telling you all this . . . nooowwww yuuuuu . . . ' His voice started to melt and became deeper and deeper and slower and slower, as he slowly melted into a shiny brown puddle with a black centre beside the sofa, leaving only a wet plastic ID card as evidence that he had ever been there. We looked at the puddle sadly as it spread over the stones, reflecting the muddy lights.

Suddenly there was a huge bang, and an enormous spinning globe appeared in front of us. It was some kind of Perspex bubble like a gyroscope and it was spinning so fast we could not look at it directly. Gradually it slowed down and came to a stop. The Perspex hatch hissed open and steam billowed out; from within emerged a woman dressed in a brown cotton suit and a bright red scarf; she appeared to float in the mist as she stepped out of the globe.

She came towards us and looked at the metallic puddle at our feet.

'I see the alternative future has had a meltdown,' she chuckled.

We stared at her. 'Who are you?' we said.

'I am coach Rosamund from another where. What is the year, please?'

'2007.'

'I really must adjust the gyroscope,' she said. 'I am late.'

'Tell us about coaching in your time.' We sat down on the sofa, which had transformed itself into a small comfortable room with three armchairs and a table lamp.

Rosamund leaned forward. 'It's wonderful!' she said. 'Coaching is everywhere. Nearly everyone is a coach. There are at least 550,761 coach-training schools, if we ever bothered to count them. Everyone is coaching and doing it their own way. There is coaching with music, coaching with the Beatles, coaching with Mozart late piano concertos, coaching with flower arranging, coaching with origami, even witchcraft coaching. There are therapist coaches, mentor coaches, manager coaches, politicians' coaches (although that is not a popular specialty), backgammon coaches, tall coaches for tall people, tall coaches for short people, and vice versa.' She paused, and looked confused. 'Whatever it is, we have it. Coaching has taken over the planet. Soon it will take over other planets as well.' She laughed. 'Coaching is too powerful not to let everyone do it.'

She got up. 'I must be off. I need to do a little time-tampering further down the line.' The globe started spinning. Only a nightmare – thank goodness.

Here is a dream . . .

THE DREAM

We were in the same junkyard as in our nightmare. The wind was blowing and then it started to rain heavily. It seemed to rain for hours before the sun came out and started to warm the ground. Steam rose from the earth. We heard a noise behind us and jumped. A man was there with an umbrella. 'Hi!' he said. 'I kept trying to offer you this umbrella but you didn't pay any attention to me.'

He was dressed in a black T-shirt and blue trousers. He had no shoes, which seemed quite natural.

'Who are you?' we asked.

He pointed to his shirt and the letters C-O-A-C-H appeared in glowing letters.

'Are you from the future?'

'That depends when we are now.'

We looked at each other and decided this was another visitant from a parallel coaching universe. We hoped he was better than the last two. At least he was better dressed.

'Do you have rules for your coaches where you come from?'

He looked up. 'Rules are our children. They come back to haunt us if we deny our parentage.'

'You didn't answer our question.'

'How do you know?'

'Are you always enigmatic?

'I am never anything *always*.'

'You are playing games. Is coaching a game?'

'A game?' He smiled. 'Perhaps. People who *must* play, cannot *play*.'

'How is coaching?'

'Very well, thank you.'

He started to fade, starting with his feet until only his face was left. He smiled hugely and vanished.

Only a dream. . .

AND REALITY?

Enough of nightmares and dreams. We don't know how coaching will be. We can make some guesses, and hope. It looks as though coaching will increase, especially with organizations, over the next five years. Managers will be trained in coaching skills, and business and executive coaching will grow. Coaching networks will expand and most large training and consulting companies will either have, or outsource, a coaching network. Coaching will become part of most corporate universities.

IS COACHING A PROFESSION?

What kind of activity is coaching? It has been described as an area, a specialization, a discipline and a field. Can it yet claim to be a profession?

A profession is usually defined by five criteria:

1   **Members of a profession have specialized knowledge or skills. This is true of coaching and, as we have seen, there are core skills, a heart and soul of coaching.**

2   Members of a profession hold themselves to a higher ethical standard than other members of society. It is important that anyone training as a coach subscribes to and holds to a charter of standards and ethics.

3   A profession is self-governing. It regulates entry into the profession, monitors performance and expels those who violate responsibilities and/or ethics. Only some coaching organizations do this.

4   They provide important benefits to society. This is true for coaching.

5   They have certain rights and responsibilities not given to every member of society. This is not generally true for coaching.

So at the moment, coaching cannot fully claim to be a profession, although it is run as a profession in some membership organizations such as the International Coaching Community. It seems likely that coaching will continue to be an unlicensed, self-regulating field for at least the next five years.

We would personally like to see several things in the next few years. First, more focus on the roots and antecedents of coaching. We understand ourselves in the present by remembering our history. By looking at the roots of coaching, coaches can discover what they are subject to in coaching and start to go beyond best practices. Best practices are only best for a short time. They evolve and should evolve all the time into better practices, through people who see the gaps in the current best practices. Uncritical acceptance of best practices will stultify a discipline, field or profession.

Second, we need more focus on the coaches' own development. Coaches cannot help clients beyond their own level. The coach's own level of development and blind spots mark the limits of their skills. There are too many coach trainings and not enough coach education. We would like to see coaches trained in and knowledgeable about developmental levels, and knowing their own level (i.e. whether they are at Stage Three, Four or Five). They will then be able to make an informed guess about the level of their clients. At the moment, much coach training is unbalanced. It gives coaches information without developing their self-awareness and personal development. Coach training is too narrow. It tends to focus too much on the behaviour of the student coach, encouraging coaches to focus too much on the behaviour of their clients. We would like to see more emphasis on coach education. The coach's presence is what makes a difference to the client. Not just what coaches can *do*, but who they *are* is critical. Coaches need knowledge, skills and self-development. Knowing, doing and being. You can suspend what you know and what you can do, but you can never suspend who you *are*.

Third, we would like to see coaching linked with other well-established areas of knowledge and professions. This will build synergy, and give coaching more credibility. Too many self-development disciplines have gone their own way, scorned other branches of psychology and academia, and withered on the vine. We hope that coaching research will continue to grow, with doctoral dissertation studies linking coaching with other established areas. We would like to see many more peer-reviewed coaching journals. We would also like to see more research and emphasis on cross-cultural coaching. This is an area that will undoubtedly grow as multinationals engage coaches for their people in different countries. Coaches who are not culturally aware will not be effective with clients from another culture.

WHAT DOES COACHING DO?

Coaching turns everyday life into self-development. This is its great strength. Everyday life can be humdrum, or it can be a series of opportunities and a call to action.

Coaching helps people to become more themselves. Coaching is society's way of moving people from Stage Three, where they are identified with social mores and introjected values, to Stage Four, where they march to their own beat, and follow their own values. Therefore, coaching will create more individuals to enrich society. It will add to the breakdown of consensus and foster niches and small communities in a way the Internet has already done.

Coaching helps people to tolerate ambiguity in themselves and therefore to tolerate ambiguity in others and deal with the world, which changes so quickly. Coaching also gives multiple and richer perspectives, fostering post-modern thinking, which is about looking from multiple perspectives at multiple contexts. It will make people think more about power – who has it and who has not. Perspective is power. Power goes to the perspective that is privileged, so people will be more aware of who decides which perspective is privileged.

Coaching helps people make new distinctions; this will help them lead a richer, happier life and also adjust to the new distinctions that are being created every day in the arts, the sciences and in business. At its best, coaching will help people see that they can create a relationship of trust, and they will be able to take this and create more such relationships in their life.

We strongly believe that we need all these skills now and in every possible future.

FUTURE RESEARCH

Coaching needs to become more evidence based. By looking at evidence for coaching from many different angles, we will understand it better. The evidence needs to be based on multiple perspectives, not just from a visible behavioural point of view. Evidence needs to be both qualitative (based on coaches' perceptions and presence) and qualitative (based on the results clients achieve that can be measured).

All good research is based on three rules:

1 **An injunction, paradigm or instruction that says, 'If you want to know this, do that.' For example: if you want to know your developmental level, you need to do a specialized developmental interview, based on the years of research that have established this area of adult developmental psychology.**
2 **Data or experience. Out of this experiment will come an experience, some data that can be evaluated and measured. This experience will shed light on what you are exploring. In this instance, the developmental interview will show you ideas about yourself that can explain some aspects of your experience, how you feel and act. It will make you more self-reflective, while giving you another perspective and set of distinctions.**
3 **Finally, you need to put this experience or data for communal confirmation or rejection. You need feedback from multiple perspectives, but particularly from those who have done the experiment that you have undergone. This gives you a much better evaluation. Your own individual subjective experience is limited.**

We hope there will be research *in* coaching – research from the inside that involves coaches looking at their practice in a critical way, learning from it, applying ideas, making experiments and reporting the results. We also hope there will be research *on* coaching – research from the outside. What does coaching do and how do the results relate to other fields? How do they fit into the broader framework of human development and change? There need to be case histories, peer-reviewed articles and measurement from the four main perspectives of the integral model:

⇨ Your internal subjective experience
⇨ The realm of measurable, visible behaviour
⇨ The impact on the external systems (the organization for business coaching and a person's relationships and/or finances in life coaching)
⇨ The cultural aspect or the extent of shared understanding between coaches

Evidence-based coaching [1] will be grounded (with explicit links to other disciplines) on an empirical (experimental and practical) and theoretical knowledge base.

EPILOGUE

Now we are at the end of our quest, at least in this book. There have been fascinating side alleys that we have been forced to leave unexplored. We hope you will go 'down the passage which we did not take / Towards the door we never opened / Into the rose-garden' [2]. We hope you will build, explore and reflect critically on all coaching theory and practice (especially your own).

A quest is a special sort of journey, a journey in search for something. And often what you find is not what you expected. In any good quest, what you find is more about yourself; you come back a different person from the one who set out. In 1977 Terry Brooks wrote a fantasy novel, *The Sword of Shannara*. It is a quest by the hero (Shea Ohmsford) to find the eponymous magical sword of Shannara in order to defeat the Warlock Lord, clearly a close relative of Sauron from *The Lord of the Rings*. Shea finds the sword, but it seems useless; it bestows no superhuman strength, no invisibility, nothing. Yet he must confront the Warlock Lord with only the sword to help him. He discovers that the sword reveals who you really are in every detail, the good, the bad and the ugly. It shows truth without pretence or excuse. It is a talisman of self-revelation. It does nothing else. Shea survives the meeting with himself. He accepts everything about himself. When the

Warlock Lord touches the sword, he too must confront who he is, and because he is evil, he does not survive that self-revelation; he is destroyed, because at the core, he is negation.

A talisman, magic or otherwise, tells you about yourself. That is the prize some seek by going far outside themselves. Others seek it by going ever deeper inside themselves. Both pilgrims meet in the same place. Each discovers that they reach one and the same end, but via different paths. We are part of the world; so self-knowledge is knowledge of the world. There is nothing else to know.

We hope that coaching will help you on your path, and we wish you good luck in your quest.

REFERENCES

1 Grant, A. (2003) Keynote Address at the Coaching Conference, University of Sydney
2 Eliot, T. S. (1935) Burnt Norton, *Four Quartets*; see online at www.tristan.icom43.net/quartets/norton.html
3 Brooks, Terry (1977) *The Sword of Shannara*

APPENDIX

HOW COACHING DIFFERS FROM OTHER APPROACHES

There is considerable confusion, especially in the business world, about what coaches are and what they do. One way to clarify is to mark the boundaries of coaching by showing what it is not. This separates it from other disciplines, and although there may be areas of overlap, it will be apparent that coaching has a separate identity of its own. The following diagram demonstrates these differences well.

On the right are professions where the professional has the experience in the discussion, on the left where the client has the experience in the discussion. At the top is when the professional operates mostly by asking questions. At the bottom is where they operate mostly by giving answers. A friend goes in the middle of the diagram. They can do anything, and you don't pay them either.

You ask questions

Coach

Facilitator
                                                    Therapist

                                                    Counsellor

                                        Friend

Client has the experience   You have the experience

                                        Mentor

                                        Trainer

                                        Teacher

Psychometrics   Manager

                                        Consultant

You give answers

Adapted from Getting Started in Personal and Executive Coaching *by*
Stephen Fairley and Chris Stout (Wiley, 2004)
Original diagram © Stephen Fairley.
Used with permission

There is always some overlap between different professions, but,
generally speaking, consultants, managers, teachers, trainers and mentors
belong in the bottom right quadrant. They are viewed as experts in their field
and they are employed to give answers.

CONSULTANTS

Consultants deal with the business system as a whole. They diagnose, make
recommendations and design answers for the whole system. Part of their
answer may involve coaching for key individuals. Consultants may give the

coaching themselves, but then they need to take off their consultant's 'hat' and put on a coach's 'hat'. (Some consultants have a large collection of 'hats'.)

Consultants are increasingly recommending coaching to help manage change. The enemy of change is inertia, and inertia comes from habits. Organizational habits are established procedures, while individual habits are the limited-thinking habits of people in key roles. Consultants may design a new system but it will fail if they try to enforce it on individuals who have retained an old, limited mindset. So, coaches are used to help jog key people into thinking differently and to implement the organizational changes.

In the same way, business trainers are recommending coaching to support their trainings and in many cases are providing follow-up coaching. The reason for this is obvious. Too often a group of managers will go away for the weekend to a wonderful hotel where they will be given an excellent training, learn new skills and new ways of thinking, and have a thoroughly great time. They come back to work on the Monday morning enthused and wanting to put their learning into action. But the workplace is not the same as the training environment. All the old associations and habits conspire to drag them back to their old patterns. Their colleagues at their workplace who have not done the training do not know anything about it. They treat the newly enthusiastic manager in the same way as they have always done. Before long (it normally takes about three weeks), the temptation to slip back into old habits is too strong. The initial enthusiasm has faded, the force of habit has set in and the managers settle back into the routine, unless they have a coach who can help them sustain their motivation and the change. This will make a long-term difference. A great deal of training is a waste of time without coaching to ensure that the lessons learned are not forgotten.

MANAGERS

There are many styles of management, but in the end, managers are responsible for results and therefore have a strong personal interest in their people working in the most effective and efficient way – in their terms. A coach does not have this interest. Managers are paid for results. They have the power to tell others what to do and their people will obey if they want to continue to work in the company. Structurally, a manager cannot be a coach. However, managers can use coaching skills in particular situations, as they have many different means to motivate, stimulate and inspire their people to get results. Increasingly, managers are also adding coaching to their arsenal of skills.

Coaching skills give managers more choice in the way they manage. In many situations they will still tell their people what to do. This is the old paradigm of management. The manager asks questions so that he or she can understand the problem in order to give the answer, instruction or hint about how to solve it. This is fine and works well in many circumstances, especially when speed is important, or there is an emergency, or the solution is technical (when management is like teaching). The new paradigm of the manager as coach is for the manager to ask questions so the *person himself or herself* can understand the problem and can solve it for themselves. Coaching makes individuals more creative and independent, and empowers them to own their work.

Management paradigms

The old management paradigm:
The manager asks questions to understand the problem in order to give the answer, instruction or hint about how to solve it.

The new paradigm for manager as coach:
The manager asks questions so individuals can understand the problem and can solve it for themselves.

Managers need to adopt a coaching approach if the issue is emotional. They may also use this approach in career development. Similarly, managers can also utilize 'coaching moments' during the day when they resist the temptation to tell employees what to do, but instead ask questions to help those people solve the problem for themselves.

It is difficult for a manager to coach, because the employee's problem may become the manager's problem, whereas a coach will not get entangled in a client's problem. There is a lot of interest now in 'the manager as coach', and it is very important to know when to wear the 'managerial hat' and when to wear the 'coaching hat'. Many managers unfortunately do not take off their manager's hat before putting on their coaching hat. Then people will see coaching only as a way of helping them do better in their work – to be a better employee. They may only get 'coaching' if they do something wrong, whereas coaching should be a reward. This means building a coaching culture, where coaching is used and valued at every level in the organization, especially from the top downwards.

MENTORS

Mentors are not coaches, although the two are often confused. Rather, they are people who have rich knowledge and experience in their field, which they pass on to those who are less experienced. The word 'mentor' has its origins in Greek mythology. Homer tells the story in *The Odyssey*, his epic poem of Odysseus' adventures during and after the Trojan War. Odysseus, King of Ithaca, was one of the Greeks who sailed with Agamemnon to destroy Troy, when Paris stole Helen (of legendary beauty) from her husband, Menelaus, Agamemnon's brother. When Odysseus left Ithaca, he put his son, Telemachus, in the care of an old man called Mentor, asking him to pass on his wisdom to his son. So the word passed into the language, meaning someone with superior knowledge, a wise teacher who teaches life skills. (Actually, it was the goddess Pallas Athene taking the form of Mentor who did the teaching; Homer portrays Mentor the man as weak and ineffectual.) Mentor meaning a trusted adviser appears much more strongly in a book by the French author François Fénelon, *Les Aventures de Télémaque*, written in 1699.

Nowadays, a mentor is usually an experienced businessperson who guides and supports younger, less experienced colleagues, so the mentor is more derived from the apprenticeship model than from the coaching model. Mentors normally have an agenda for their clients, whereas coaches do not.

TEACHERS AND TRAINERS

Coaching is neither teaching nor training. Teachers and trainers are experts in their subjects and are expected to pass on knowledge and skills. Coaches deal in process, but do not pass on content. Training or teaching usually has a clear goal and expectations defined by the teacher. You expect to get something you want and you are there to learn it.

When Joseph wanted to learn Portuguese, he engaged a teacher named Leandro, who was fluent in English, Portuguese and French, and he and Joseph spoke only in Portuguese during the lesson (except when Joseph was stuck for the right words). Leandro wrote down the key vocabulary and grammar as they went along. Other teachers might use a different methodology, like going through a book, or studying grammar or rote learning of Portuguese words or phrases. When Joseph consulted a coach about learning Portuguese, the coach didn't teach him and didn't suggest anything, but helped him explore what learning Portuguese meant, how he would judge when he was fluent in Portuguese, and what was important to him about learning Portuguese. They explored external and internal resources Joseph already possessed and those he needed and how he could learn in the quickest and easiest way – Joseph defined all.

Teaching shades into coaching only at the more advanced levels where a teacher might explore a subject with a student in a more open-ended way, helping the student think it through, without imposing their own answers. This could happen in a university seminar.

THERAPISTS AND COUNSELLORS

Moving to the upper right of the diagram, a coach is neither a therapist nor a counsellor. Therapy deals with the client's mental *health*. Coaching deals with the client's mental *growth*. Coaching clients are adults who function adequately, and are not clinically depressed. The coach does not deal with health problems directly, although coaching may help the client to decide how to deal with them. Most forms of therapy have clients who are predominantly motivated to get away from pain and discomfort. The client's way of coping is under great stress, and may have broken down significantly. Therapy is remedial. The client wants something fixed and knows there is something wrong.

Imagine a scale of well-being measured from 1 to 10, where 1 represents great unhappiness, with the client barely functioning. A score of 10 means they are feeling great and getting great results. The midway point, 5, means 'Can't complain' and 'Not too bad'. Therapy clients tend to fall between 1 and 4. They want to get to 5. Once they are functioning normally, then a therapist might work to get them further up the scale. No one turns up on a therapist's doorstep saying, 'I feel great; help me feel even better.' But this is often what coaching clients say. They tend to start at least on 4 or 5; sometimes they start on 7 or 8. The coach aims to move them up to 9 or 10 or *expand the scale*, because 10 is only the clients' *perceived* limit of their happiness.

1----------2----------3----------4----------5----------6----------7----------8----------9----------10

Very unhappy	Very happy
Very poor results	Very good results
Therapy	Coaching

The scale of well-being

Also, many therapies look for causes in the past. Coaching deals mostly with exploring the present and designing the future. How the client got to where they are is less important than dealing with it now. Therapy will also pay more attention to the clients' feelings, and clients will usually go through a gamut of emotions. There is often a focus on exploring painful emotions in order to resolve them. Coaches will not do this. Emotions may emerge in coaching but they are not the primary focus. Coaching focuses on actions and new behaviours; emotions are created from new insights rather than being relived or released, and clients are invited to think more about the present and the future rather than the past.

In therapy it is often assumed that insight alone will bring change, but for coaches, awareness is only a first step. Awareness without action can simply lead to a client who knows all about their problem, its history and dynamics, but still feels powerless to change it (and so they stay stuck).

FACILITATORS

A coach is not a facilitator. Facilitators work with groups to help them make a decision. An ideal facilitator helps the process, but stays out of it, seldom making suggestions. Once the group has come to a decision or consensus, the facilitator's job is done. The word comes from the Latin, meaning 'someone who makes it easy'. A coach is more likely to work one to one (which a facilitator never does), and also a coach will bring far more of his or her own personality into the coaching.

PSYCHOMETRIC TESTS

The bottom right quadrant is the realm of psychometric tests. The client has the expertise (in their own life) but the psychometric still gives answers, by taking the information the client gives them and putting it into another form that is meant to be helpful. In previous times, astrology was the main psychometric.

BIBLIOGRAPHY

COACHING

For all books listed below, where publishers differ between territories, US publishers are shown in brackets. First editions are cited wherever possible.

Auerbach, J. (2005) *Seeing the Light: What Organizations Need to Know About Executive Coaching*, College of Executive Coaching

Dilts, R. (2003) *From Coach to Awakener*, Meta Publications

Doyle, J. (1999) *The Business Coach: A Game Plan for the New Work Environment*, Wiley

Downey, M. (1999) *Effective Coaching*, Orion

Flaherty, J. (1999) *Coaching: Evoking Excellence in Others*, Butterworth-Heinemann

Fortgang, L. (2001) *Living Your Best Life*, Thorsons

Fournies, F. (2000) *Coaching for Improved Work Performance*, McGraw-Hill

Gallwey, T. (1974) *The Inner Game of Tennis*, Bantam Books

Hargrove, R. (1995) *Masterful Coaching*, Pfeiffer

Hunt, J. & Weintrub, J. R. (2002) *The Coaching Manager: Developing Top Talent in Business*, Sage Publications

Kauffman, C. (2007) *Pivot Points: Small Choices with the Power to Change Your Life*, Evans Press

Landsberg, M. (1999) *The Tao of Coaching*, HarperCollins

Logan, D. & King, J. (2004) *The Coaching Revolution*, Adams Media

Laske, O. (2005) *Measuring Hidden Dimensions*, IDM Press

Lyle, J. (2002) *Sports Coaching Concepts: A Framework for Coaches' Behaviour*, Routledge

O'Connor, J. & Lages, A. (2004) *Coaching with NLP*, Thorsons

O'Neill, M. B. (2000) *Executive Coaching with Backbone and Heart,* Jossey-Bass
Rossinski, P. (2003) *Coaching Across Cultures,* Nicholas Brealey
Sieler, A. (2003) *Coaching to the Human Soul,* Newfield Publishing
Skiffington, S., & Zeus, P., (2003) *Behavioural Coaching,* McGraw-Hill
Stober, D. & Grant, A. (2006) *Evidence-Based Coaching Handbook,* Wiley
Whitmore, J. (2002) *Coaching For Performance,* Nicholas Brealey
Whitworth, L., Kimsey-House, H. & Sandahl, P. (1998) *Co-Active Coaching,* Davies-Black
Zeus, P. & Skiffington, S. (2000) *The Complete Guide to Coaching at Work,* McGraw-Hill
Zeus, P. & Skiffington, S. (2002) *The Coaching at Work Tool Kit,* McGraw-Hill

GENERAL

Argyris, C. (1990) *Overcoming Organisational Defences,* Prentice-Hall
Austin J. (1973) *How to Do Things with Words,* Harvard University Press
Bandler, R. and Grinder, J. (1975) *The Structure of Magic Volume 1,* Science and Behaviour Books
Bandler, R. and Grinder, J. (1976) *The Structure of Magic Volume 2,* Science and Behaviour Books
Bandura, A. (1997) *Self Efficacy,* W. H. Freeman
Barrett, R. (1998) *Liberating the Corporate Soul,* Heinemann
Basseches, M. (1984) *Dialectical Thinking and Adult Development,* Ablex Publishing
Bateson, G. (1972) *Steps to an Ecology of Mind,* Ballantine Books
Beck, D. and Cowan, C. (1996) *Spiral Dynamics,* Blackwell
Berne, E. (1964) *Games People Play,* Penguin.Block, P. (2000) *Flawless Consulting,* Jossey-Bass Pfeiffer
Chuang Tzu, *Basic Writings,* (Translated by Burton Watson, 1964), Columbia University Press
Cialdini, R. (1998) *Influence,* HarperCollins
Cook-Greuter, S. *Post Autonomous Ego Development,* available from cookgsu@comcast.net
Csikszenthmihalyi, M. (1991) *Flow,* Harper
Csikszentmihalyi, M. & Csikszentmihalyi, I. (eds.) (2006) *A Life Worth Living: Contributions to Positive Psychology,* Oxford University Press
The Dalai Lama & Cutler, H. (1998) *The Art of Happiness,* Hodder (Riverhead)
De Ropp, R. (1968) *The Master Game,* Dell Publishing Company
Drucker, P. (1989) *The New Realities,* HarperCollins
Ekman, P. & Davidson, R. (1994) *The Nature of Emotion: Fundamental Questions,* Oxford University Press
Gardner, H. (1993) *Frames of Reference,* Fontana Press
Gebser, J. (1985) *The Ever Present Origin,* Ohio University Press
Gilligan, C. (1982) *In a Different Voice,* Harvard University Press
Fisher, R. and Ury, W. (1983) *Getting to Yes,* Penguin
Fitz-enz, J. (2000) *The ROI of Human Capital,* American Management Association
Flores, F. & Solomon, R. (2001) *Building Trust,* Oxford University Press
Friedman, T. (2005) *The World Is Flat,* Penguin (Farrar, Straus & Giroux)
Gladwell, M. (2002) *The Tipping Point,* Little, Brown and Company (Back Bay Books)
Goffee, R. & Jones, G. (1998) *Character of a Corporation,* HarperCollins
Goleman, D. (1995) *Emotional Intelligence,* Bloomsbury (Bantam)
Hall, E. and Hall, M. (1990) *Understanding Cultural Differences,* Doubleday
Herrigel, E. (1953) *Zen and the Art of Archery,* Random House
Hofstede, G. (1997) *Cultures and Organizations,* McGraw-Hill
Kanter, R. Moss, (1983) *The Change Masters: Innovation for Productivity in the American Corporation,* Simon & Schuster
Kauffman, S. (1995) *At Home in the Universe,* Penguin
Kegan, R. (1994) *In Over Our Heads: The Demands of Modern Life,* Oxford University Press

King, P. & Kitchener, K. (1994) *Developing Reflective Judgment*, Jossey-Bass

Kirkpatrick, D.L. (1994) *Evaluating Training Programs: The Four Levels*, Berrett-Koehler

Kohn, A. (1993) *Punished by Rewards*, Houghton Mifflin

Kolb, D. (1984) *Experiential Learning Experience As the Source of Learning and Development*, Prentice-Hall

Koplowitz, H. (1990) *Unitary Consciousness and the Highest Development of Mind*, Praeger

Korzybski, A. (1994) *Science and Sanity*, Institute of General Semantics (first published 1933)

Laing, R.D. (1999) *The Politics of the Family*, Routledge

Loevinger, J. (1987) *Paradigms of Personality*, Freeman

Lyotard, J.-F. (1993) *The Post Modern Explained*, University of Minnesota Press

Maslow, A. (1998) *Towards a Psychology of Being*, Wiley

Maturana, H. & Varela, F. (1987) *The Tree of Knowledge: The Biological Roots of Human Understanding*, Shambhala

Morgan, G. (1986) *Images of Organisation*, Sage

O'Connor, J. (2000) *The NLP Workbook*, Thorsons

Peterson, C. & Seligman, M. (2004) *Character Strengths and Virtues: A Handbook and Classification*, Oxford University Press

Piaget, J. (1952) *The Origins of Intelligence in Children*, Norton

Pinker, S. (1997) *How the Mind Works*, Penguin

Rogers, C. (1980) *A Way of Being*, Houghton Mifflin

Searle, J. (1969) *Speech Acts: An Essay in the Philosophy of Language*, Cambridge University Press

Schein, E. (1999) *Process Consultation Revisited*, Addison-Wesley

Schein, E. (1988) *Process Consultation, Lessons for Managers and Consultants Volumes 1 and 2*, Addison-Wesley

Seligman, M. (2003) *Authentic Happiness*, Nicholas Brealey

Senge, P. (1992) *The Fifth Discipline*, Random House (Currency)

Toffler, A. (1971) *Future Shock*, Pan

Torbert, W. (1991) *The Power of Balance: Transforming Self, Society and Scientific Enquiry*, Sage

Trompenaars, F. (1997) *Riding the Waves of Culture*, Nicholas Brealey (McGraw-Hill)

Waldrop, M. (1993) *Complexity*, Simon & Schuster

Wilber, K. (2006) *Integral Spirituality*, Integral Books

Wilber, K. (1996) *A Brief History of Everything*, Shambhala

PAPERS AND ARTICLES CITED IN THE TEXT

Anderson, M. (2001) *Executive Briefing: Case Study on the Return on Investment of Executive Coaching*, Metrix Global LLC

Brock, V. (2006) *Who's Who in Coaching – Executive Summary*

CIPD Survey March 2005 *Who Learns at Work?*

Condon, W. (1982) *Cultural Microrhythms* in Davis (ed.), *Interactional Rhythms: Periodicity in Communicative Behaviour*, Human Sciences Press

Douglas, C. & McCauley, C.D. (1999) 'Formal Developmental Relationships: A Survey of Organisational Practices', *Human Resource Development Quarterly* 10

von Foerster, H. (1994) 'Ethics and Second Order Cybernetics', *SEHR*, 4 (2): *Constructions of the Mind*

Frederickson, B. & Losada, M. (2005) 'Positive Affect and the Complex Dynamics of Human Flourishing', *American Psychologist* 60

Grant, A. (2003) Keynote Address at the Coaching Conference, University of Sydney

Graves, C. (1981) 'The Emergent, Cyclical Double Helix Model of the Adult Human Biosocial System', handout for presentation to World Future Society, Boston, Mass., May 1981 (compiled for Dr Graves by Chris Cowan)

Graves, C. 'Levels of Existence: An Open System Theory of Values', *Journal of Humanistic Psychology*, November 1970

Hicks, M., & Peterson, D. (1999) 'The Development Pipeline: How People Really Learn', *Knowledge Management Review* 9

Jarvis, J. (2004) *Coaching and Buying Coaching Services – A CIPD Guide*, Chartered Institute of Personnel Development

Laske, O. (2004) 'Can Evidence Based Coaching Increase ROI?', *International Journal of Evidence Based Coaching and Mentoring*, 2 (2)

Losada, M. (1999) 'The Complex Dynamics of High Performance Teams', *Mathematical and Computer Modeling* 30

Peterson, D. & Hicks, M. (1999) 'Strategic Coaching: Five Ways to Get the Most Value', *Human Resources Focus* 76 (2)

Peterson, C. & Seligman, M. (1984) 'Causal Explanations as a Risk Factor for Depression: Theory and Evidence', *Psychological Review* 91 (3)

Peterson, C. Seligman, M. & Valliant, G. (1988) 'Pessimistic Explanatory Style Is a Risk Factor for Physical Illness: A Thirty-Five year Longitudinal Study', *Journal of Personality and Social Psychology* 55

Sheldon, K. and Elliot, A. (1998) 'Not All Personal Goals Are Personal', *Personality and Social Psychology* Bulletin 24 (5)

Western, D. (2006) 'Confirmation Bias', (unpublished) paper presented to the 2006 Annual Conference of the Society for Personality and Social Psychology

ABOUT THE AUTHORS

JOSEPH O'CONNOR

Joseph O'Connor is an internationally recognized author, trainer, executive coach and consultant. He is a Master Trainer of coaching, co founder of the International Coaching Community (ICC), and a leading author in the field of communication skills, leadership and coaching.

He is the author of 17 books, which have been translated into 29 languages. He has trained in Europe, North and South America, Asia and New Zealand, and was awarded the medal of the Singapore National Community Leadership Institute for his work in training and consultancy in 1996. He has trained coaches in 15 countries and is co-founder of the International Coaching Community.

Joseph's clients include BT, The Panama Canal Authority, UNIDO, BA, Citibank and HP Invent.

He lived for many years in London, and now lives in São Paulo, Brazil. You can contact Joseph at joseph@lambentdobrasil.com

ANDREA LAGES

Andrea Lages is one of the most respected coaching trainers in the world.

She has giving executive coaching and training in coaching, including the International Coaching Certification Training, to people from more than 20 countries.

She is co-founder of the International Coaching Community (ICC) and an ICC Master Trainer, co-founder and CEO of Lambent do Brasil, an International Training and Consulting company based in São Paulo.

Andrea works internationally as an executive coach and business trainer running courses and seminars on coaching, communication skills, systemic thinking and leadership. Andrea is fluent in English, Spanish and Portuguese and gives coaching and courses in all three languages.

Andrea has worked at many different venues in the Americas, Asia and Europe, including the UK. Her clients include Petrobrás, GlaxoSmithKline and the Secretary of Development of Rio de Janeiro. You can contact Andrea at andrea@lambentdobrasil.com

Joseph and Andrea founded the International Coaching Community in 2001. They also founded Lambent do Brasil, their coaching, training and consulting company in Sao Paulo in 2001. They currently live in Sao Paulo with their young daughter, Amanda.

The first book they wrote together was *Coaching with NLP*, published in 2004, and now available in ten languages.

THE INTERNATIONAL COACHING COMMUNITY (ICC)

The ICC is one of the largest professional membership organizations for coaches in the world. All the members of the ICC have successfully completed the International Coaching Certification Training. The ICC has Core Competencies and Standards and Ethics that all members agree to follow.

The ICC runs over 60 training courses in 14 different countries every ear.

The ICC has advanced trainings in corporate coaching, executive coaching, life coaching and team coaching.

The vision of the ICC is the creation and support of an effective coaching profession governed by clear standards and ethics

See www.internationalcoachingcommunity.com

LAMBENT DO BRASIL

INTERNATIONAL COACHING SERVICES

Lambent do Brasil trains coaches through the ICC and specializes in providing professional coaches for business at every level. An international specialist in business coaching, it manages coaching projects worldwide for companies in many different countries with its international network provided by the ICC. Because all coaches have the same training, the coaching has the same methodology internationally.

TRAINING SERVICES

Lambent do Brasil runs ICC coaching training sessions internationally.

It also provides trainer's training in neuro-linguistic programming to international standards.

CONSULTANCY

Lambent do Brasil provides consultancy through the systemic audit process to identify leverage points for business development.

For details, see: www.lambentdobrasil.com

Contact: info@lambentdobrasil.com

INDEX

transformational coaching 187–8
transition 191–2
trust 17–18, 162–3

Unestähl, Lars-Eric 52
United States, coaching in 57–72

values 118–19, 182–4
    see also concerns

values in action (VIA) survey 118–19
virtues 118–19

Whitmore, Sir John 27, 62, 76
Whitworth, Laura 26

Zen in the Art of Archery 27
zone 116–18, 127